CONFLICTED MISSION

Conflicted Mission

FAITH, DISPUTES, AND DECEPTION ON THE DAKOTA FRONTIER

Linda M. Clemmons

MINNESOTA
HISTORICAL
SOCIETY PRESS

For Margaret Clemmons

**CLEAN
WATER
LAND &
LEGACY**
AMENDMENT

www.mhspress.org

The Minnesota Historical Society Press is a member of the Association of American University Presses.

Manufactured in the United States of America

10 9 8 7 6 5 4 3 2 1

♾ The paper used in this publication meets the minimum requirements of the American National Standard for Information Sciences—Permanence for Printed Library Materials, ANSI Z39.48–1984.

International Standard Book Number
ISBN: 978-0-87351-921-2 (paper)
ISBN: 978-0-87351-930-4 (e-book)

Library of Congress Cataloging-in-Publication Data available upon request.

This and other Minnesota Historical Society Press books are available from popular e-book vendors.

Portions of this work originally appeared in Linda M. Clemmons, " 'Leagued together': Adapting Traditional Forms of Resistance to Protest ABCFM Missionaries and the Treaty of 1837," *South Dakota History* 37 (Summer 2007): 95–124, © 2007 by the South Dakota State Historical Society.

Image credits: The map on p. 37 was drawn by David Deis, Dreamline Cartography. All photographs are from the Minnesota Historical Society's collections; the pipestone tablet on p. 79 is item 68.52.1107, Fort Renville Box 158AY.

Book Design by Wendy Holdman.

Contents

CONFLICTED MISSION

Introduction

In *Old Rail Fence Corners,* a compilation of Minnesota settlers' remembrances, Mrs. John Brown tells a story about an encounter between Samuel Pond, an American Board of Commissioners for Foreign Missions (ABCFM) missionary, and a Dakota man. Brown writes, "Mr. Pond once met a Shakopee Indian on the trail and neither would turn out for the other. They ran into each other 'bump.' [The] Indian said 'Ho.' Mr. Pond said, 'Ho.' Each continued on his way." Of course, it is likely that this encounter did not happen as told. Whether true or not, the story is an important allegory that highlights several aspects of missionary interaction with the Dakota. Most times, the missionaries and Dakotas walked on parallel paths, both committed to their own ways, never coming together or truly understanding the other. Throughout the history of the mission, however, both sides continuously bumped into each other, faced resistance, and then continued on. After their meeting, Pond and the Dakota man were probably each moving in the same general direction as they had before, but their overall trajectory might have changed as a result of the contact. While the Protestant missionaries never shed their evangelical identities or stopped believing that all Dakotas needed to adopt Christianity and change their culture, interaction with the Dakota pushed the missionaries in unintended, and frequently unwelcomed, directions.[1]

What follows is the story of the ABCFM Dakota mission in Minnesota from 1835 to 1862. A chronological history of the Dakota mission sheds light upon the dual themes of change and conflict embedded in this mission's history. As the missionaries worked to Christianize and civilize the Dakotas, they themselves changed in ways that caused both internal and external stress and conflict. Simply put, antebellum missionaries were not supposed to change; indeed, the very nature of missionary work in the early nineteenth century was designed to be unidirectional, with superior missionaries ministering to and changing supposedly inferior heathens. The Dakota missionaries were painfully aware that the reality of life on the Minnesota frontier did not match the heroic image portrayed by the evangelical press. To maintain the façade, they did their best to hide these changes from their sponsoring organization, the government, and even each other.

Focusing on examples of change and conflict within the Dakota mission both adds to and challenges the commonly accepted view of antebellum missions to American Indians. Recently historians have argued that missionaries were changed by the very people they came to convert. Missionary religious beliefs, cultural assumptions, and relations with antebellum society were challenged and occasionally altered as a result of the mission process. Conversion—broadly defined—was not a one-way process. As Jay Riley Case noted, missionary work "also involved cooperation, negotiation, conversation, reassessment, and transformation, from all parties." The experience of the Dakota missionaries adds a further dimension to this scholarship, illustrating how interaction with native peoples changed the missionaries in both small and more substantive ways.[2]

While these histories add new insight into the process of cultural and religious exchange for both natives and Euro-Americans, scholars often portray change for the missionaries as unthinking. Historians use words such as "unconscious," "beyond their control," "inadvertent," "unwitting," "unrecognized," and "unknowing" to underscore that change was unwelcome, unanticipated, and counter to the natural order of how Indian–missionary relations were supposed to proceed. For example, historian Richard Pointer argues that interaction with Native Americans impacted colonial missionary David Brainerd's "emotional and spiritual health, sense of calling and ministerial worthiness, preaching style and content, [and] understanding of missionary success." However, Brainerd "could not acknowledge such borrowing, even to himself, given typical Christian fears of being tainted by any type of pagan idolatry."[3]

The Dakota missionaries had a different experience; the changes that occurred after years of interaction with the Dakotas were not unconscious, unrecognized, or uncontested. Indeed, their actual experience with the Dakotas led to internal turmoil for the missionaries and created external conflict with the ABCFM, the federal government, and eventually Minnesota settlers, which increased over the course of the mission. Indeed, conflict was one of the defining features of the Dakota mission during its thirty-year existence in Minnesota.

Much of this conflict arose because the Dakota missionaries—in their own minds and in the collective evaluation of the antebellum public—failed to live up to the ideals promoted by the evangelical press. During the antebellum era, an assertive evangelical press published and distributed materials to gather funds and workers for "the Salvation [of] the whole world." These promotional materials focused on the glory and self-sacrifice of missionary work and the imminent conversion of vast numbers of non-Christians around the world. Articles, religious tracts, and sermons all portrayed male and female missionaries as heroic, self-sacrificing, romantic—even as martyrs. The Dakota missionaries quickly learned it was impossible to live up to these exalted standards, especially when the Dakotas failed to match the stereotypes promoted in the mission press. The difference between the published ideal and life in the field compelled the missionaries to attempt to hide many of their daily accommodations as well as their internal and external struggles.[4]

In the end, the Dakota missionaries had much to hide. Throughout their thirty-year tenure in Minnesota, they experienced continuous tension and discord. The majority of conflicts fell into three categories: internal conflicts, external conflicts, and friction over their diverging evaluations of race and language, each merging with and reinforcing the others. For instance, internal conflicts could lead to external tension with the ABCFM or the Dakotas' Indian agent. Likewise, the missionaries' changing views of the Dakota language led to tension with the new settlers streaming into Minnesota in the 1850s and 1860s.

Throughout the following chapters, different examples of conflict and change are examined from the missionaries' point of view. As such, this book does not purport to examine the Dakotas' interpretation of events. Although the missionaries offered biased interpretations of Dakota history, religion, and culture, their writings also provide insight into some of the challenges the Dakotas faced in the early to mid-nineteenth century. The missionary publications, reports, and letters also explore the formative years of Minnesota's development as a territory and state, and antebellum evangelical culture in general. John Peacock, in his afterword to *The Dakota Prisoner of War Letters,* calls the events leading up to and through the Dakota War of 1862 "an enormous, difficult, and painful puzzle that we all must put together." The missionaries' story—with all of its limitations and inherent biases—is one piece of this puzzle.[5]

Internal Conflicts

Although all missionaries entered missionary work holding fundamental biases, Richard Pointer notes that during their time in the field colonial missionaries often experienced "theologizing moments," which led them (often unconsciously) to reflect on their own religious beliefs, talents, and culture. Jay Riley Case also discussed this process with regard to world Christianity, noting that indigenous peoples "compelled missionaries to give serious attention to issues they had never previously considered." Some of these topics included theology, educational theory, and church admission policy. Missionaries also examined, and occasionally rethought, American conceptions of civilization.[6]

Throughout their time in Minnesota, the men and women of the Dakota mission consciously experienced numerous and reoccurring "theologizing moments." Many of these moments arose when Dakotas forced the missionaries to question, and reflect upon, their Christian beliefs. Most important, interaction with the Dakotas compelled the missionaries to question what it meant to become and remain a Christian. For instance, could Dakotas who were involved in polygamous marriages become church members? Could Dakotas travel and hunt on the Sabbath and remain within the church? Could Dakota converts retain any of their old religious beliefs? The ABCFM offered unambiguous answers to all of these questions. Tension arose, however, when life in the field challenged the missionaries to reconsider—and even subvert—these clear-cut directives.[7]

Occasionally, these theologizing moments led the missionaries to worry about their own religious convictions. If their entire identity was linked to converting the Dakotas, what happened if and when they failed? Indeed, these moments of self-doubt led some of the missionaries to question their own beliefs, moral character, and abilities. This especially was true for women, whose dreams of independent missionary work often failed to materialize in the field. An extreme manifestation of this self-doubt occurred following the treaties of 1851, when the majority of missionaries resigned from the Dakota mission.

In addition to creating religious tension, the mission experience also led the Dakota missionaries to question several aspects of the sacrosanct division between what they termed civilized and uncivilized behavior. According to the thinking of the time, the missionaries came from a civilized society, and the Dakotas from an uncivilized one. As such, the missionaries were the teachers, and the Dakota their students. However, life on the Minnesota frontier occasionally inverted this supposed truism. The missionaries found that the Dakotas were better able to survive in Minnesota than they were. In some cases, the missionary men, and especially the women, became dependent on Dakotas. At other times, the missionaries questioned whether hunting was an uncivilized activity and even began to use "savage" gift-giving practices to entice Dakotas to their meetings and schools. The missionaries also were embarrassed when their own conduct—for example, bickering with each other—failed to provide the proper model of "civilized" behavior for the Dakotas. In the aftermath of 1862, several of the missionaries were publicly criticized for questioning whether the actions of military officials and some settlers were "uncivilized."

In sum, contact with the Dakotas "often provoked these evangelical missionaries to reconsider their positions." However, the amount and direction of change was deeply personal and "did not unfold in a uniform or inevitable manner." Some missionaries were more susceptible to change and self-doubt than others (Thomas Williamson and Mary Riggs, for example). Other missionaries, however, resisted accommodation (Stephen Riggs). But even the most intractable missionaries were forced to consider new positions and ideas, even if they ultimately rejected them as invalid. In most cases, the missionaries were keenly aware of these "theologizing moments" and attempted to keep them to themselves or within the small mission community.[8]

External Conflicts

As the men and women of the Dakota mission struggled with the reality of life among the Dakotas, they attempted to hide their challenges and changing views from their home board. The ABCFM had one set of conversion criteria and policies for its widely divergent missions, which ranged from the American frontier to China, India, Hawaii, Burma, and beyond. In the mid-nineteenth century, many of these policies were developed by Rufus Anderson, the ABCFM's most influential corresponding secretary of the era.

First and foremost, Anderson argued that promoting Christianization, as opposed to cultural change, needed to be the focus of every missionary action. As historian Paul Harris noted, "To preach the gospel pure and simple became the ideal of missionary practice." Second, Anderson argued that missionaries were not to compromise with "heathenism"; rather, native converts needed to follow the same church admission standards as any member of a New England congregation. Third, the missionaries needed to limit expenditures in the field; in other words, to run their missions with "New England simplicity." Finally, while female missionaries were important to the success of each mission, they would take care of the home so that their husbands could focus entirely on proselytizing. Anderson's directives did not always translate well to the Dakota mission. The missionaries' failure to follow these orders produced tension on both sides and led the missionaries to edit their official correspondence to the Board.[9]

During the first years of the Dakota mission, conflicts with ABCFM were foremost in the minds of the missionaries. As time progressed, however, tension with the ABCFM decreased while conflicts with the government increased in intensity. Frequently, scholars depict missionaries as working hand in hand with the government to achieve the same ends. Historian Neal Salisbury summarizes this point of view: Protestant missionaries are frequently depicted as "advancing . . . the political goals of the white conquerors." In his article on the relationship between the Dakota missionaries and the federal government, Robert Craig explicitly linked Christianity with imperial ideology and empire building.[10]

While the Dakota missionaries certainly had strong ties with the federal government, the relationship was more conflicted than Craig and other historians have acknowledged. Indeed, the experience of the Dakota missionaries closely mirrored that of their Cherokee brethren. Several historians have noted that some ABCFM missionaries openly fought against Andrew Jackson's Indian removal policies, especially with regard to the Cherokees. These challenges to the federal government came at a price. One week after enactment of the Indian Removal Act, Secretary of War John Eaton terminated the ABCFM's allotment of nearly $3,000 for the southern Indians, stating that the loss of funds stemmed from the Board's challenges to removal.[11]

The experience of their Cherokee colleagues taught the Dakota missionaries that criticism of federal Indian policy came with a price, and in some cases they consciously remained silent in order to receive government funds, federal farming, teaching, and medical positions, and money from the Dakota treaties of 1837 and 1851. Because of the close relationship between the Dakota missionaries and the federal government, the Dakotas saw the ABCFM missionaries and the government agents as one and the same. As time passed, however, this close—but conflicted—relationship was strained, as missionaries criticized the treaties of 1837, 1851, and 1858 (although for different reasons than the Dakotas). They also divided with government agents over the best way to civilize Indians, whether funds should go to Catholics, and whether Dakota was a civilized language. Moreover, they were highly disparaging of the Indian agents' characters and abilities. As tension grew on the frontier, the Dakota missionaries attempted to follow their long-standing rule of remaining silent. In the 1850s and 1860s, however, they became increasingly open in their criticism of government policies. Of course, this created conflict with government officials as well as the newly arrived settlers.

Conflict over Race and Language

The missionaries' views on race and language further divided them from many government officials and Minnesota settlers. In the eighteenth century, most Euro-American commentators (such as Thomas Jefferson) believed that Indians were racially equal to Europeans. According to the "monogenetic theory," all peoples had the same origin and were fundamentally alike. This belief in inherent equality, however, did not include the idea that all societies were equal in the present day. Commentators argued that some peoples, like Native Americans, had developed inferior cultures and religions. This belief led many people to see Indians as "biologically admirable but socially abhorrent." Two theories emerged as to why some cultures had degenerated over time. One held that environment and education had produced inferior cultures, whereas another argued that the Indians represented a fallen society. Even if tribes had declined over time, the monogenetic theory assumed that if the Indians' environments were changed, they "would respond as whites did and quickly become productive citizens." Or, as one antebellum missionary promised, converted Indians would become "white and delightsome."[12]

The Enlightenment focus on the inherent equality of Native Americans sharply contrasted with the antebellum era's growing belief that some peoples were biologically inferior. Called polygenesis, this theory posited that different races had separate (and inferior) origins. Thus, changing Indian culture would not allow them to participate equally in American society. Many U.S. Indian policymakers came to believe in the immutable inferiority of Indians, which meant that no amount of preaching or civilizing would change their degenerate nature. The idea that Indians could become "white" was replaced by the adage, "Once an Indian, always an Indian." The upshot of this government policy was the removal, or relocation, of Indians, which was justified by the belief that Indians were inferior and should give up their lands to more "advanced" citizens.[13]

Changing ideas of race in antebellum America were also applied to language. In the sixteenth through the eighteenth centuries, most people believed that languages had a common origin. Philosophers of language maintained that all languages were the same at the beginning, just as the monogenetic theory of race argued that all peoples had a common origin. Over time, however, some societies—like Indians—had developed inferior cultures, religions, and languages. Because languages had a common origin, it was believed that with proper instruction "deficient" Indian languages could eventually convey Christian knowledge.[14]

By the early nineteenth century, many antebellum Americans began to reject the idea that languages shared a common origin, just as many renounced the monogenetic theory of race. Unlike European languages (specifically English), Indian languages were described as defective and incapable of conveying abstract ideas. Indeed, some theorists likened Indian speech to infant babble. Indians were seen as being like children, capable of thinking only in terms of their immediate wants. English, on the other hand, was the language of civilization. Without knowledge of English, Indians could never become citizens and participate in government.[15]

The Dakota missionaries' response to the antebellum debate over Indians' race and language was certainly influenced by their interaction with the Dakotas. This finding adds to the historical debate on missionary ideas about race and language. With regard to missionaries and race, historians have offered conflicting opinions; some have argued that missionaries resisted the growing racism of the antebellum era, while others have found that after extensive interaction with Indians, some missionaries began to abandon Enlightenment ideals of race in favor of scientific racism. This study of the Dakota missionaries follows those historians who have argued that even after extensive interaction with the Dakotas, the missionaries continued to follow the older Enlightenment ideas about race.[16]

While historians disagree over missionary conceptions of race, they concur that, like government officials, most antebellum missionaries continued to characterize Indian languages as inferior, uncivilized, and deficient. As such, historians argue that missionaries adhered to the common antebellum idea that Indians must learn English to become Christian and civilized even after studying the native language. The experience of the Dakota missionaries, however, shows a different outcome. Over time, the missionaries came to see Dakota as a civilized language, equal to English. Stephen Riggs even began an ill-fated and long-running campaign to have Dakota-speaking men declared citizens of Minnesota.[17]

The men and women of the Dakota mission had not expected to participate in the debate over race and language; life with the Dakotas, however, forced them to confront and question their own assumptions. Their changing views of the Dakota language, as well as their staunch adherence to older notions of race, ultimately divided them from other antebellum government officials and settlers. The most extreme manifestation of this ideological conflict appeared in the aftermath of the Dakota War of 1862.

Dakotas and ABCFM Missionaries

The Dakotas probably would have found the antebellum debate over race and language largely academic. It ultimately did not matter to the Dakotas whether they were "civilized" first or Christianized first, as the result was the same—both the missionaries and the federal government targeted their religion, their culture, and, eventually, their lands. Because the missionary and Dakota perspectives were so different, this book does not purport to study history from the Dakotas' perspective, nor does it chronicle their interpretations of events on the frontier. While the missionaries unwittingly documented Dakota resistance to their mission in their correspondence, they never attempted to understand the roots of this opposition; indeed, they interpreted Dakota actions through the lens of their own cultural and religious ideologies. For instance, when Dakotas killed mission cattle, the missionaries believed that this act stemmed from the Dakotas' antipathy to their proselytizing. While this belief may be true, there could be other reasons that had little to do with Christianity and more to do with the loss of land, the missionaries' refusal to participate in gift-giving practices, their close ties to the federal government, or various other factors.[18]

As the thousands of missionary letters attest, the Dakotas were the center of the missionaries' universe, but the reverse was not true. During much of the ABCFM mission's time in Minnesota, most Dakotas lived the majority of their lives apart from the missionaries. They probably did not think about the missionaries unless they needed something, or the missionaries' actions became especially intrusive, or Dakota anger over federal Indian policy spread to the Protestants. What was important to the Dakotas, however, was the missionaries' (albeit conflicted) association with the government, settlers, issues of removal, and warfare. The historical issues and events that influenced the missionaries intersect with Dakota history and would have been important to the Dakotas at the time, but it is up to other historians to tell the Dakotas' story without the missionaries as the central characters.[19]

Missionaries and the Development of the United States and Minnesota

The story of the ABCFM mission to the Dakotas speaks to issues of both national and local importance. On the national level, the story of the Dakota missionaries provides insight into evangelical culture that stood at the center of antebellum society. Their story also touches on how one group of missionaries dealt with and thought about issues important to antebellum Americans, including race, language, gender, cultural change, and the relationship among religion, removal, and the government.

The story of Minnesota's development as a territory and state cannot be told without reference to the ABCFM missionaries. The missionaries were among the first Euro-American settlers in the region and paved the way for further settlement. Although other missionary organizations proselytized to the Dakotas in the antebellum era—including representatives of the Methodist, Catholic, and Episcopalian churches—the ABCFM organization was the best funded and had the largest sustained presence in Minnesota prior to the Dakota War of 1862. Through their mission work, the Dakota missionaries witnessed and participated in the main events of early Minnesota history, including Indian treaties, the transition from territory to state, the influx of settlers, and the Dakota War of 1862.

The ABCFM missionaries' influence in local and national Indian affairs persisted into the post-1862 period. A few of the original missionaries, and their children, continued the ABCFM's missionary work and followed the Dakotas to their new reservation as they were removed from Minnesota. One missionary, Moses Adams, was even appointed Indian agent to the Sisseton as part of President Grant's "peace policy." Stephen Riggs wrote numerous ethnologies and Dakota dictionaries in the late nineteenth century, which he published through the Minnesota Historical Society and the Smithsonian Institution. Riggs's publications exposed another generation to the missionaries' view of the Dakotas, although under the guise of dispassionate scientific studies.[20]

Aside from missionary work, many of the Dakota missionaries played prominent roles in the development of the Minnesota Territory. They helped bring government and religion to the white settlers who flooded the region beginning in the 1840s. Gideon Pond, for example, served as a representative in the first territorial legislature, worked in various local governmental positions in Bloomington, Minnesota, and started the first Presbyterian church for white settlers. His brother, Samuel, also founded a Presbyterian church for white settlers. Moses Adams ministered to white settlers in Nicollet County and later opened a Presbyterian church at Traverse des Sioux. He also served as the American Bible Society agent for Minnesota.

This book focuses on the conflicted ABCFM Dakota mission from its settlement in 1835 until its disbandment in Minnesota following the Dakota War of 1862. The Dakota mission was conflicted on many levels. The missionaries clashed with each other, the ABCFM, the American government, and the Dakotas. They struggled over what it meant to convert and civilize Dakotas and how to build a simple, perfect, but cost-effective society on the frontier. The missionaries found that work with the Dakotas was rarely heroic, romantic, unidirectional, or as successful as the mission press had promised. At the same time, they attempted to keep these conflicts from the evangelical press and the people who eagerly followed their exploits on the Minnesota frontier.

Antebellum Missionary Language

The missionaries wrote thousands of words discussing their conflicted experience and intricate deception on the Minnesota frontier. Many of the words that they used are deeply problematic and offensive. This point was brought home to me by my eleven-year-old son. I left a draft of this introduction on the kitchen counter, and my son picked it up and started reading it. A few minutes in, he stopped and asked me why I was using words that I hated and that he would get in trouble for saying. He unknowingly hit upon one of the difficult issues involved in writing antebellum mission history: how to use and frame the missionaries' language. I was silent for a few minutes, with different responses running through my head, none of which would have satisfied the black-and-white mind of my eleven-year-old. If words are offensive you do not use them. Case closed. I finally came up with a response that I still feel was inadequate but satisfied him: I study the meanings of these words to help understand people who lived in the past and to show why the words are unacceptable today.

Many of the words used to describe the beliefs and conflicts of the ABCFM missionaries, such as "civilization," "barbarism," and "savagery," are in current usage harmful, and represent an ideology that has thankfully been challenged. While each of these problematic and derogatory terms has a history, a few comments about the term "conversion" help to illustrate the problem of working with antebellum missionary language in general. In recent years, historians have cautioned against using the term "conversion" when discussing missionaries, Native Americans, and Christianity, as it "perpetuates ... [evangelicals'] understanding of the process of religious change as the total and unilateral displacement of native spiritual error by universal religious truth." Historians argue that conversion never proceeded in this "either/or" fashion, nor was conversion a "one-way process whereby supine native religions were totally transformed by a more active, dynamic force."[21]

Despite its obvious limitations and biases, I have chosen to use "conversion" throughout this book because the missionaries themselves used this term. Indeed, "conversion" encapsulated their worldview, religious faith, and evaluation of the Indians' religion and culture. At least initially, the missionaries viewed conversion as an all-or-nothing affair, with no room for negotiation or accommodation: being a Christian meant no longer being a Dakota. In other words, the missionaries unapologetically wanted to entirely do away with Dakota culture and religion, which present-day historians rightly condemn. One of the arguments of this book, however, is that interactions with the Dakota occasionally forced the missionaries to question, and even redefine, their definition of what it meant to convert to Christianity.

Other nineteenth-century words, such as "civilization" and "savagery," are used in a similar way throughout this book; they are included in missionary quotations and some of my commentary to provide insight into the missionaries' initial mindset and to show how some of the parameters of their definitions changed, evolved, or were reinforced after extensive contact with Dakotas. Despite my decision to use these terms to examine the missionaries' way of thinking about the Dakotas and themselves, I am mindful of my son's reminder that they are not words to be taken lightly.

CHAPTER 1

"Waging War ... against the Powers of Darkness"

An Idealized Vision of Missionary Work, 1830-35

In 1880, Stephen Riggs published an inspirational version of his life as a missionary to the Dakota entitled *Mary and I: Forty Years with the Sioux.* According to Riggs, his book was intended to motivate "those interested in the uplifting of the Red Men." In his introduction to *Mary and I,* the Reverend S. C. Bartlett echoed the same thesis, noting that Riggs's book would "quicken the piety at home" and kindle "holy ambition ... in the hearts of many other young men." Riggs was a model missionary because of his "faith and zeal ... wisdom and patience ... self-sacrifice and Christian peace"; he also was intelligent, pious, and utterly devoted to his cause. Indeed, Riggs never doubted "the righteousness of [his] decision" to become a missionary; he remained devoted to converting the Dakota from his arrival in Minnesota in 1837 until his death in 1883.[1]

Each chapter of *Mary and I* was intended to inspire the evangelical public with Riggs's piety and devotion to missionary work. The book begins with the birth of Stephen Return Riggs in Steubenville, Ohio, in 1812. During his childhood Riggs studied the Bible and attended a log-cabin school. He chose missionary work after having a conversion experience: "the Lord appeared to me in a wonderful manner," he remembered, and "from that time and onward my path lay in the line of preparation for such service as he should call me unto." Instead of hammering "on the anvil" like his father, a blacksmith, Riggs chose to strike "a strong and steady stroke for God and man."[2]

Riggs studied to become a missionary at Jefferson College and then graduated from Western Theological Seminary. After receiving his license to preach, he dreamed of working in China, which was considered a prestigious posting, rather than undertaking domestic missionary work. Indeed, David Greene, one of the corresponding secretaries of the ABCFM, complained that "[c]andidates for the Indian missions are lamentably few." Riggs chose

Stephen R. Riggs,
about 1865.

to join the small number who ministered to Indians after talking to Thomas Williamson, a fellow Ohioan who had been affiliated with the ABCFM Dakota mission since 1835. Riggs married Mary Ann Clark Longley before he left for Minnesota in 1837, because the ABCFM disapproved of unmarried missionaries. As he set out for Minnesota with his new wife, Riggs was deeply committed to evangelical Protestantism, missionary work, and the righteousness of his cause. The rest of his book detailed his forty-year commitment to living up to the ideal set out in the book's introduction, although the reality of life in the field was far more conflicted and challenging than what he depicted.[3]

Inspiring Missionaries: The Antebellum Evangelical Press

The men and women of the Dakota mission had an idealized vision of missionary work before they arrived in the field. Much of the romanticized imagery came from the evangelical literature of the era, which was designed to encourage evangelism around the world. These texts collectively created ideal—and often impossible—standards for American missionaries to emulate.

The early nineteenth century saw what David Paul Nord has called the "industrialization of evangelism." Using new printing technology, religious organizations published and disseminated thousands of religious tracts to promote their "righteous empire." As David Morgan noted, "belief was converted into graphic information [and text] and disseminated cheaply over great distances by virtue of a mass-produced medium and an ever-expanding infrastructure of distribution." These widely distributed religious tracts were a way to "galvanize the faithful as well as to convert the ignorant."[4]

One of the mainstays of this burgeoning antebellum evangelical literature was the missionary memoir. Indeed, over seventy works featuring American missionaries were published before 1870. One of the first and most famous of these biographies featured David Brainerd, a colonial missionary who died in 1747 while working to convert the Delaware to Christianity. Brainerd's missionary work became known through Jonathan Edwards's *The Life of Brainerd*. Nearly 70,000 copies of *The Life of Brainerd* were distributed in the nineteenth century alone. In his biography, Edwards provided "a detailed account of [Brainerd's] spiritual life, his devotional exercises, his physical afflictions . . . and his quest for Indian souls." He is depicted as saintly, heroic, pious, and an inspirational model for those thinking of devoting their lives to missionary work. As zealous young divinity students read Brainerd's memoir, they were motivated to become, according to historian Joseph Conforti, "heroic Christians in their own right."[5]

Evangelical women had female missionaries to read about and emulate. One of the most prominent works was based on the life of Nancy Judson, a missionary to Burma who died in the field. Judson's memoir, first published in 1829, was reprinted every year until 1856. Over fifteen biographies were written about Judson, at least three of which sold more than 26,000 copies by the 1850s. Judson's story, which touched on themes of "self-sacrifice, spiritual dedication . . . religious activism . . . [and] evangelical martyrdom," became a staple among evangelical readers.[6]

Readers were also fascinated by the story of Harriet Newell, a woman who died in 1812 during her first year of missionary work in India. Newell's memoir was published in 1814, and a new edition was printed almost every year for the next twenty-five years. According to historian Amanda Porterfield, in death Harriet Newell "became a major religious figure; no other woman in the second decade of the nineteenth century was so widely eulogized or emulated." Likewise, Mary Kelley called Newell, "an icon of evangelical Protestantism." Like Brainerd, Newell inspired evangelical women to undertake mission work. Among them was Narcissa Whitman, an assistant missionary with the ABCFM's Oregon mission. According to biographer Julie Roy Jeffrey, "Narcissa had found the story of Harriet Newell ... particularly compelling." Whitman saw Newell as a "lovely saint" and as a model for her own missionary ambitions. As it turned out, Narcissa Whitman also died young in the mission field, and her story was retold to influence another generation of missionaries.[7]

While historians view these memoirs as hagiographies, evangelical men and women read them as the literal truth. The biographers depicted missionaries as saints and missionary work as romantic and heroic, and as a way to help bring about the millennium—the thousand-year reign of Christ (also known as the Second Coming). Other media also promoted this message. Missionary organizations published monthly magazines and annual reports that detailed their efforts to convert non-Christians around the world. In 1860, the ABCFM's magazine, *The Missionary Herald,* had a circulation of 16,241 copies, which reached an estimated 292,000 Presbyterians and Congregationalists. The *Annual Report of the Board of Foreign Missions,* a publication of the Old School Presbyterian Board of Foreign Missions, started with 36 pages in 1838 and grew to 128 pages by the eve of the Civil War. The Baptist mission proudly proclaimed that it used "2,500 reams of paper" and "produced 7,000,000 pages" for the reading public. Evangelical men and women eagerly read these magazines and closely followed missionary exploits in various fields around the world.[8]

Evangelical Protestants also attended lectures by returning missionaries and read missionary literature at ladies' clubs, Bible study groups, and Sunday school classes. During these talks speakers gave "shocking portraits of life outside the Protestant world," including "[v]ivid detail and horrible anecdote" that gave enthralled listeners "a sense of immediacy" about the pressing need to establish more mission stations. Weekly sermons at local churches often featured visiting missionaries. When Dakota missionary Gideon Pond returned to Connecticut in 1843, he attended a sermon in his old church. The minister "prayed for the heathen and for the Missionaries with feeling," he wrote in a letter to his brother, and after the sermon members of the congregation asked many questions about Pond's missionary work.[9]

Missionary memoirs, magazines, lectures, and sermons all disseminated the same themes to potential missionaries: missionary work was heroic, selfless, and one of the most worthwhile pursuits that a committed Christian could undertake. If problems ensued, missionaries simply needed to redouble their efforts. According to Mary Lyon, the founder of Mount Holyoke women's college, foreign missions were "our nation's great feature of the morally sublime." The governing board of the ABCFM described missionary labor in the same exalted terms. Missionary work was "one of the greatest, most benevolent, and most successful enterprises ever undertaken by man . . . We glory in . . . the approaching conversion of the world."[10]

Ideal Religious Beliefs

At the center of all the literature was the missionaries' faith. It depicted their religious beliefs as all consuming, inflexible, and strict, influencing every aspect of their lives. These exacting beliefs grew out of the religious fervor of the Second Great Awakening, a general Protestant revival movement which swept through antebellum America. Historians typically date its beginning to the late 1700s and early 1800s. During this time, scattered revivals, mainly in the form of camp meetings, took place on the frontier. For instance, in 1801 a large camp meeting held at Cane Ridge, Kentucky, drew approximately 23,000 worshippers and led to numerous conversions. After these initial revival meetings in the western areas of the United States, the movement gathered momentum, and by 1810 a general rekindling of interest in religion had occurred across the nation. Revivals continued in waves throughout the antebellum period. The Second Great Awakening included most Protestant denominations and became so successful that, according to historian Richard Carwardine, evangelical Protestantism became the principal subculture in antebellum America. As religious historian William McLoughlin states, during the antebellum period "[t]he story of American Evangelicalism is the story of America itself."[11]

The ABCFM missionaries belonged to the Presbyterian, Congregational, Dutch Reformed, or Associate Reformed church, all of which were deeply influenced by the Second Great Awakening. At first glance, it seems counterintuitive that the antebellum evangelicals affiliated with these churches would choose missionary work. Theologically these denominations were grounded in the sixteenth-century Calvinist doctrine of limited atonement, which held that Christ, by dying on the cross, had absolved a select few of their sins and ensured their salvation. This doctrine was directly related to the idea of predestination. Calvinists believed that God alone had chose those who would be saved, and humans did not have the power to influence their own salvation. Men and women responded to God's initiatives; they could not make their own move to God. Thus, missionary work and traditional Calvinist doctrine seemed antithetical. If men and women could do nothing to save themselves, what motivation would they have to join a church or turn from sin?[12]

As the fervor of the Second Great Awakening swept across the nation, however, many Presbyterian and Congregational theologians challenged the concept of predestination. Although followers of the Calvinist tradition stressed the sovereignty of God, they argued that humans could perfect themselves and the society around them. Increasingly, theologians contended that men and women, although deeply sinful, could accept God's grace if they truly believed in Jesus Christ. Ministers based their changing ideas on the belief that Christ had not died to save only a small number of the elect (limited atonement); rather, Christ had died to save all who accepted salvation (general atonement). According to this theology, known as New Divinity, men and women could choose, in a limited way, whether to accept God's offer of salvation. Thus these new theological interpretations inspired a need for missionaries who could help people repent their sins and give their lives to Christ.[13]

Although many Presbyterians and Congregationalists embraced these innovations, tensions arose between congregations that adhered to the new ideas and those that remained committed to the orthodox theology. In 1837 the debates became so acrimonious that the Presbyterian Church divided. The more conservative branch of the church remained committed to predestination and suggested that the new ideas bordered dangerously close to Catholicism—one of the worst charges that could be leveled against a Protestant at the time. The conservatives feared that soon the difference among Presbyterians, Methodists, and Catholics would be minimal. This division also affected missionary work. Adherents to old-school ideas formed their own missionary organization, known as the Board of Foreign Missions, to promote their version of Calvinist theology. Followers of what became known as the New Divinity allied themselves with the more liberal and interdenominational American Board of Commissioners for Foreign Missions (ABCFM). As religious historian David Kling summarizes it, the

ABCFM was "a New Divinity creation, rooted in New Divinity theology, inspired by New Divinity revivals, and staffed by a well-established New Divinity social and institutional network."[14]

Although the ABCFM missionaries mainly adhered to the revised theology, they continued to follow many of the ideas of their Calvinist ancestors. For example, ABCFM missionaries believed that God spoke through the scriptures and that the Bible alone had the authority to regulate their daily and religious lives. Because the scriptures contained everything a person needed to know to live his or her life, they believed that Christians should diligently read and study the Bible daily. To understand the "great truths which the Scriptures contain," Presbyterian and Congregational parents taught their children their letters at an early age so that they could read from the Bible. As one of their first goals, missionary men and women hoped to teach native peoples to read so that they could study the scriptures.[15]

The ABCFM missionaries also believed, like their Puritan forebears, that full membership in the church required a conversion experience. A conversion experience was "an internal transformation in which they feel the power of God's redeeming grace cleansing their souls." In other words, an outward profession of faith was not enough; "rather, the inner, palpable work of the Holy Spirit had to be confirmed." Although the responsibility of conversion ultimately rested with the individual, evangelical Protestants believed that true conversion experiences followed a series of discrete steps that required the assistance of a diligent minister. Once a person had mastered each step, church authorities judged the validity of the conversion experience. If the person was truly awakened, he or she was "born again" and became a full member of the church. If not, he or she needed to revisit the different steps. In sum, a typical conversion consisted of "conviction of sin, severe depression, joyful conversion, and subsequent assurance punctuated by periods of spiritual deadness."[16]

Newly awakened men and women could not rest on their laurels following their conversion experience, however. Converts needed to continue their religious education by reading the scriptures, saying prayers, attending weekly church services, and practicing evangelism. They also needed to live a just and holy life, which involved abiding by the Ten Commandments; refraining from sinful activities, such as card playing and drinking alcohol; keeping the Sabbath holy by not traveling or working; and showing their obedience to God. The ideal missionary was not supposed to deviate from these strict standards in any way, either personally or in their standards for native conversion. The missionaries were expected to apply these same strict rules to all native converts.

Finding the Ideal Missionary

The ABCFM made sure that each of its missionaries had a conversion experience and adhered to exacting standards of morality and piety before being granted an appointment. The Board upheld these demanding standards by having all potential missionaries submit application materials to a selection committee. Candidates sent evidence of their educational background, age, and marital status. Most important, applicants forwarded testimonials about their piety from local church officials or theological professors. In the selection process, the potential missionary's piety, faith, devotion, and formal theological schooling received precedence over any secular training, such as experience living on the frontier, constructing cabins, raising cattle, farming, or managing budgets. As corresponding secretary David Greene commented, the "values of true holiness of heart and life" were the most important factors.[17]

Because of the importance placed on spreading evangelical theology, the ABCFM, unlike its Baptist or Methodist counterparts, required its missionaries to have a formal theological education. They believed that a well-educated clergy would help people understand and follow the dictates of the Bible. Ministers would be required to explain Bible passages, highlight important readings, guide their congregation to consider details they might have missed, and guard against heresy. Moreover, educated ministers could influence their congregations to consider their relationship with God by presenting thought-provoking sermons. Because of the importance the Board placed on education, the male missionaries spent four years at college and three years at prominent Presbyterian or Congregational theological seminaries such as Andover, Lane, Western, and Union.[18]

Female missionaries were also highly educated for the time. Many of the women attended female seminaries, such as Mount Holyoke, Ipswich, Troy, and Hartford, which were dedicated to training young women to become teachers and missionaries. They offered women the equivalent of a college education, and many of their courses mirrored those of their male counterparts. For example, the curriculum during the girls' senior year at Ipswich

(Massachusetts) Female Seminary, run by Zilpah P. Grant and Mary Lyon, included algebra, ecclesiastical history, natural theology, philosophy of natural history, and religion.[19]

In addition to education and theological training, the selection committee gave preference to candidates who had not yet reached thirty years of age, arguing that younger missionaries were better suited to deal with the rigors of missionary life. Moreover, younger missionaries would learn the native languages more easily. According to an ABCFM treatise, as missionaries aged, their "organs [became] too rigid, and the power of ceaseless attention to sounds [became] difficult to acquire." In 1851, the average male missionary began his career at age twenty-seven, whereas female missionaries generally were in their early twenties.[20]

Finally, although the selection committee did not necessarily prefer a specific geographic region, the majority of ABCFM missionaries came from New England, New York, and the old Northwest, especially Ohio, Indiana, and Illinois. Only a handful came from southern states. Many factors contributed to this geographic disparity. First, the ABCFM was unabashedly a northern organization. It was headquartered in Boston, grew out of New England Congregationalism, and drew its members from revivals that influenced the northern sections of the country, especially western New York, which often has been called the "burned over district" due to the large number of revivals and religious fervor which swept across the region during the antebellum period. Second, and more important, the issue of slavery kept many southerners from joining the organization. Although the ABCFM became mired in the issue of Cherokee and Choctaw converts who owned slaves, the Board officially condemned the institution. An 1845 Board report called slavery a debased system that violated the natural rights of man and demanded "its entire and speedy removal." The Board's location and rhetoric, and the ardent support of abolition by many of the missionaries and executive board members, kept many pro-slavery southerners from accepting the ABCFM as a legitimate organization.[21]

On paper, the men and women affiliated with the Dakota mission fit the ABCFM's strict standards—they were educated, were young, hailed from northern states, and belonged to churches heavily influenced by the Second Great Awakening. They also strongly supported the numerous reform movements of the era which were closely associated with the religious revivals, especially the temperance and abolition movements. Most important,

Table 1. Summary of Missionary Demographics

Missionary	Religion	Education	Age Joined the Dakota Mission	State of Origin
Thomas Williamson	Presbyterian	Jefferson College/Yale/ Lane Seminary	35	Ohio
Stephen Riggs	Presbyterian	Jefferson College/Western Theological Seminary	25	Ohio
Mary Riggs	Presbyterian	Buckland Female School/ Ipswich Female Seminary	24	Massachusetts
Moses Adams	Presbyterian	Ripley College/Lane Theological Seminary	26	Ohio
Robert Hopkins	Presbyterian	Hillsborough/South Hanover College	27	Ohio
Gideon Pond	Congregational	—	24	Connecticut
Samuel Pond	Congregational	—	26	Connecticut
Jedediah Stevens	Congregational	Studied with Rev. Samuel Mills	35	New York
Lydia Huggins	Presbyterian	—	22	Ohio

they all had experienced conversion and were deeply committed to spreading Christianity around the globe.[22]

The Ideal Missionary Woman

Both men and women were required to submit to the Board evidence of their piety and devotion. Missionary memoirs and Board directives, however, explicitly stated that women were expected to play different—but still significant—roles in missionary work than their male counterparts. First and foremost, the ideal missionary woman served as a helpmeet to her husband. The ABCFM informed potential female candidates that "the chief role of missionary wives was to free their husbands from domestic concerns so they could concentrate on their work." Women would accomplish this goal by creating efficiently run homes on the frontier and raising pious children. Moreover, women's "inherent" traits of piety, serenity, and morality would help to counteract the more volatile male personality and keep their husbands focused on their work. Samuel Pond, a Dakota missionary, complained to Thomas Williamson that he had less time to spend on his missionary duties after marrying. Williamson consoled Pond by explaining that Pond's wife would actually help his missionary efforts, as a "more tranquill [sic] state of mind may enable you to do more in less time."[23]

Missionary women also were expected to keep their husbands from inappropriate relationships with native women. In a letter to ABCFM secretary Selah Treat, Stephen Riggs explained the benefits of marriage in missionary work on the frontier: "The men connected with the [fur] trade both as principals and clerks . . . have their squaws." Missionary wives would serve as "a safeguard against [this] temptation." The ABCFM also noted that missionary wives would keep their husbands from seeking "solace in a native woman" because the "perpetual cheerlessness" of the mission field would greatly "strengthen the natural desire for female companionship."[24]

In additional to protecting their husbands' morality, missionary women would help to convert native women and children by transferring the values of domesticity to the mission field. Through their own model, they would show native women how to run an orderly home and raise Christian children. ABCFM secretary Rufus Anderson described the ideal missionary woman as a "moving commentary on the Bible; everything she says or does should remind the hearer or beholder of something in the Bible; her whole life should be altogether a New Testament life." Missionary women also would teach school and run prayer meetings and Sunday schools for native women and children. By focusing their talents on women and children, missionary women allowed their husbands "to do more than he could do *alone*."[25]

Although women contributed to the success of each mission, they could not pursue a missionary appointment without the sponsorship of a man. For instance, the ABCFM refused applications from married women if they did not have a corresponding request from their husbands. Married women could encourage their husbands to apply but had little recourse if this avenue failed. By the 1830s, unmarried women worked as teachers and assistants at Indian missions, but they almost universally received their positions because of family ties to male missionaries. Moreover, single women always traveled under the sponsorship of a male missionary and lived with his family once they reached their destination. Even with the protection of a family member, antebellum missionary organizations rarely allowed single women to travel overseas to work in China or India (although this would become common by the latter decades of the nineteenth century), instead assigning them to missions closer to home.[26]

Following the general pattern of ABCFM appointments, the majority of women affiliated with the Dakota mission were the wives of the male missionaries or had close family ties. For example, Jane Williamson, who taught at mission stations in Minnesota for twenty-eight years, was the sister of Thomas Williamson. Another teacher, Sarah Poage, was the sister of Margaret Williamson. More often than not, the single women married soon after they arrived in the mission field. Fanny Huggins (the sister of Alexander Huggins) married Jonas Pettijohn, an ABCFM farmer, while Cordelia Eggleston, the younger sister of Julia Stevens, married Samuel Pond, the single man who had begun his mission the year before the arrival of the ABCFM in Minnesota. Widowers often remarried one of the single assistants. After the deaths of their wives, Joseph Hancock married Sarah Rankin, a teacher originally from Ohio, while Stephen Riggs married Anna Ackley, another instructor. The experience of women connected with the Dakota mission confirms that antebellum evangelical women had few opportunities for missionary work independent of a husband or family member.

Despite the ABCFM's restrictive policies, numerous women dreamed of becoming missionaries after reading memoirs of martyrs like Newell and Judson. Because marriage served as a gateway to missionary work, some actively sought to marry a man who had applied to the ABCFM. Historian Patricia Grimshaw, in her study of missionary women to Hawaii, opens her book with the story of two women—Lucy Goodale and Laura Fish—who agreed to marry strangers so they could work at the ABCFM's Sandwich Island mission. Grimshaw argues that the women's decision to marry was "the outcome of an independently acquired ambition for an unusual career as Christian teachers on a distant, non-Christian frontier." Women, like their male counterparts, desired to engage in mission service, and marriage allowed them to achieve this objective. In a biography of Narcissa Whitman, who worked with the ABCFM's Oregon mission, Julie Roy Jeffrey also argues that Whitman married a relative stranger to fulfill her dreams of becoming a missionary. Missionary women, according to historian Leonard Sweet, married to achieve their callings.[27]

Women associated with the Dakota mission also parlayed marriage into missionary work. Mary Ann Clark Longley, for instance, participated in an "arranged" marriage to Stephen Riggs. Longley had all the requisite background necessary for missionary work—an excellent education, experience as a teacher, a commitment to her church, and a desire to spread Christianity. As Mary Longley wrote her mother, "I am willing to be separated from you all, if I can thus do most either directly or indirectly to advance the cause of Jesus." Knowing of her interest in missionary work, Reverend Dyer Burgess wrote to Longley asking her if she would meet with Stephen Riggs, then an aspiring missionary about to finish his religious training. Longley agreed to the meeting, but things did not go well. Riggs did not impress her despite his obvious piety and enthusiasm. In a letter to her brother, Alfred, Longley described Riggs as "smaller than middle stature, plainer than mediocrity, even very homely if you please." More important, they did not make a romantic connection. "You know I despise the affectation of romance and desire to bring my views down to the sober reality," she told Alfred. "[Y]et I cannot think of forming such a sacred and unalterable connection without evidence of an interchange of affection, a congeniality of soul."[28]

After reading about her initial impression of Stephen Riggs, Longley's family must have been surprised when she announced her engagement to the aspiring missionary a few weeks later. She attempted to explain her

Stephen and Mary Ann
Clark Longley Riggs,
about 1860.

change of heart to her mother. Longley recounted that soon after the un-favorable interview she received a letter from Riggs. In the letter, which she forwarded to her mother, Riggs praised her commitment to missionary work but understood her reluctance to marry. Although he promised not to pressure her, he asked for an answer as soon as possible because he knew that she "love[d] the poor, the perishing heathen too much to cause any unnecessary delay." In his letter, Riggs linked Longley's desire to become a missionary with marriage. His appeal to her sense of religious duty was successful. Despite her misgivings, Longley agreed to follow the guidance of the "inclinations of Providence" and marry Riggs. She resolved to content herself with the fact that Riggs was a "kind and devoted Christian."[29]

Women like Mary Riggs sacrificed their romantic ideals to fulfill their dreams of missionary work, and they certainly wanted to play an integral role in the ultimate success of each mission. However, the Board also made clear that women's most important role was within the home. Could women perform independent and important work from the confines of their homes and in a challenging frontier setting? From the beginning, there was a strong likelihood of a disconnect between the promised ideal and the reality of mission work.

This issue has led to a debate among historians about the nature of mis-sionary work for women. Some historians argue that women fulfilled their dreams of independent missionary work and even translated their experi-ences into more freedoms once they were in the field. Joan Brumberg ar-gues that missionary work promoted "an identifiable, albeit truncated, form of religious feminism." Others historians, however, contend that women's dreams of independent missionary work were crushed by the daily reality of their domestic duties. The experience of women missionaries to the Dakotas contributes to this debate.[30]

A Stereotyped Vision of the Dakotas: "Heathenism" and "Savagery"

In addition to promoting an idealized version of missionary work to evan-gelical men and women, the antebellum evangelical press depicted Indian religion and culture in stereotyped ways. From colonial times forward, com-mentators characterized Indian religions as false and as worshipping Satan. Like other colonial, and then antebellum, commentators, the Dakota mis-sionaries uniformly described Dakota religion as "demon worship." Samuel

Pond called Dakota villages "strongholds of the prince of darkness," where "[f]or many ages Satan has reigned." Gideon Pond entitled his 1860 treatise on Dakota religion *Paganism, a Demon Worship.* The missionaries derided the Indians for worshipping "everything they see," instead of one god. Stephen Riggs explained that "if a man desires fair weather, he is quite as likely to present his obligations and prayers to a *tortoise* or a *stone* as to the *Great Spirit.*" Samuel Pond summarized the missionaries' view of Dakota religion: "Their religious beliefs," he wrote, "were a strange medley of silly whims and abominable falsehoods; and their superstitious practices were a compound of ludicrous follies and disgusting absurdities."[31]

Because Indian religion was termed "demon worship," the missionaries believed that they played an important role in helping to win the cosmic war between Christianity and heathenism. Indeed, the belief that the missionaries were fighting a war against heathenism was so pervasive that most of the missionary letters and sermons evoke images of war, soldiers, weapons, or battles. Samuel Miller, a Presbyterian clergyman and author, preached in an 1836 sermon that "[t]here is a great battle yet to be fought with these opposing powers. How violent and long continued the conflict may be, I presume not to calculate." Evangelical ministers like Miller called the missionaries soldiers who valiantly waged war against the powers of darkness. The missionaries used the scriptures, sermons, and prayer meetings as their weapons, for "God's truth has sharp arrows in it, and the Holy Spirit knows how to use them in piercing even" heathen hearts. In the end, the Lord's battle would be won with the help of God, who would use his power to "give effect to every well-directed stroke of the weapons of his appointment." When they arrived in Minnesota, the ABCFM missionaries worked to draft the Dakotas into their holy war, not only for the Indians' sake but also for the good of the world. This mission was not for the faint at heart. As Jedediah Stevens commented, a Christian missionary "should not be a 'novice' in the [c]hristian warfare." Rather, he needs to know "the enemies that he has to meet . . . [and] how to defend himself from their attack."[32]

Although battling heathenism took precedence, the Dakota missionaries ultimately hoped to change various Dakota cultural practices as well. According to Samuel Pond, the Dakotas "were as savages, while they still retained the customs of their ancestors." The missionaries criticized the Dakotas' gender roles, homes, living conditions, subsistence patterns, kinship relations, and child-rearing practices, which they viewed as "savage" and "uncivilized" and leading to character flaws. Throughout their early correspondence, the missionaries described the Dakotas using a host of negative terms that included lazy, warlike, intemperate, savage, polygamous, thieves, indifferent, and sottish. Mary Riggs wrote that the Dakotas' "indolence and filthiness are enough to make the heart sick, but their ignorance and degradation [are] enough to make it bleed." Stephen Riggs summarized his view of the Dakotas when he first arrived in Minnesota: "There are bad smells and bad sights and bad sounds. There are bad words and bad actions. There is gross sensuality as well as devilish wickedness."[33]

Although the missionaries harshly criticized the Dakotas' religion, cultural practices, and character, they firmly believed that with proper instruction and an acceptance of Christianity, the Indians could be fully integrated into American society. In this respect the missionaries' views of Indians ran counter to the growing scientific racism of the antebellum era. In the early nineteenth century, racist ideology was becoming increasingly common. Many antebellum politicians believed Indians were racially inferior. "By the 1820s," Theda Perdue writes, "white Americans increasingly saw individuals as fixed in their cultures, and cultural practices became a component of race—inborn traits that could not change." Thus Indian "savagery" did not stem from the environment, but from inherent physical and intellectual inferiority. Indians were a separate, and inferior, race. This ideology helped to justify Jackson's policy of Indian removal during the 1830s and beyond.[34]

Historians have argued, however, that antebellum missionaries resisted the rising tide of scientific racism in America. While a growing number of antebellum commentators came to see Indians as inherently inferior, the missionaries continued to see purported native failings as a product of the environment, not race. Thus if Indians accepted Christianity and its civilized ways, they could participate equally in the political and social life of the nation. According to historian Michael Coleman, "No matter how repulsive their heathen ways or how racially deficient other whites might judge them to be, to the missionaries Indians were human beings of full spiritual, intellectual, and social potential." David Kling agrees, stating that "evangelicals divided the world into heathen and Christian without regard to social status or geographic residence." Everyone had potential "spiritual equality."[35]

At the beginning of their enterprise, the Dakota missionaries' attitudes toward race support Coleman's and Kling's findings. In their early diaries and letters, the missionaries described the Dakotas as racially equal to

Euro-Americans, despite their harsh evaluations of Dakota culture and religion. Samuel Pond noted that "the complexion of the Dakotas is considerably darker than of the Europeans, but is not very dark. Their cheek bones are not particularly prominent... and many of them are good looking. Taken together the race cannot be characterized as a homely race." As Samuel Pond succinctly commented, the Dakota Indian had "all the elements of true manhood; let us not regard him as though he did not belong to the same race with ourselves... As a man, he is by nature equal to the white man." ABCFM missionary Joseph Hancock even informed the U.S. commissioner of Indian affairs that "in intellectual capacity I do not consider the North American Indian inferior to the Anglo-Saxon race."[36]

Although the Dakota missionaries rejected the growing scientific racism of the era when they first entered the mission field, it remains to be seen whether they retained these ideas after extensive interaction with the Dakotas. Few scholars have examined how people who had daily encounters with Native Americans dealt with the issue of race. Most of the current literature on race and Indians relies on observers who had little day-to-day contact with Native Americans. Gray Whaley, one of the few scholars who have written on this issue, argued that Methodist missionaries in Oregon increasingly came to define natives in terms of racialized thinking, which served as a principal rationale for abandoning their mission. Likewise, ABCFM missionaries in Africa "failed to live up to the egalitarian aspect of their theology and to the promise of Christian solidarity they preached." The following chapters examine how the Minnesota missionaries viewed race after close interaction with the Dakotas. Two questions are posed in that discussion. First, did the missionaries continue to accept Indians as potential racial equals after their extensive contact with "real" Indians? Second, if the missionaries' ideas about race remained stable, how did other Americans, many of whom accepted the new ideas of scientific racism, react to the missionaries' enterprise?[37]

The Founding of the Dakota Mission

Secure in their original belief that the Dakotas desperately needed to be Christianized, the first contingent of ABCFM missionaries left for Minnesota in 1835. The ABCFM delegation, however, were not the first Protestant missionaries to arrive in the region. In 1831, Samuel W. Pond and Gideon H.

Pond decided to devote themselves to missionary work. As evidence of their deep commitment to spreading the gospel, the Pond brothers began their work without the financial backing of a missionary society and with no formal theological training. Using their own funds and donations collected from their church, Samuel traveled west on a scouting expedition. Once he had chosen a mission field where "they might be useful," Samuel promised to send for Gideon. Following their plan, Samuel Pond left Connecticut in March 1833, traveling to Galena, Illinois, where he questioned the townsfolk about potential mission sites. After many conversations, Samuel wrote to Gideon, saying that they would proselytize to the Dakota in southern Minnesota. "Soon after my arrival here, on becoming acquainted with the condition of the surrounding Indians," Samuel wrote, "my interest was excited on behalf of the Sioux, a large nation west of the Mississippi, and on the Missouri and its branches."[38]

Upon Gideon Pond's arrival in Galena in April 1834, the brothers boarded a steamship to take them to Fort Snelling (in present-day St. Paul). Because the War Department forbade private citizens from living in Indian country without a permit, the Ponds worked out a compromise with Lawrence Taliaferro, the Dakotas' Indian agent from 1819 to 1840. In return for permission to reside in Indian country, Gideon and Samuel promised to teach the Dakota men gathered at Eatonville, near Lake Calhoun (in present-day Minneapolis), how to farm.[39]

At the same time the Pond brothers arrived in Minnesota, the ABCFM sent an expedition to assess the formation of mission stations west of the Mississippi River and north of the state of Missouri. Thomas Williamson, a physician and theological student at Lane Seminary in Ohio, led the group. In May 1834, Williamson traveled up the Mississippi River as far north as Fort Snelling. Along the way, he visited Dakota, Sac, and Fox villages and talked with other missionaries, Indian agents, military commanders, and representatives of the Indian nations. Upon his return, Williamson suggested that the ABCFM open a mission among the Dakota people of Minnesota. Although Williamson described the Dakotas as "extremely poor, ignorant, and wretched, and strongly disinclined to abandon their present course of life," his report also stressed the ability of the Dakotas to improve themselves under the ABCFM's tutelage. In defending his choice of the Dakotas, Williamson argued that they seemed "more inclined to receive teachers and missionaries among them [than the Sac and Fox], and more desirous

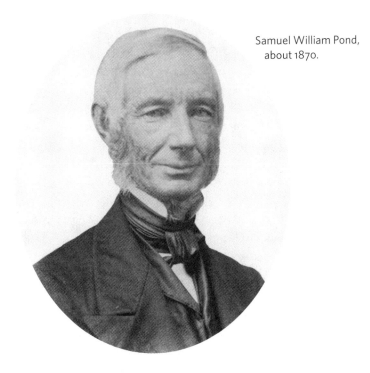

Samuel William Pond, about 1870.

to avail themselves of the advantages to be derived from the knowledge and arts of civilized life."[40]

The executive committee accepted Williamson's recommendation and approved a mission among the Dakotas. In 1835, the Williamson, Stevens, and Huggins families arrived in Minnesota and presented themselves to Taliaferro, just as the Ponds had done a year earlier. Unlike the Ponds, however, the three new mission families were assured of their acceptance because the ABCFM had secured permission from the War Department prior to their departure. After consulting with Agent Taliaferro, the Stevens family moved to establish their mission near Lake Harriet, in present-day Minneapolis, about seven miles northwest of Fort Snelling. A French-Dakota trader named Joseph Renville invited the ABCFM missionaries to establish a station in the Minnesota River Valley near Lac qui Parle, about 150 miles west of Fort Snelling. With Taliaferro's support, the Williamson and Huggins families agreed to locate their second station near Renville's trading village. Although the Pond brothers quickly joined the ABCFM stations, it would be years before they would be officially appointed as full missionaries, as they did not have formal theological training.[41]

From the two original stations, the ABCFM mission to the Dakota eventually expanded to include eleven different stations throughout southern Minnesota. Over the next twenty-eight years, the ABCFM established a semi-permanent station near Fort Snelling (1841–43) and more permanent stations at Traverse des Sioux (1843–53), St. Peter's (1844–47), Kaposia (1846–52), Prairieville (1847–53), Oak Grove (1843–53), Red Wing (1848–54), Yellow Medicine/Pajutazee (1852–62), and New Hope/Hazelwood (1854–62). The ABCFM appointed dozens of missionaries to aid in converting the Dakota people to Christianity. Some of the more prominent missionaries assigned to the Dakota nation included Stephen and Mary Riggs (who arrived in 1837), Robert and Agnes Hopkins (1843), Moses and Nancy Adams (1848), and John and Nancy Aiton (1848).

As these missionaries converged on Minnesota, they believed that all signs were favorable for the Dakotas' conversion. The men and women of the Dakota mission were committed to their cause, well educated, and supported by the most prominent missionary organization of the era. They had the government's blessing to build their stations in Minnesota. What the missionaries failed to take into account was that the Dakotas had not asked for missionary stations. The fact that the missionaries proceeded without Dakota approval was immaterial, as historian William McLoughlin pointed out. "No one asked whether the [Indians] needed or wanted Christianity. That seemed like asking whether a starving man needed food or a drowning woman a boat."[42]

This mindset allowed the missionaries to ignore the fact that they knew little or nothing about the Dakotas. From the local Indian agent, they learned that the Dakotas (also known as the Sioux and Santee Sioux) were divided into four bands—the Mdewakanton, Wahpekute, Wahpeton, and Sisseton. In the mid-1830s, according to the local Indian agent, the Mdewakantons were the largest band, with about 1,658 people residing in seven villages near present-day St. Paul. The Wahpekute were the smallest band, with 325 people; they resided along the upper Cannon River and west along the Blue Earth and Des Moines rivers. The Sissetons numbered 1,256 and the Wahpetons around 750; both lived farther west, along the Minnesota River and on the shores of Lake Traverse and Big Stone Lake.[43]

At the time, the missionaries did not know that the Dakota were part of a larger group known as Oceti Sakowin, or Seven Council Fires. In ad-

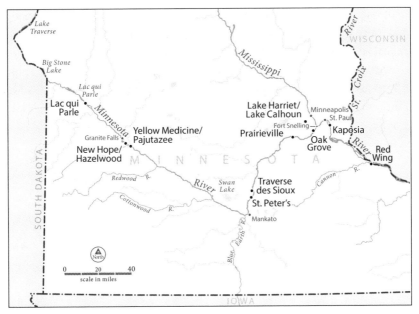

ABCFM missions to the Dakota in Minnesota.

dition to the four bands of the Dakota, the Oceti Sakowin consisted of the Ihanktown/Lower Yanktonai and Ihanktowana/Upper Yanktoni (also known as the Nakota) and the Tetonwan (Teton or Lakota). While the missionaries would later travel to meet with other bands of the Oceti Sakowin living west of Minnesota, they never established any permanent missions with these bands prior to 1862.[44]

In addition to knowing little about the Oceti Sakowin or its history, the missionaries also did not understand the Dakotas' religious or cultural patterns beyond general antebellum stereotypes and assumptions about Indians. Moreover, while they realized that they were not the first white men and women to interact with the Dakotas—explorers and fur traders had entered Minnesota long before the ABCFM built their first cabin on Lake Harriet—they did not take into account the long-term effects of interaction with French Catholic traders on the Dakotas.

In sum, the ABCFM missionaries had little practical knowledge of the Dakotas or how to begin life on the Minnesota frontier when the first contingent arrived in 1835. However, they had their faith and they believed that faith was enough (as Gideon Pond commented, the missionaries originally had "faith that [could] move mo[u]ntains"). Based on their reading of evangelical missionary literature and stereotyped information about Indians, the men and women of the Dakota mission arrived in Minnesota ready to vanquish heathenism among the Dakota. Their plan to win this "war," however, did not take into consideration the reality of life on the Minnesota frontier or the fact that the Dakotas were not passively waiting to be saved.[45]

CHAPTER 2

"We are not without heartfelt trials in this heathen land"

Conflicts within the Mission Community, 1835-39

In 1837, when Stephen and Mary Riggs left for what they called the "far West" to proselytize to the Dakota, they realized from their studies of evangelical literature that they would face privation and self-sacrifice. They admitted, however, that they had "very little appreciation of what its difficulties might be." As they traveled from Massachusetts to Minnesota by a combination of stagecoach, wagon, and steamship, Stephen Riggs slowly recognized some of the difficulties he would experience; indeed, he depicted their journey as a gradual movement from the "civilized" east to the "savage" west. When he arrived in Minnesota, he described a "wild and almost uninhabited region" with "nothing but Indians and military." He informed his relatives back home that he and Mary were "in the wilds of the West, beyond the cabins of the pioneer."[1]

Of course, Dakota people, as well as present-day historians, would take exception to Riggs's characterization of Minnesota as a wild and uninhabited place. By Riggs's standards, however, Minnesota stood outside the pale of Euro-American civilization. Statistically speaking, he was correct: very few settlers of European descent lived in Minnesota in the 1820s and 1830s. Indeed, the Euro-American population when Minnesota became a territory in 1849 was only 4,852, and the first sizeable number of immigrants would not arrive until the 1850s. Likewise, when the ABCFM first came to Minnesota, Minneapolis and St. Paul had not been established. Riggs and the other ABCFM missionaries encountered small communities of fur traders of both Dakota and European descent. They also interacted with military officers associated with Fort Snelling, which was constructed by the U.S. government in the early 1820s. As they talked with members of the Fort Snelling garrison and the Indian agent, the missionaries sought information about the location and size of Dakota villages to plan their stations. In order to reach as many Dakota villages as possible, the ABCFM missionaries decided that at least one of their stations needed to be located on the prairie, further removed from Fort Snelling.[2]

Because of the frontier setting, the missionaries quickly realized that a number of ABCFM policies did not translate to the field. The Board's selection process privileged piety, theological knowledge, and devotion to the mission cause. These attributes, however, did not help the missionaries build homes, clear land and plant crops, hunt and gather food, produce products they had once purchased back east, or survive in general on the Minnesota frontier. The missionaries asked the Board to hire "secular" laborers to allow them to focus on proselytizing; tensions arose when the Board denied their requests for financial reasons. The missionary literature failed to discuss how to live and survive on the frontier, especially without the full financial support of their governing board.

The missionaries also faced conflicts with members of the garrison at Fort Snelling, the Indian agent, and federal Indian policy in general. While the Dakota missionaries had not given much thought to surviving on the frontier, they were at least forewarned about potential problems with government officials based on the experiences of other ABCFM missions, especially those stationed with the Cherokees. When conflicts arose with federal Indian agents over the focus of their program, their use of the Dakota language, and other issues, the missionaries attempted to keep their complaints within the mission community. The missionaries' changing evaluation and use of the Dakota language further divided them from government officials and the antebellum public. As the missionaries struggled to learn Dakota, they began to question whether Dakota actually was an inferior language, as most antebellum commentators on language believed. Indeed, they slowly began to see Dakota as a difficult, complex language that even had the potential to become equal to English.

Missionary women faced unique conflicts on the Minnesota frontier, conflicts which differed from those of their husbands. Indeed, such unexpected stress led Mary Riggs to comment that while she "experience[d] many joys," she was "not without heartfelt trials in this heathen land." Riggs's sentiment sharply contrasted with her initial optimism, which led her to enter into a hastily arranged marriage so that she could help to convert the "poor Indians" in the "far [W]est."[3]

Finally, both male and female missionaries experienced conflicts with other members of the Dakota mission. For example, several missionaries became embroiled in disagreements with Jedediah Stevens, one of the first Dakota missionaries. The tensions escalated until all members of the mission community were drawn into the dispute. These internal conflicts challenged the image of missionaries as role models of "civilized" behavior. As such, the missionaries glossed over these disputes in their official correspondence, and the *Missionary Herald* omitted any references to discord among its Dakota missionaries. In sum, at many different levels the reality of mission life on the Minnesota frontier revolved around themes of conflict and deception which were noticeably absent from evangelical literature at the time.

Conflict with the ABCFM

Prior to joining the ABCFM, the missionaries did not give much thought as to how they would survive on the Minnesota frontier. Indeed, ABCFM orders explicitly stated that the missionaries should not concern themselves with material issues. Unfortunately, life on the Minnesota frontier did not mesh well with this directive. Because frontier settlements were not established during the early years of the Minnesota mission, the ABCFM missionaries could not rent homes or utilize existing churches. Their own prejudices also did not allow them to use Dakota structures or integrate with Dakota villages. Instead, mission ideology and policy dictated that the missionaries needed to construct their own "civilized" enclaves—modeled on New England farming villages—to contrast with the "uncivilized" Dakota communities. To follow this order, the missionaries constructed their mission settlements from scratch, including homes, churches, schools, and rudimentary shelters and fences for their cattle. They also cleared land for crops.

Most male missionaries, however, had little or no knowledge of farming or constructing homes. Because of their lack of skills, the missionaries took an inordinate amount of time to build cramped and utilitarian homes; many of the structures also served multiple purposes. For example, at the Lake Harriet mission station near Fort Snelling, Jedediah Stevens built two log structures; one housed his family, while the other served as a school and church. At Lac qui Parle, Joseph Renville, a French-Dakota trader, initially lent the Williamson family a temporary shelter. Williamson, however, quickly built a "log house a story and a half high." When Stephen and Mary Riggs arrived, the two families shared this small structure for five years. The log house originally served as the school and church as well. Mary Riggs referred to her living quarters at Lac qui Parle as her "little chamber"; three of her children were born in this room, further straining the small space. Private homes for each mission family and a separate church would not be built until years later.[4]

While the men struggled to construct homes and churches, the women lacked skills to make clothing or find food on the frontier. For instance, it took Cordelia Pond an inordinate time to make "pantaloons and vests" from the cloth sent to her by relatives because she had never done this before. Likewise, while Mary Riggs succeeded in making her first "pair of pantaloons" and a dress, it "required much . . . time." After one year in the mission field, Mary Riggs informed her brothers, who were considering missionary work, to learn more practical skills—including how to make glass-powder and how to cure beef and pork—before applying to the ABCFM.[5]

The missionaries universally complained that these unfamiliar and time-consuming chores interfered with preaching and studying Dakota. They pleaded with the Board to hire workers so that they could focus on teaching and converting the Dakotas. In an 1837 letter to the ABCFM, Jedediah Stevens asked the Board to send him a farmer "who will . . . attend to the secular concerns of the Mission." Despite the missionaries' requests, the ABCFM did not authorize additional laborers, especially during the mission's early years. This issue was a major source of contention and disillusionment because the missionaries expected the Board to fully support their work.[6]

Despite making frequent requests for funds and laborers, the missionaries kept the extent of their frustration from the Board. Private letters, however, harshly criticized the Board's lack of support for the Dakota mission. In a letter to his uncle, Gideon Pond wrote that he "was often led to wonder why it is that while the Christians of the U.S. are praying for the conversion of the heathen, the ABCFM must hold so many men waiting so long who are ready to . . . go on this errand of mercy for want of funds." He called this an "embarrassment." The evangelical press encouraged missionaries to devote their lives to "converting the heathen," but the ABCFM did not provide the funds to support those who were willing to proselytize.[7]

The Board had legitimate reasons for withholding financial support. In 1837, a severe financial panic swept the nation, drying up the Board's funds. As a result of the Panic of 1837, Secretary Greene asked the missionaries to economize. He warned that the ABCFM's "treasury is deeply in debt, and the receipts fall short from month to month." This meant that the missionaries needed to "curtail and reduce their expenses." In monetary terms, economizing meant that the Dakota mission could only spend $1,000 for the entire year of 1837 (Williamson received $550 for Lac qui Parle, and Stevens $450 for Lake Harriet).[8]

Financial problems also curtailed the expansion of the Dakota mission. The Board members were not able to open new stations and did not appoint new missionaries, except for Stephen and Mary Riggs, who left for Minnesota before the ban was instituted. Because of the finite number of missionaries—which included the Pond brothers, the Williamson, Riggs, Huggins, and Stevens families, and two female assistant teachers—only a small number of Mdewakanton and Wahpeton Dakotas interacted with the missionaries during their first five years in Minnesota. Thus, while the missionaries attempted to center their lives around the Dakotas, the reverse was not true. According to Thomas Williamson, "very few of the Indians beyond this station [Lac qui Parle] . . . have even had any opportunity of hearing the gospel."[9]

Even if the financial crisis had not occurred, Board policy still exhorted its missionaries to practice a "cheerful . . . Christian self-denial." According to Board directives, missionaries were expected to create simple, ideal communities that would serve as models for the Indians. Every resource was to be directed at converting Indians and creating a self-sustaining native clergy. What the Board did not realize was that creating a simple religious community on the frontier was an expensive project. Even though they were living as frugally as possible, most Dakota missionaries could not survive on the Board's funds and had to supplement their incomes. Some missionaries accepted government farming positions, while others requested supplies and clothing from family members or their congregations back east. Missionary women also planted gardens or made essential items themselves, even though they initially lacked the requisite skills.[10]

Many of the missionaries had joined the ABCFM because it was one of the best-known and -funded organizations of the antebellum era. The missionaries expressed disappointment over the inadequate funds and privately complained that the lack of support hindered their efforts. While there were many other reasons for the small number of converts (as discussed in subsequent chapters), the lack of funds certainly did not help their efforts. As Thomas Williamson lamented, "I have no evidence to the present hour that I have been instrumental in the conversion of a single soul." Although

Williamson blamed himself, other missionaries (quietly) placed some blame on the ABCFM's lack of financial support.[11]

Conflict with the U.S. Government

The missionaries also disagreed with the U.S. government over various issues during the early years of the mission. Most of the missionaries' criticism of the government, however, was not publicized out of concern that any complaints could jeopardize the entire missionary project. As ABCFM corresponding secretary David Greene warned, "a bird of the air may carry your remarks to [government officials] and you may soon feel the consequences of your impudence . . . By all means keep clear of any quarrel or any disagreement with the officers or agents."[12]

Although even quiet criticism of the federal government was risky, the missionaries frequently complained to the Board, and each other, about various aspects of federal Indian policy. One of the first disputes arose over differing philosophies of conversion. Federal Indian policy officially stated that civilization—including practicing farming, speaking English, attaining literacy, and living a settled existence—should come first, after which an acceptance of Christianity would naturally follow. Accordingly, federal Indian agents hired men to teach Indians to plow, purchased looms so women could learn to weave, and built permanent homes so Indians would give up their seasonal rounds.

The ABCFM inverted the government's order: they believed that Christianity must supersede civilization. Once a person or group had accepted Christianity, civilization would follow. As Thomas Williamson stated, "The object of missions to heathen such as the Dakotas is first to make them a [c]hristian and secon[d]ly a civilized people. The full benefits of civilization have never been enjoyed by any people without the gospel." The missionaries' focus on Christianization, however, created problems with government agents. Indian agent Lawrence Taliaferro complained that he needed to constantly remind the missionaries about their role in the Dakota communities. "I have endeavored to impress all missionaries . . . that Christianity must be preceded by civilization among the wild tribes." Taliaferro criticized the Pond brothers for failing to follow the government's agenda, calling their actions "the height of extravagance, and folly."[13]

Criticism went both ways on the Minnesota frontier. The missionaries privately accused the federal agents of intemperance, laziness, and, most important, unchristian behavior, and did not consider them proper role models for the Indians. Stephen Riggs complained to the Board about the character of Indian agent Lawrence Taliaferro, calling him "neither a man of talents nor of moral honesty. He is not respected by the Indians, nor can he be."[14]

The soldiers stationed at Fort Snelling received more disdain than the Indian agent. The missionaries described the soldiers as drunkards, lazy, gamblers, and poor models for the "impressionable" Indians. Some of the soldiers even held slaves, which challenged the missionaries' strong abolitionist beliefs. When Jedediah Stevens hired a soldier to help at his station, he worried that the man's "example before our children and the Indians is not such as is desirable." Similarly, Williamson warned that the laziness of the soldiers increased "the aversion to labour which is natural to savages." Mary Riggs called the military "a sink of iniquity, a school of vice." As such, she vowed to avoid the men of the garrison and refused to invite them into her home.[15]

Even if the missionaries did not agree with federal policies and criticized the character of federal agents and soldiers, the ABCFM warned them to keep their opinions to themselves. If they angered the Indian agent or the commander of Fort Snelling, they risked losing their permit to reside in Indian country. Thomas Williamson, for one, was reminded that his residency in Minnesota depended on the good will of the local Indian agent. In 1835, Taliaferro asked him to "watch over the Indians and traders and give him information of any thing it might concern the government to know." Williamson's compliance was clearly not voluntary. In the same letter, Taliaferro warned Williamson that "in consequence of recent orders . . . it will be necessary for [the missionaries] to have more express permission and authority from the government of the U.S. to reside here," even though the ABCFM had already obtained a permit from the War Department. Although Taliaferro did not specifically link compliance with the missionaries' permission to reside in the area, Williamson could not help but see the implied threat. Whether they liked it or not, the missionaries served as government auxiliaries and even as informants in Indian country.[16]

Taliaferro and subsequent Dakota agents also kept the missionaries in check through disbursals of federal money. The so-called Civilization Fund, created by Congress in 1819, originally appropriated $10,000 annually to various benevolent organizations to instruct Indians "in the mode of agriculture suited to their situation; and for teaching their children in reading, writing, and arithmetic." Over time, Congress increased the amount of the annual appropriations and expanded the number of organizations receiving funds. Although the ABCFM continued to provide the majority of the yearly budget, the Dakota mission benefited from the Civilization Fund. In 1834, the government set aside $2,200 from the fund for the Dakotas. Likewise, in 1839, the Dakota mission received $1,000 from the "now ample civilization fund," and in 1840, the Lac qui Parle mission secured $300. For a perpetually underfunded mission, these payments provided an economic incentive to support government requests and programs.[17]

The ABCFM missionaries also benefited financially from government farming positions. In return for an annual salary, the Indian agent hired missionaries to teach Dakota men to farm using government-issued plows, seeds, and other supplies. In 1839, Taliaferro offered Samuel Pond $500 per year to fill the position of government farmer. Members of the Board in Boston initially were reluctant to allow Pond to accept the government position. They worried that farming chores would interfere with his more important work of proselytizing. However, the Board eventually approved Pond's appointment. Financial considerations assuredly influenced their decision. With the $500 stipend, Pond could cover all of his family's expenses, and most of his brother's, without additional assistance from the ABCFM.[18]

Because government agents issued permits for residence in Indian territory, disbursed Civilization Fund monies, and controlled lucrative farming positions, the missionaries needed to cultivate a positive relationship with government officials. Before he left for Minnesota, Stephen Riggs received a letter from Secretary Greene defining his obligations to the federal Indian agents. Greene warned that government officials could "do more or less to favor or hinder your work; and nearly every one of them you may make your friend or opposer, according as you treat them respectfully and courteously, or the reverse." Riggs would undoubtedly find the government officials, agents, and soldiers "profane, Sabbath breakers, or addicted to vicious courses," Greene continued, but he needed to overlook their faults because "this class of persons have [sic] great influence" over the Indians. Similarly, Greene issued a warning to Jedediah Stevens when he seemed to be on the verge of angering the local Indian agent over his repeated requests for funding and aid. "I regard it as of great importance that we should by a course of kind, respectful, and courteous proceeding," Greene admonished, "make the agents of Government and all public officers our friends " If Stevens did not temper his requests, Greene warned, he might "awaken a prejudice against yourself and your cause which would be very injurious."[19]

Working closely with the government, however, frequently impeded the missionaries' relations with the Dakotas. If the Dakotas did not like government policy, the missionaries received the brunt of their anger. This would become abundantly clear over the next three decades when the federal government negotiated a series of unpopular and, in some cases, fraudulent treaties with all four bands of Dakotas. Even if the missionaries disagreed with federal policy, they rarely aired their misgivings in a public forum. Thus, the Dakotas did not distinguish between government officials and the missionaries. Conversely, the government officials were never completely happy with the missionaries' goals and practices.

On one hand, the Dakota missionaries publicly supported federal Indian policy and directives. They agreed with the Indian agent that the Dakotas needed to be changed and accepted federal funds and appointments to achieve this goal. On the other hand, the missionaries privately questioned the morality and piety of government agents and soldiers. They also fundamentally disagreed with the government's focus on civilization over Christianization. Dakotas, however, did not see these fine distinctions; they only saw the missionaries' public support of U.S. Indian policy—and the desire of both parties to change their religion and culture.

Conflicts over the Dakota Language

The missionaries' use and changing evaluation of the Dakota language further divided them from government officials and, increasingly, the majority of the antebellum public. When they first arrived in Minnesota, the missionaries believed that all Dakotas should learn to speak and read English. Indeed, they followed the general thinking of the era, which described all Indian languages as inferior. Although converts should learn to speak English, Board missionaries were instructed to learn the native language, as it would allow them to begin proselytizing more quickly. Preaching would be expedited because missionaries supposedly could learn Dakota (an inferior, infantile language) faster than Dakotas could learn English (a superior and more difficult language). Samuel Pond summarized the importance of learning Dakota to the success of their mission: "We were convinced from the first that our influence over the Indians would depend . . . on the correctness and facility with which we spoke their language, we wished to speak like Dakotas and not like foreigners."[20]

As the Dakota missionaries worked to fulfill the Board's directive, however, it quickly became apparent that learning Dakota would not be the simple process described in the evangelical press. The missionaries were not linguists, were not trained in transcribing and learning a language; most did not even speak a second language. Likewise, few Dakota men or women spoke English. Some of the traders spoke French and Dakota, but the missionaries did not speak French. Despite these problems, the missionaries found ways to fulfill the Board's order to learn Dakota. Thomas Williamson, for example, first began to study French. After learning enough of the language, he laboriously translated a chapter of the Bible into French. Williamson then read the French passage, sentence by sentence, to Joseph Renville, a French-Dakota trader, who gave the Dakota translation. Gideon Pond wrote down Renville's translations of the passages.[21]

In addition to the long chain of translation, the missionaries struggled to develop a system for writing Dakota, which had never been a written language. The missionaries used the "Pond alphabet," developed by Samuel and Gideon Pond, during their first year with the Dakotas. The Pond brothers found that all of the vowels in the Dakota language, and most of the consonant sounds, corresponded to the Roman alphabet, so they attempted to transcribe Dakota using the same letters as English. However, the Ponds noted that Dakota had several sounds that were unknown in English and did not correspond to any letter. Because Dakota did not use the letters *c*, *q*, *x*, *g*, and *r*, these were assigned to the unique Dakota sounds. This system was relatively simple and had the added benefit of not needing any new type for printing presses when the missionaries published their translations.[22]

While the system of notation was relatively simple, translation problems continually plagued the missionaries. For one thing, they faced the daunting issue of translating Christian terms into Dakota, which usually had no corresponding words or concepts. As historian Monica Siems writes, "What could 'God,' or a host of other Christian theological terms, mean in the language of a culture that had no corresponding referents?" In his book *Sacred Language,* anthropologist William Powers discussed the problems Catholic and Episcopal missionaries had in translating just one phrase, "Lamb of God, you take away the sins of the world, have mercy on us" into Lakota. After translation, the sentence became something like "Wakantanka's little

In 1839 Riggs wrote to Samuel Pond, who was then at Lake Harriet, encouraging the Ponds to do more translations of biblical texts: "I wish to do something at this but find I have a great deal to learn of the language yet."

mountain sheep suddenly puts badness in another place, pity us." The translation is ungrammatical and awkward, but more important, it lacks any reference to meaningful Lakota cultural experiences. At that time, their society did not have lambs, God was not singular, and sin did not exist. The ABCFM missionaries encountered the same difficulties translating "lamb of God" into Dakota. As Stephen Riggs wrote, "'The *lamb* of God,' an expression perfectly at home in our ears, is exceedingly strange to a Sioux."[23]

In addition to their problems with Christian terminology, the missionaries found that other translation issues hampered their ability to communicate with the Dakota. Joseph Nicollet, a French explorer who visited Lac qui Parle, reported that the missionaries originally had decided not to translate the name Moses because the Dakotas could readily pronounce the name. Unfortunately, as they discovered when they delivered their sermons, *Moze* or *Monze* in Dakota, although it sounded like Moses, meant "my rear end." After realizing their mistake, they quickly translated Moses as "Mowis," a word they said had "special meaning to the savages." Another time, Mary Riggs reported that she once angered her students by calling them "her lambs." Instead of taking this as a term of endearment, the students were deeply offended and told the rest of the village that Riggs had called them "the children of sheep." Stephen Riggs also was embarrassed when he thought the Dakota word for fish was *pish*. It turned out that a Dakota boy had just been trying to say the English word. In addition to problems with Dakota syntax and vocabulary, the missionaries had difficulty reproducing many of the Dakota sounds. Mary Riggs admitted that her Dakota students laughed at her due to her mispronunciations.[24]

Although the translation process was laborious, problematic, and inexact, the missionaries produced an astounding number of translations over the years. From 1836 until 1860, the missionaries collectively translated and published a dictionary containing over 15,000 words, classroom materials for children, the entire Bible and other religious texts, and hundreds of hymns. Some of these works included the *Dakota Spelling Book* (1836), *The Dakota First Reading Book* (1839), the third chapters of Proverbs and Daniel (1839), *The Second Dakota Reading Book: Consisting of Stories from the Old Testament* (1842), *Wowapi Mitawa* (1842), the Acts of the Apostles and the Epistles of Paul with the Revelation (1843), *Grammar and Dictionary of the Dakota Language* (1852), *The Pilgrim's Progress* (1858), and *Dakota Odowan* (comprising 113 hymns).[25]

This body of translated work shows how much effort the missionaries put into translation. Their letters reflect an obsessive desire to learn Dakota and produce accurate translations, a pursuit that consumed most of their waking hours. Williamson calculated that he spent more than half his time learning the language. He spent at least half of every day studying Dakota and full days in the winter. Likewise, Samuel Pond commented that he "spen[t] most of my time studying Sioux." Missionary letters to each other (especially from Stephen Riggs) were filled with technical translation questions.[26]

Indeed, the male missionaries' study of Dakota became so consuming that at times they ignored both the Dakotas and their own families to work on translations. One morning, Samuel Pond was looking forward to reading the Bible and working on his translations when he was interrupted by some Dakotas who wanted to borrow items, asked for help splitting logs, and invited him to join their ball game. Pond passed up these opportunities to interact with the Dakotas, however, in favor of working on his translations. Another time, Mary Riggs described how she left her infant son with her husband when she went to visit the nearby Dakota village. When she returned home hours later, she was surprised to find her son in the same position and her husband hunched over his translations, from which he seemed not to have moved. Riggs's desire to learn the language was, according to his wife, "indefatigable."[27]

As the missionaries devoted more and more time to studying Dakota, cracks began to appear in their blanket condemnation of the language as simple and primitive. The Board—and the public at large—continued to view Dakota as a deficient language. The Minnesota missionaries, on the other hand, contrary to their own Board, government officials, and the larger antebellum public, increasingly found Dakota to be a complex language. According to Samuel Pond, "[i]t has often been represented by persons having but a superficial knowledge of Indian languages that they are imperfect and defective, and can be made to express but a very limited range of ideas." He noted that this might be true for other Indian languages, but "it is certainly not true of the Dakota." Likewise, Stephen Riggs, Mary Riggs, and Thomas Williamson all stated that they found the Dakota language "uncommonly difficult to learn."[28]

More important, as the missionaries struggled to learn Dakota, they began to question whether it was inherently inferior to English. As Thomas Williamson commented, "How far the language of the Dakotas is defective

xa xe xi xo xu
ya ye yi yo yu
za ze zi zo zu

,ca ,ce ,ci ,co ,cu

,pa ,pe ,pi ,po ,pu
,ta ,te ,ti ,to ,tu

---

an en in on un
ix om

Tipi.   Xunka.

can	den	hda
cen	dus	hde
cin	gan	hdo
con	gin	hdu
cun	han	hen
dan	hba	hin

Xina watopekiyapi.

Wakpa mini xbe.	Can hanska wan
Nina tateyanpa.	bosdan ehdepi.
Taja rinca.	Miniruha ska
Wata kin dus ya.	watopekiyapi.
Wata kin sam-	Haronta suksuta
yapi tuka tete kin	on iyakaxkapi.
ska.	

Wata caje kin he wiyokihedan ekta un.
"Swan" eciyapi. Maga'tanka he kapi.
Wicaxta xakpe wata kin en opapi.
Tipi ska wandake cin he ohna tipi.
Watokapa tanhan yanke cin he hokxiyoqopa.
Ecadan iye tipi ekta kipi kta.

JESUS.

Wanyagpica xni yaun qon,
   Waonxida on yahi,
Wicacerpi iyacu qa,
   Wicaxta hecen yaun ;

Marpiya kin en yaki qa,
   Wowitan hduha yaun :
Marpiya kin owancaya,
   Nitowaxte yuhapi.

Pages from *Dakota Tawoonspe, Wowapi I* (Dakota Lessons, Book I, 1850),
Dakota Odowan (Dakota Hymns, 1879), and a catechism, 1882.

DAKOTA ODOWAN.

ODOWAN 1.

1. Owihanke Wanica
Itonmayape cin,
Mioran kin tonakiya
Iwanmayaka wo,
Nitawakonze kin
Ionximada wo.

2. Nitowaxte wakan wan
Duhe cin he wacin;
Yati waxte nanke cin,
Cantowakpani ce.
Nitawiyokiye kin,
Tanyan wanyag mayan wo.

3. Canku wan owotanna,
Yaonpe cin ohna,
Misiha kin opeya,
2

DAKOTA
WIWICAWANGAPI KIN.

DAKOTA CATECHISM.

BY S. R. RIGGS, A. M.
MISSIONARY OF A. B. C. F. M.

AMERICAN TRACT SOCIETY,
150 NASSAU AND 13 FR. ST. NEW YORK.

I am not prepared to say. I am inclined to believe that it is less so than interpreters would have us to suppose." Stephen Riggs concurred, stating that the Dakota language was "full and rich in some respects . . . the Dakota verb is quite complex, and capable of expressing shades of meaning and forms of action in much greater variety than the English verb." Riggs was even "humiliated" to find that "The Dakotas [were] better acquainted with the names and habits of these inhabitants of the waters, air, and earth, than we are."[29]

The missionaries also noted that the Dakota language possessed "great flexibility" and was "capable of vast improvement." Because of its flexibility, they speculated, perhaps, over time, Dakota could even become a civilized language. Although the missionaries believed that Dakota was *initially* inferior to English, their work in the field led them to consider that it was not an inherent deficiency. Indeed, they believed that the Dakota language was "inferior" because the Dakotas initially had an "inferior" culture and religion, echoing earlier Enlightenment ideas about race and language. As Thomas Williamson commented, the Dakota language was "as complete as their present mode of life require[d]." Their "knowledge of words cannot be more extensive than [their] knowledge of things." Thus, because they did not have "civilized" concepts like a king, courts of justice, or domesticated animals, they obviously did not have corresponding words. Likewise, Dakota was currently "barren of words to convey religious instruction" because they had not been exposed to evangelical Christianity.[30]

As Dakotas became familiar with civilization and Christianity, words would be added to their language to express this new knowledge. Riggs commented, "New words will be coined to meet the mind's wants; and new forms of expression, which at the first are bungling descriptions only, will be pared down and tucked up so as to come into harmony with the living language." Likewise, Samuel Pond stated that "[i]n its present state, [Dakota] could not be used as the language of a civilized people, for it would require many additions before it could represent all the ideas that are readily expressed in any of the languages of Europe; but it is probably as susceptible to improvement" as any language "spoken by savages." Stephen Riggs summarized the process by which Dakota could become a "civilized" language: As "men become purified and elevated in heart and life, the impurity disappears from their conversation. Thus are the barbarous languages of the world brought up into the Christian household."[31]

In the early years, the Dakota missionaries were not willing to state that

Dakota was a language of civilization, only that it had the *potential* to become equal to English, just as the Dakotas in general had the potential to adopt civilized ways and Christianity. As the missionaries learned Dakota and experienced its complexity, it became part of their mission, as Stephen Riggs commented, "[t]o put God's thought into their speech." Even tentative comments about the complexity and potential equality of the Dakota language, however, put missionaries at odds with government officials and the public at large, who increasingly believed that Indians and Indian languages could never be civilized.[32]

Conflicts for Missionary Women

Like their male counterparts, missionary women eagerly began to learn Dakota. From her post at Lac qui Parle, Mary Riggs reported that she spent her days writing and studying translations and "listening to the Dakota which I cannot understand." The missionary women and the female teaching assistants, such as Jane Williamson, studied Dakota so they could teach Dakota women and children in their own language. As their devotion to learning the Dakota language illustrates, the women wanted to play an integral role in converting the Dakotas. They threw themselves into missionary work from the time they arrived in Minnesota.[33]

In addition to learning the language, missionary women taught domestic tasks to Dakota women and children. Soon after her arrival in Minnesota, Mary Riggs showed some Dakota girls and women how to sew, even though Dakota women always had made garments, footwear, and shelter for their families. The irony was lost on Riggs that the Dakota women she taught were probably more experienced seamstresses than she. Despite their relative inexperience, Riggs and the other missionary women also taught spinning, weaving, and knitting and held cooking demonstrations. Missionary women also attempted to convert Dakota women and children to Christianity by holding prayer meetings and Bible study groups. They modeled Christian behavior by not working or traveling on the Sabbath and refraining from alcohol. In all cases, the women's interaction with the Dakota women was intended to "enlighten their untutored minds and lead them into all truths."[34]

Missionary women also taught in the schools at each station. They instructed the children in reading, writing, and mathematics and concluded the lessons with singing. While many of the women wanted to teach full time, most were only able to teach part of the day, generally in the morning. After dismissing their Dakota students, the women spent their time performing chores in their homes, although many times they asked the female students to stay to watch or help them work. Because of the overwhelming nature of their many duties, the women frequently shared the labor in the classroom if several families lived at one station.[35]

Some of the more adventurous women traveled to visit Dakota villages. Fanny Huggins proudly informed Cordelia Pond that she had crossed the river to teach in a Dakota village. Likewise, Mary Riggs walked to a nearby village and visited with one of the chief's daughters. The missionary women occasionally provided medicine to the Dakota women and children. Once a Dakota woman with a sick child visited Mary Riggs and asked for medicine. Riggs gave the child a dose of rhubarb (the same treatment she had given her own sick son), and the child improved. After her initial success, Riggs continued to be "asked very frequently for medicine . . . though I have confined myself to castor oil and rhubarb, I believe they have been quite efficacious."[36]

Each of the missionary women also "adopted" Dakota children into their families with the idea that immersion into civilized Christian families would speed their conversion (the same philosophy—albeit on a much larger scale—informed the late-nineteenth-century federal boarding school system). In all, approximately fifty Dakota children boarded with the mission families; at any given time, each family had at least one and sometimes as many as six native children living with them. Mary Huggins Kerlinger, daughter of Alexander and Fanny Huggins, recalled that fourteen Dakotas resided with her family at various times during her childhood. Some remained only a few months, while others stayed for years.[37]

Because most of the boarders were young girls (only nine of the fifty boarders were males), missionary women performed most of the labor related to the boarders' care and education. When the children first arrived, the missionary women bathed them (the women wrote that they were "dirty" and filled with "vermin"), cut their hair, and dressed them in donated clothing. Once the boarders were "remade," the missionary women quickly integrated them into the daily rhythm of the mission. In the morning, the women taught the boarders at the mission school. After school, the boarders returned to the missionaries' living quarters, where they performed domestic chores—including washing, cleaning, sewing, and cooking—alongside the missionary women. The boarders received more religious instruction than the day students and attended more prayer meetings and Sunday services. Nancy McClure, who boarded with three different mission families over the years, described her days at the mission. "At these missions we girls were given religious instruction and taught reading, writing, and something of the other lower branches, and how to sew, knit, and, as we grew older, to spin, weave, cook, and do all kinds of housework. We were first taught in Indian, then in English."[38]

The myriad of activities performed by the women seems to indicate that Mary Riggs, Fanny Huggins, Cordelia Pond, Sarah Pond, and others associated with the Dakota mission had achieved their goal of independent missionary work. Certainly, the women's early letters show that they made important contributions to the mission community. Despite the evidence of the women's extensive missionary work—at least in the early years—the women themselves filled their letters with remorse about the lack of time they devoted to the Dakotas.

All of the women complained that their heavy domestic chores drastically curtailed their ability to proselytize. Mary Riggs wrote her mother that "I sometimes feel that I am doing nothing and can do but little for their benefit. The various little domestic duties, which seem to claim attention, take up more time than I anticipated, or at least than I hoped would be the case." Cooking, cleaning, washing clothes, making butter, and sewing kept women like Riggs from focusing their full attention on studying the language, traveling to Dakota villages, and holding prayer meetings. As Mary Riggs summarized to her mother, it was a "woman's lot" to "take charge of domestic affairs—to do a thousand things that require time and patience." As Jedediah Stevens commented, these domestic chores "wor[e] down [the women] with ha[r]d Labour."[39]

Missionary women like Mary Riggs and Cordelia Pond were disillusioned by the limited time available to devote to proselytizing. More fundamentally, however, the missionary women's experience living on the frontier challenged the essence of missionary ideology: missionaries were supposed to teach and the natives were supposed to learn. In the case of the Dakota mission, the instructor-student relationship was sometimes inverted, and the Dakota women became the missionary women's teachers and helpers. This especially occurred during the early years of the mission, when the missionary families lived far from other white communities. To fill the void left by the absence of a strong community support system, Dakotas frequently stepped in to take care of the missionary women and their families. By and large the missionary men did not experience this inverted relationship, as they did not prepare food, give birth, and nurse the sick.

When the missionaries arrived in Minnesota, they knew little about sustaining life on the frontier. Trained to be preachers, not hunters or farmers, the missionaries lacked the knowledge needed to survive in isolated areas. Mary Riggs wrote to her brother, "We do not often have a fresh morsel, for Mr. Riggs has neither the time or the skill requisite." Although Mary Riggs planted vegetable gardens, learned to process indigenous plants from her Dakota neighbors, and received periodic shipments of supplies from the Board, her family's diet often lacked meat and other staples. Furthermore, the supplies provided by the Board often arrived late and were frequently spoiled. Agnes Pond reported, "Our flour was sent to us from way down the Mississippi. When we got it, it had been wet and was so mouldy [sic] that we had to chop it with an ax." Without help from the Dakotas, the missionaries' diet was bland and unsatisfying; typically, they ate potatoes and weak coffee for breakfast, milk and mush or bread for lunch, and bread and butter and milk for dinner.[40]

Nearby Dakotas helped to supplement this bland diet by providing the missionary women with meat, berries, syrup, and vegetables (especially corn) throughout the year and emergency provisions when they had exhausted their supplies. When the Riggs family moved to a new mission station, they had used up their food and winter was upon them. When the Dakotas learned about the Riggs's situation, they presented them with more than fifty ducks. The Dakotas also supplied the missionaries with difficult-to-obtain products, such as fresh strawberries, sugar, venison, and eggs, many of which they "had not seen since leaving the states."[41]

In addition to lacking some foods, the missionary women did not have a community of Euro-American women to help with childbirth or to care for their newborns. Thus, they often turned to Dakota women for help. Mary Riggs gave birth to her first child a few months after her arrival at the Lac qui Parle mission. Although the birth went well, Riggs suffered from "sore breasts in consequence of taking cold I suppose. One is now very much better, being affected only externally, the other is still swollen & most painful especially when drawn." When Dr. Williamson, the mission physician,

Women and children guarding corn, Pajutazee mission, August 1862.

failed to remedy the situation, Riggs improved under the care of Dakota women. Riggs praised the Dakota women for their skill in making her well again and for their "ability to perform so difficult a part of nursing."[42]

Likewise, Fanny Pettijohn turned to Catharine, a Dakota woman, after the birth of her daughter Laura. Like Mary Riggs, Pettijohn suffered from "full breasts." To solve the problem, Catharine brought her son Lorenzo to be nursed along with Laura. Catharine would "come at night and let the child draw at my breasts . . . She stayed awhile in our house & then she set her tent close by & would bring it three or four times a day . . . I feel much better than I did."[43]

Certainly, Fanny Pettijohn needed Catharine's help. However, her reliance upon a "savage" woman gave her great anxiety. Women like Pettijohn did not want to accept aid or depend upon those who were supposed to be their students. When this occurred, they took action to reassert their authority. During her illness, Fanny Pettijohn lamented that she came to rely on Catharine so much that "she has got the up[p]erhand of me so completely that I have to give her every thing she asks for." This inversion of the teacher-student relationship bothered Pettijohn so much that she sent Catharine away because she came to "love Katharine [sic] & cannot help shewing [sic] her favors that I do not to anyone else."[44]

Pettijohn and the other women of the ABCFM initially assumed that the Dakota people could not survive without their help. They believed, along with most nineteenth-century Euro-Americans, that the Indians would perish without the benefits of Christianity. The women's letters and diaries, however, show that they relied on the support of the same people they declared unable to care for themselves. During their first years in Minnesota, the missionary women depended on the Dakotas to help them adapt to an unfamiliar terrain, to provide food and goods, and to replace the female community they left behind when they joined the ABCFM. The missionary women, however, voiced their concerns only to each other or to their sisters and mothers back east. Their conflicted relationship with the Dakota women remained a private concern, as it challenged some of the essential tenets of missionary beliefs.

The fact that their dreams of missionary work did not match the reality of life on the frontier led some women into despair. Mary Riggs wrote, "For a fortnight past our sea has been rather rough for pleasant sailing. Agitation of spirits has unfitted me for writing, and even now, notwithstanding all my efforts to the contrary, I fear that mental depression arising from a variety of causes will weigh me down." However, a few sentences later, she noted that if the Dakotas become children of Jesus, "we shall be repaid a thousand fold, for all our anxious and wearisome hours." If she could be instrumental in the conversion of one Dakota, she promised to "bear the thousand little trials incident to missionary life." Despite Riggs's unhappiness, she remained committed to the ABCFM's overall goal and put up a stoic façade of soldiering on. Indeed, Riggs was very careful to only express her disillusionment to her family members. She wrote to her sister Henrietta that it was necessary to be "careful, very watchful over our words, thoughts, and actions."[45]

Conflict within the Missionary Community: The Stevens Affair

Individual missionaries like Mary Riggs attempted to keep the difficulties of missionary life for women from becoming public knowledge. Likewise, the entire mission community downplayed and even tried to hide the internal strife and bickering that consumed the small mission community throughout the 1830s. During the early years of the Dakota mission, Jedediah Stevens's abrasive personality and questionable actions precipitated a crisis that consumed the mission community and distracted them from their work. The conflict also challenged the image the missionaries had of themselves as role models of "civilized" behavior.

Although the details are murky, Stevens employed a Mr. and Mrs. Brown to work at his mission so Mr. Brown could "devote [his] whole time to the secular business of the station." After only a few months, however, Mr. Brown filed a complaint with the ABCFM against Stevens, alleging that he and his wife had "been ill-treated." He charged that Stevens used "threatening and harsh language, & endeavored to injure him in other ways." Further, he accused Stevens of refusing to pay their travel expenses and wages. Finally, Brown stated that other missionaries found Stevens to be "unworthy of the patronage of the Board."[46]

Secretary David Greene, who handled domestic missions, took the matter seriously. While cautious of falsely accusing a devoted Christian, Greene was equally worried about retaining a missionary "whose reputation or conduct is such as to discredit . . . the Christian or missionary cause." Therefore, he asked the Pond brothers, Stephen Riggs, and Thomas Williamson to respond to Brown's charges. Their respective answers, as well as Stevens's defense, highlight the nascent divisions within the mission community.[47]

Samuel Pond, who had worked closely with Stevens, replied first. Although he later retracted some of his harshest comments, Pond criticized Stevens in no uncertain terms. He wrote that Stevens "is utterly unfit to be at the head of a mission station." Pond derided Stevens's "love of display . . . and his disregard for the feelings of those associated with him." Moreover, Stevens had "not learned and will not learn Sioux," and finding a farmer who could work with the man was "not likely." Stephen Riggs concurred with Pond's harsh evaluation, writing that he did not wish "to be associated with him . . . under any circumstances." Riggs never retracted any of his criticisms.[48]

Unlike his more combative colleagues, Thomas Williamson sought to mediate between the two factions. Upon receiving the Board's request to evaluate Stevens, Williamson traveled more than 150 miles to talk with Stevens. In his evaluation letter, Williamson stated that he had always been on friendly terms with Stevens and found him to be "eminently useful as a minister of the gospel & a missionary." He did, however, confirm that Stevens had failed to learn Dakota and admitted that he was "rather unpopular . . . both among Indians and others." Indeed, he noted that the Pond brothers and Stephen Riggs had not been "able to live & labour comfortably in immediate connection with . . . [Stevens's] family." Williamson concluded on a conciliatory note, saying that "it is strange if there was not some fault on both sides" and that "they all give good evidence of piety as industrious as I could wish them."[49]

Even before learning of his "betrayal" by several of his colleagues, Stevens wrote a rambling letter defending his actions; dozens of other letters followed over the next several months also proclaiming his innocence. In these letters, Stevens admitted that he had not paid the Browns for their work. However, he stated that it was Brown's fault. Despite his anger at the Browns, Stevens directed the bulk of his ire at the Pond brothers and Stephen Riggs for writing the Board instead of "convers[ing] with me on the subject as they had abundant opportunity." He also accused them of having "some obliquities or eccentricities of character," including impulsivity. Stevens especially criticized Samuel Pond for allegedly making unwanted advances on his niece and "urging her to break her engagement." Finally, Stevens fired back (unfairly) that the Ponds had failed to learn the Dakota language.[50]

At this time, Stevens did not lose his appointment. However, the Board refused to expand his station and send more laborers. They strongly admonished him to "avoid collisions of this kind, as . . . they give occasion for much talk, much reproach, and to a greater or less[er] extent [lead to] alienation and prejudice against the Board and its missions." An internal conflict was not meant to become public knowledge, as it contradicted the image of missionaries selflessly working together. The dispute with Stevens was never mentioned in any public Board publications at the time; it remained an internal issue.[51]

The Board was hopeful that the Stevens issue had been resolved. Unfortunately, another crisis involving Stevens arose several months later. Stevens accepted a paid position as a government farmer for another Dakota community. He asked the Board for additional funds to start his new station and to supplement his government wages. Thomas Williamson supported Stevens. The Pond brothers and Riggs, however, thought that Stevens should not receive additional Board monies and, indeed, should leave the ABCFM. The situation eroded further when Stevens took mission property to his new station. After this incident, even Williamson supported the removal of Stevens from the Board's service.[52]

Again, Stevens defended himself in a lengthy letter, promising that "all the hidden things of dishonesty shall be revealed." He called the other missionaries "anti-Christian" and reiterated that the charges against him had no foundation. The entire debacle was settled when the Board members voted to sever their connection with Stevens, noting privately that they wanted put to rest the "notoriety" that the case had garnered. For this reason, the Board attempted to keep the real reason for his dismissal from the public. The *Annual Report* from this year simply stated that Stevens had received a government farming position that "called him to labor in a field separate from the mission." Even the Dakota missionaries withheld the true motive for Stevens's dismissal from their private correspondence. Samuel Pond, who had clashed numerous times with Stevens, simply informed his sister that Stevens had left the Board "at his own request."[53]

In retrospect, this crisis seems petty—simply an expression of conflicting personalities. The incident, however, sheds light on the inner workings of one mission community. Most important, resolving the Stevens situation took an inordinate amount of time. Indeed, the missionaries' correspondence during this dispute focused more on Stevens than on proselytizing. The conflict also illustrates that the missionaries were not always the virtuous, selfless paragons portrayed by the evangelical press. Of course, this was not published in the *Missionary Herald* or the ABCFM's *Annual Report*.

Moreover, although the missionaries did not mention the Dakotas' response in their letters, the Dakotas assuredly witnessed and discussed the petty bickering that consumed Stevens, the Pond brothers, and Riggs. Indeed, Stevens deliberately brought the Dakotas living near his station into the conflict. In response to the other missionaries' charge that the Dakotas did not like him, Stevens invited a "chief" to his home to talk on the subject. According to Stevens, the chief appeared friendly and criticized the Ponds for being "fickel [sic] minded" with "no fixed purpose of mind." Stevens also had the government agent ask the Dakotas to choose sides between himself and the Ponds. Although Stevens did not record all of his comments, perhaps the "chief" noted the irony of missionaries offering moral guidance at the same time they could not keep their own house in order.[54]

The incident also reveals the missionaries' personalities. As will become apparent in the following chapters, the characteristics highlighted during this conflict manifested themselves in other interactions with the Dakotas. For example, Stephen Riggs consistently took a harder line and rarely changed his mind. The Pond brothers, however, initially offered strong criticism of Stevens but then became more conciliatory. Williamson, in contrast, was more willing to compromise and find a middle ground. These characteristics continued to define the missionaries into 1862 and beyond. Although the missionaries went through the same selection process and held the same religious beliefs, they also were individuals who responded in ways consistent with their personalities.

Finally, although the Board knew about the internal bickering in Minnesota, the missionaries persisted in portraying their community as united and working with devotion toward their goal. In 1837, Thomas Williamson informed Secretary Greene, "The members of this mission have been enabled thus far to live in . . . utmost peace and harmony." In 1838, in the midst of the Stevens debacle, Samuel Pond echoed these words, writing, "All the missionaries at this station are harmoniously and industriously endeavoring to do good." These statements highlight the missionaries' desire from early on to conceal problems at their stations.[55]

Amid Conflict, Optimism

Given the troubles the missionaries faced during their first years, it would seem likely they would give up and return home. However, with the exception of Jedediah Stevens, the original missionaries continued to work for the ABCFM for at least the next decade. The missionaries remained committed to their work for several reasons.

First, some of the initial problems resolved themselves. Jedediah Stevens left the service of the ABCFM in 1839 and became the government's problem when he assumed his new federal farming post. Certainly personality conflicts and differences of opinion continued to plague the mission, but the level of acrimony never reached that seen during the Stevens affair. The Panic of 1837 eventually ended, and in the 1840s, while continuing to practice frugality, the Board invested money in expanding the Dakota mission and finally appointed new missionaries. Despite continued conflicts with the government over the direction of the Dakota mission, the federal government funneled much-needed money to the mission through farming positions and the Civilization Fund. All of the men and women—despite their overwhelming domestic duties—eventually learned enough of the language to converse with and proselytize to the Dakotas.

Second, the missionaries continued to believe in the inherent equality of the Dakotas and their ability to change their ways, despite the growing scientific racism of the time. The missionaries' writings about the Dakota language illustrate this point. Many antebellum commentators used the supposed inferiority of Indian languages to bolster their claims about the inequality of the Indian race. After attempting to learn the Dakota language, the missionaries found the opposite: the Dakota language was complex and difficult to learn. Even more controversial was their evolving claim that Dakota had the potential to become a "civilized" language.

Third, and most important, the missionaries continued to have faith that all Dakotas would convert to Christianity. Strong and unyielding faith had propelled the missionaries to Minnesota in the first place, and that faith did not retreat at the first signs of conflict. The metaphor "planting seeds for the future" appears throughout the missionaries' writings during this time period. Looking back, Stephen Riggs wrote that the early years were "seed-sowing time. Many seeds fell by the wayside or on the hard path of sin. Most fell upon thorns. But some found good ground" and would spring up decades later.[56]

Finally, the missionaries would not give up their calling because the eyes of the evangelical world were watching the Dakota mission. In 1839, Thomas Williamson noted that "There is a vast responsibility resting on us missionaries to the Sioux. None of the other Indian missions is now looked to with more interest. In consequence of the abandonment of some of them the Christian Public is now becoming faint hearted in respect of them all."[57]

While the missionaries kept their faith when faced with challenges from the government, the ABCFM, and each other, it remains to be seen how they would respond when they clashed with the Dakotas. The conflicts that occurred between the missionaries and the Dakotas over religious and cultural practices during the first five years of missionary work proved much more difficult to resolve than internal squabbles between the missionaries or their conflicts with the ABCFM and government officials. At least these groups spoke the same language and had the same cultural and religious reference points.

CHAPTER 3

"We could not make them see with our eyes"

Early Conflicts with the Dakotas, 1835-40

During the first five years of their work, the Dakota missionaries quickly learned that the Board's widely publicized strategy for converting Indians to Christianity did not translate well to the reality of life in the field. Rufus Anderson, one of the most influential secretaries of the Board (1832–66), developed a strategy for converting the world to Christianity; under his plan, missionaries simply would preach the gospel. He argued that "civilizing" Indians was secondary to proselytizing and, therefore, should not be the focus of the ABCFM missions. The primary job of the missionary, Anderson believed, "was to plant the gospel, build a native church, and then go home. Anything else was a distraction." Reverend David Magie of the ABCFM summarized Anderson's plan for conversion: "The gospel, preached with the Holy Ghost sent down from heaven, is all we need to recover men from their sins."[1]

Despite the fact the Dakota missionaries parroted Anderson's words, the secretary's policies did not translate to the mission field on many levels. First, and most important, preaching the gospel alone did not produce results during the ABCFM's first five years in Minnesota, except for a small pocket of converts at Lac qui Parle. Language factors initially limited the missionaries' ability to preach to the Dakotas, as did the lack of funds provided by the Board. Most important, the ABCFM's strict requirements for conversion and continued church membership made it extremely difficult for Dakotas to become, and remain, church members. Additionally, those few Dakotas who joined the church refused to play a subservient role; rather, they demanded to have a voice in church policy and membership.

Second, missionaries in the field found it nearly impossible to separate Christianization from civilization, as Board policy required. The missionaries quickly learned that it was difficult to admit Dakotas as church members without first changing some of their cultural practices. The Dakota missionaries became embroiled in disputes over Dakota warfare and gift-giving, which alienated potential converts. The missionaries also clashed with the Dakotas over whether church members could be involved in polygamous marriages, travel on the Sabbath, and continue to hunt. For their part, Dakotas who interacted with the missionaries strongly defended their cultural practices and refused to join the church if they were forced to give up all, or even some, of them.

Finally, Board policy forbade any compromise with so-called savage or heathen practices; Indian church members were required to adhere to the same strict conversion standards as Euro-American members. However, life in the field militated against this uncompromising policy. If the missionaries wanted anyone to consider joining the church, some accommodation was necessary. The missionaries, for their part, worked to hide the extent of their accommodation from both the ABCFM and the evangelical public.

During their first five years in Minnesota, the missionaries' problems in converting the Dakotas generally came under four main categories: warfare, gift-giving, mission converts, and mission schools. In each of these areas the missionaries experienced "theologizing moments" when they were forced to confront and potentially rethink some of their preconceived notions about Dakota culture and religion, as well as their own religious and cultural beliefs. These experiences also illustrate how the black-and-white directives of the ABCFM—conceived by Rufus Anderson in Boston—were challenged by the reality of life on the Minnesota frontier.

Woven throughout are the stories of two Dakotas: Wambdiokiya (Eagle Help) and Joseph Renville. In their voluminous correspondence, the missionaries generally referred to the Dakotas only in the aggregate: for instance, "Sioux are remarkably fond" of music; the Dakotas are "very much attached to their own superstitions"; the Pond brothers were "liked by most of the Indians." In the first five years of correspondence, Wambdiokiya and Joseph Renville stand out as two notable exceptions to this pattern. The personal stories of these two men speak to the larger issue of missionary efforts to convert all Dakotas to Christianity.[2]

Wambdiokiya was a noted Wahpeton and a full-blood Dakota and Joseph Renville a mixed-blood (Dakota-French) trader. Both men lived near the Lac qui Parle mission, and although they interacted with the missionaries and promoted the ABCFM's agenda, Wambdiokiya and Renville also

challenged mission policy by pushing the missionaries toward accommodation. They also strongly voiced their opinions and refused to play subservient roles in the mission. Samuel Pond commented that Wambdiokiya
"had much to say about our labors here, other missions, wars, etc." Likewise,
Pond noted that Renville was not shy about expressing his views and was
somewhat "dictatorial in his manners." In sum, these two men, and countless others only referred to as "Dakotas" by the missionaries, failed to act
like the simple heathens portrayed by the mission press.[3]

Conflict over War: The Case of Wambdiokiya

Despite the ABCFM's directive to focus on preaching, the missionaries (especially Stephen Riggs) became embroiled in a dispute over warfare. After
witnessing Dakota war parties and scalp dances, the missionaries demanded
that the Indians cease attacking their enemies and stop the savage displays
that invariably followed. Stephen Riggs wrote, "War in all of its forms and
circumstances, is a dreadful demon." Secretary Greene agreed, challenging
Riggs to "transform these bloodthirsty and revengeful warriors into meek,
and inoffensive followers of the Lamb." Riggs in effect made ending "savage"
war practices a requirement for conversion.[4]

The missionaries had lectured the Dakotas about war parties from the
time they arrived in Minnesota in 1835, but the issue of warfare escalated
to a fever pitch in the late 1830s when Wambdiokiya planned an expedition
against an Ojibwe village at Leech Lake. Although the missionaries condemned all Indian warfare, they were particularly incensed at Wambdiokiya's leading role. Wambdiokiya was one of the first Dakotas to learn to read
and write at the Lac qui Parle mission. Although he never indicated that he
wanted to accept Christianity, the missionaries believed that his conversion
was imminent. Their hopes were bolstered when the warrior sent his daughter to board with the Riggs family and attend the mission school. Because
the mission had few potential converts, Wambdiokiya's role in the war party
was especially distressing. As Mary Riggs lamented, "I greatly fear Wambdiokiya, who probably has more knowledge of gospel truth than any other
Sioux, is given over to the service of Satan."[5]

Led by Stephen Riggs, the missionaries strongly condemned Wambdiokiya's war plans. Riggs explained, "The thought that a war party of reckless
and merciless savages should go from this place with the fiendish purpose of

killing and scalping men women and children was one which was too dreadful to entertain for a moment." Riggs explained that it was his "duty to testify against their offensive wars and to teach them that vengeance belongs to God." Riggs did everything in his power to discourage the expedition. He informed Wambdiokiya that he would pray that no one would be killed, and refused to use the mission mill to grind corn for the war party. He attempted to convince Indian Agent Taliaferro and the commander of Fort Snelling to intervene, but both officials told him that "nothing could be done."[6]

Finally, when the local agents failed to act, Riggs wrote—but never sent—a memorial to Congress claiming that government measures in place to stop Indian warfare were inefficient. In a private letter to his brother-in-law, Riggs further explained his petition, calling the U.S. government "lamentably defective in peace principles and practices and even in the exercise of common justice to the poor and degraded." Despite Riggs's anger at the government's Indian policy, it is likely that the ABCFM's strong warning not to anger government officials influenced his decision not to send the memorial.[7]

In retaliation for Riggs's interference, members of the war party, led by Wambdiokiya, killed two mission cows at Lac qui Parle. Wambdiokiya also removed his daughter from the Riggs family and the mission school. The war party then left for Leech Lake. However, after several days, the warriors returned to Lac qui Parle starving and having failed to accomplish their objective. The famished warriors blamed the missionaries for their misfortunes. According to Riggs, "[t]hey believed all this happened to them in consequence of our prayers, and so they vowed destruction to every thing belonging to the mission." Partially acting on this threat, the men killed a mission bull and shot at several others. Some Dakota parents also removed their children from the Lac qui Parle day school. In the end, the warriors' actions cost the missionaries about $150, temporarily closed the Lac qui Parle school, and "so excited" Stephen Riggs's "nervous system that [he] did not recover from it for several days."[8]

Before the incident escalated further, both sides attempted to end the disagreement. After killing the mission cattle, the Dakotas suggested that Riggs hold a feast so that the two sides could resolve their differences or, as an alternative, provide them with "powder and lead." Initially, Riggs refused to act on either suggestion, arguing that he would not compromise with savagery. As the events reached an impasse, however, Riggs invited some principal men to a feast, "[w]ishing to conciliate them as much as possible." Despite the efforts on both sides, the feast did not have its intended effect. Stephen Riggs would not admit that he was wrong, nor would he give the men powder and lead. The stalemate was finally broken when Joseph N. Nicollet, a French scientist and cartographer who was visiting Lac qui Parle, arranged "on behalf of the Indians to pay for the mission cattle destroyed." Both sides agreed to Nicollet's compromise.[9]

Although the crisis was resolved, the disagreement over the war party illustrates aspects of the missionaries' and Dakotas' conflicted early interactions. First, it shows that a vast cultural gulf separated the two people. Wambdiokiya and Stephen Riggs adhered to different definitions of warfare. For Wambdiokiya, warfare represented a way to gain honor and status. He attempted to explain the importance of warfare to Dakota men in a letter to the missionaries: "But only such as have killed an enemy are entitled to wear feathers from the royal eagle. Therein [the wearing of eagle feathers] lies the greatest glory in their opinion." Despite Wambdiokiya's explanation, Riggs did not see glory in war; he saw only a violation of Christian morality.[10]

In this and other instances the Dakotas strongly defended their point of view and refused to assume the subservient roles assigned to them by the evangelical press (and American society in general). While the missionaries lectured the Dakotas about avoiding war, Dakotas lectured the missionaries about the necessity of warfare. When Riggs informed Wambdiokiya that Christians did not go to war, the warrior told him that he "wishes to be a [c]hristian but cannot and he does not believe any of the Dakota men can. 'They cannot leave off their wars.'"[11]

Moreover, Dakota warriors pointed out the hypocrisy of the missionaries' uncompromising stance on warfare. In a letter to her parents, Mary Riggs noted that when she "talk[ed] to the Indians about putting a stop to their quarrels, the answer . . . most commonly receive[d] makes me blush . . . 'Well, say they, you long-knives,' as they call Americans, 'have the bible, and know everything yet you are always making war.'" At times, the Dakotas' observations compelled the missionaries to take a hard look at their own culture's beliefs and actions. In the case of Mary Riggs, the Dakotas' comments forced her to confront some of the contradictions between American warfare and her own evangelical religious beliefs.[12]

Despite the Dakotas' strong defense of their right to go to war, potential existed for compromise on both sides. Both Wambdiokiya and Riggs attempted to reconcile their opposing viewpoints. Before leaving for Leech Lake, Wambdiokiya wrote a letter to the missionaries acknowledging that he understood their aversion to war. He asked them, however, to understand his position: he must protect his community from its enemy. At the end of the letter, Wambdiokiya suggested a compromise. "My friend," he wrote. "I will tell you just what I think... From my boyhood I have made war very much. But the Great Spirit forbids it and on that account I will leave it off. Just this once I will go to war and then I will stop... When I have done this I will teach my friends very much."[13]

Although Riggs never toned down his rhetoric, he did make an effort to use Dakota means to resolve a disagreement by holding a feast. Later, Riggs also admitted that he may have been overzealous in his condemnation of the war party and intimated that his immoveable position could have made the situation worse. In the end, Riggs had not intended harm. Rather, he wanted "to keep... [the war party] from shedding human blood... but we could not make them see with our eyes."[14]

While Riggs tentatively questioned his response to the war party, other missionaries openly indicated that his response was in fact overzealous. Williamson informed Secretary Greene that "perhaps... [Riggs's] zeal in a good cause may have lead [sic] him to say more than was consistent with the best policy." Samuel Pond went further, defending the Dakotas' right to go to war in general. Although he categorically stated that he opposed war, he equated Dakota warfare with wars fought in America and Europe. The Dakotas "did not make war on each other because they were Indians, but because they were men... their wars were necessary as wars generally are." They defended their country just like the British, French, or Americans. Pond's statement echoed the Dakotas' claim of white hypocrisy—why did Indians need to give up their wars when whites fought each other (and Indians)? Life at the Dakota mission led some missionaries—like Williamson, Pond, and Mary Riggs—to ruminate on the definition of "savage" warfare and how they, as Christians, should respond.[15]

Conflict over Gift-giving

The missionaries also became embroiled in disputes with the Dakotas over the proper way to use property, goods, and resources. Like other Euro-

Americans of the time, the missionaries valued private property. They believed that almost everything could be bought, sold, and owned. The missionaries, and other immigrants to Minnesota who arrived in later decades, had their acreage surveyed, registered the plot with the local land office, and built fences to physically delineate the boundaries of their property. Because of the importance attached to the legal possession of land or goods, the federal and local governments enacted laws to punish anyone who stole, harmed, or trespassed on another's property. Indeed, federal officials believed that the best way to civilize Indians was to first teach them the value of private property.[16]

Unlike their Euro-American counterparts, many Dakotas, like other Native American peoples, valued giving away, rather than accumulating, private property. While the Dakotas understood Euro-American definitions of property ownership, they often chose to ignore laws, boundaries, and legal contracts because these did not fit into their value system. These two notions of property frequently came into conflict. The missionaries called the Dakotas' ideas about property wasteful, dangerous, and uncivilized. By Dakota standards, the missionaries showed a callous disregard for anyone but themselves.[17]

Missionary Views of Dakota Gift-giving

Ironically, given their complaints about Dakota gift-giving, the missionaries viewed Christian charity as a positive trait. They solicited donations of clothing and supplies from their home communities to help equip their missions. Likewise, the ABCFM collected monetary contributions from churches across the East and Midwest. Throughout their time in Minnesota, the missionaries distributed medicine, supplies, reading materials, and clothing to the Dakotas. Although the missionaries accepted and gave gifts, several key issues caused them to see their Christian charity as fundamentally different from Dakota gift-giving practices. Although the missionaries viewed Christian charity as a positive trait, they argued that the Dakotas shared their property and food "to an injurious extent." If the Indians gave away all of their property, they would have nothing left to care for their children or the elderly. Ultimately, the missionaries believed that Dakota gift-giving would lead to the impoverishment of their villages, unclothed children, starving elders, and even death.[18]

The missionaries also linked gift-giving with "heathen" religious practices. Feasting played an integral role in many Dakota rituals and dances. During the medicine dance, for example, the missionaries reported that "the dance . . . was kept up from morning till night, and then came the feast. The food was of the best they could procure." The missionaries complained that during this dance "food . . . needed in the family was often lavishly expended." In their view, Dakota spirituality put communities in danger of starvation, poverty, and dependence.[19]

Likewise, the missionaries condemned Dakota kinship practices because of their relationship to gift-giving. According to Ella Deloria, a Dakota anthropologist, "[k]inship was the all-important matter . . . Its demands and dictates for all phases of social life were relentless and exact; but, on the other hand, its privileges and honorings and rewarding prestige were not only tolerable but downright pleasant for all who conformed." Dakotas were enmeshed in a far-reaching array of kinship relations that extended beyond their immediate family. Each of these relations involved certain responsibilities, including, among other things, sharing food. Thus, like their spiritual practices, the missionaries worried that Dakota kinship obligations would impoverish their communities.[20]

Finally, the missionaries were concerned that honoring the Dakotas' requests for aid could bankrupt their mission. The missionaries complained that Dakotas arrived at all hours "begging" (as they called it) for food, medicine, clothing, and blankets. Mary Riggs wrote to her brother about her frustration with Dakota requests. "We have been for three days overrun with visitors from sunrise to sunset. Our patience had been tried not a little—beg—beg—beg . . . !" Stephen Riggs encapsulated the missionaries' feelings about the Dakota's begging: it "was worse than annoying—it was vexatious." If the missionaries honored all the requests, they would not be able to feed and clothe their own children. As Mary Riggs commented, "If we make a practice of giving there will be no stopping place."[21]

Dakota Defense of Gift-giving

The Dakotas staunchly defended their gift-giving practices. They argued that gift-giving would not lead their villages into dependence or starvation. According to Dakota cultural practices, food was divided among the group. In this way, all community members helped each other through lean times and assured that those who could not hunt or care for themselves had enough to eat. If everyone gave, everyone would eventually receive when they were in need. If people refused to share, the system would break down. The Dakotas believed that individuals who hoarded goods would force the entire community into dependence, not the opposite, as the missionaries contended.

The Dakotas also pointed out that the missionaries did not always follow their own teachings. In a letter to the Ponds, Wambdiokiya reproached the brothers because the missionaries "teach that we should love others as ourselves, and do not share with them what we ourselves possess." On another occasion, two Dakota men similarly challenged Mary Riggs during a Bible meeting. According to Riggs, the men told her that "they, having nothing, are so liberal, they think it strange that we who have, in their estimation, so many things, should withhold anything which they ask us for. And when we say the Bible says we should love our neighbors as ourselves, they ask why then do we not divide what we have with them, 'that would be loving them as well as ourselves.'" Because missionaries like Mary Riggs refused to follow Dakota traditions, the Dakotas nicknamed them "The stingy."[22]

The missionaries also were "stingy" because they failed to justly compensate the Dakotas for the resources they used to build and maintain their missions. If the missionaries followed their own teachings, the Dakotas argued, they "ought to pay for the logs they used in building their houses, and the rails that fenced their fields, and even for the hay they cut." Instead, the missionaries took what they wanted without offering compensation or suffering any legal consequences. The laws the U.S. government implemented to protect property ignored Indian claims to land and resources. From the Dakotas' perspective, the missionaries stole from them with the government's blessing. In the context of missionary disregard for Indian resources, their lectures on the sanctity of property seemed tainted with hypocrisy.[23]

The missionaries' religious practices also created confusion and anger with regard to gift-giving. For example, one Sabbath, a Dakota woman traveled "a considerable distance" to the Lac qui Parle mission to deliver freshly picked strawberries. Because it was the Sabbath, Mary Riggs refused to accept the strawberries. Not surprisingly, her refusal made no sense to the Dakota woman; Riggs undoubtedly appeared rude and ungrateful. It came as a surprise to Riggs (but not the modern reader) that the next time she requested strawberries "no one brought any."[24]

When the missionaries acted rudely and broke Dakota customs, the

Dakotas responded by attempting to teach them the proper way to share and distribute goods. In their letters home, the missionaries frequently reported that the Dakotas instructed them about the importance of generosity and sharing. For instance, Wambdiokiya lectured Riggs to "[b]e very liberal of food. As many men as come to visit you, give them something to eat . . . And if anyone is without something which you have[,] give it to him and make him glad . . . The Dakota custom is not to deny their own people anything."[25]

Accommodating Gift-giving Practices

In their public letters, the missionaries strongly criticized Dakota gift-giving practices and ignored Wambdiokiya's lessons. Behind the scenes, however, the missionaries began to hand out gifts to attract students to their schools and churches. At the Lake Harriet mission, Jedediah Stevens gave cornbread to children who attended school, while Stephen Riggs and Thomas Williamson began their meetings at Lac qui Parle with "kettles of boiled pumpkins, turnips, and potatoes." Stephen Riggs reported that he and Thomas Williamson "made a feast for the big men of the village that we might have an opportunity of delivering to them our message." By giving away food at the churches and schools and holding feasts, the missionaries followed traditional Dakota cultural practices to promote their overall goal of conversion. However, the missionaries made sure to distinguish between their gift-giving and that of the Dakotas. While Mary Riggs admitted to her mother that the mission gave out turnips and potatoes to the Dakotas, she promised her that "she need to not fear . . . that we have not reserved enough for ourselves." Riggs clearly made the distinction between Dakota actions, which impoverished families, and her actions, which promoted Christianity. On the ground, however, both practices looked the same.[26]

Another time, Thomas Williamson accompanied a group of Dakota men on a hunt. Williamson packed provisions for the entire trip. The first day, however, Williamson shared his supplies with the group "in accordance with Dakota custom." He did so because "he thought best to give the most of what he had to those with whom he went." Realizing, however, that his actions might be controversial and not sit well with the Board, Williamson begged Riggs that all records of his gift-giving during the expedition be kept quiet and all information "which relates to his tour with the Indians, not be published."[27]

The clash over gift-giving practices provides further insight into the cultural misunderstanding that underlay all Dakota-missionary interaction. The missionaries believed the Dakotas should adopt Euro-American views of property, while the Dakotas remained equally committed to following their own gift-giving practices. As anthropologist Bruce White commented, "from a white point of view, [to] destroy someone else's property was vandalism. To help yourself to another's food was theft. To be insistent in asking for anything was begging." For the Dakotas, according to historian Rebecca Kugel, "Gift giving, both as a philosophical concept and as a physical act, was considered central to every human interaction by all of the Native peoples of the Great Lakes area." From the beginning of the Dakota mission, this lack of understanding created conflicts and tension.[28]

It is not surprising that the missionaries' actions in the field sometimes undermined their uncompromising rhetoric. The Dakotas commented on their hypocrisy and chided them for their inconsistencies. As with the war party incident, Dakotas were active agents in the debate over gift-giving and refused to defer to the missionaries. Thus, in the early years of the Minnesota mission, two equally paired rivals struggled to control key cultural practices. Indeed, the Dakotas seem to have had the upper hand. If the missionaries failed to do as they wished, they could engage the missionaries in debate, refuse to take them on hunts, or simply stay away from the mission altogether. The missionaries were aware of this dilemma and quietly struggled over how much to accommodate Dakota practices.

Conflict with Dakota Church Members: The Case of Joseph Renville

During the first five years of the Dakota mission, conflict also arose between the few Dakota converts and the ABCFM missionaries. Following Board policy, the missionaries initially defined conversion as an all-or-nothing proposition—the Dakotas either met their stringent criteria for church membership or they were not counted as converts. As Stephen Riggs commented, "[O]ur God is a jealous God, and the religion of the Bible is an uncompromising religion." The few Dakota converts, however, found it difficult to follow these rules. Within the small Christian community, conflict arose over what it meant to become and remain a Christian. The case of Joseph Renville, the French-Dakota trader from Lac qui Parle, illustrates some key challenges the missionaries experienced in attempting to convert the Dakotas to Christianity.[29]

Joseph Renville and Converts at Lac qui Parle

At the Lac qui Parle station—arguably the most successful ABCFM mission in the early years—most of the converts were linked in some way to Joseph Renville. Renville was born in 1779 to a Mdewakanton woman from Kaposia and a French trader. For the first several years of his life, Renville lived with his mother at Kaposia. When Renville turned ten, his father sent him to Canada to study with a Catholic priest and to learn "elements of the Christian religion." After his father died, Renville returned to Minnesota and began to work in the fur trade, first with the Hudson's Bay Company and then with the Columbia Fur Company. Finally he joined the American Fur Company and ran a trading post at Lac qui Parle. Renville married a Mdewakanton woman named Mary and had eight children, although only six lived into adulthood. He died in March 1846, leaving behind a large family and a great deal of debt.[30]

Missionary hagiographies of Renville's life stressed that he had been interested in Christianity long before the arrival of the ABCFM. These writers point to several incidents that illustrated his naïve (as they characterized it) interest in Christianity. First, they focus on Renville's marriage. Because there were no clergymen in Minnesota at the time, Renville traveled to Prairie du Chien, where he was married "with Christian usage, by a priest of the Romish church." Second, the missionary biographers noted that the trader's prize possession was a "large folio Bible in the French language." Because he was illiterate, he constantly asked "his employers in the fur-trade to send him a clerk who could read it." The culmination of these stories was, of course, the arrival of the ABCFM missionaries, who nourished the seeds of Christianity that had been planted, but never properly fertilized, over the years. Because Renville had shown an interest in Christianity and desired further instruction, Thomas Williamson, Alexander Huggins, and their families agreed to accept Renville's invitation to build a station near his trading post at Lac qui Parle.[31]

Joseph Renville supported the ABCFM missionaries when they first moved to Lac qui Parle, providing the families with a temporary home, a place for their school, and food and other provisions. Renville also served as the missionaries' main interpreter and translator. Most important, Renville "was active in persuading those under his influence to attend the religious meetings" and the school. As a result of Renville's efforts, the missionaries counted Renville's wife Mary as the first full-blood Dakota convert; she also had the dubious distinction of being the first "Dakota who died in the Christian faith." The ministers baptized Renville's children and taught them at the Lac qui Parle day school. Some of his children boarded with mission families. After attending the mission churches and schools for most of their lives, four of his children remained close to the ABCFM church into adulthood. His youngest son, John B. Renville (also called Jean in some records), lived and studied with the missionaries when he was a boy, attended Knox College in Illinois, and eventually became a church elder and an ordained minister. Renville's elderly mother also became part of the mission church.[32]

Joseph Renville also influenced his extended family to convert. Two women—known to the missionaries as Rachel and Catherine—joined the Lac qui Parle church; they were the wives of Tachanhpetanineya (Left Hand), Mary Renville's brother. The children of these two women also had close ties to the ABCFM church, including Lorenzo Lawrence, Joseph

This pipestone tablet, shown here at full size, was excavated from the ruins of Joseph Renville's trading post in 1940. Other fragments of carved and inscribed pipestone found within the building's walls suggest that someone who lived there regularly carved the stone. Although the tablet resembles a sampler, it is not possible to know how it was used.

Kawanke, Sarah Hopkins, and Joseph Napesniduta, one of the first full-blood male converts. Wambdiokiya also was related to Renville. Thomas Williamson summarized the importance of Joseph Renville's family to the Lac qui Parle mission: of the approximately twenty people who regularly attended his Sabbath meetings, "nearly half... come from Mr. Renville's [family] and more than half of our native members now in this neighborhood and in good standing are in some sense members of his family." When he died in 1846, the missionaries lamented that the Lac qui Parle church lost over half of its members. It is unclear whether the missionaries acknowledged the irony that their success at Lac qui Parle was supported by a kinship system that they condemned as wasteful and destructive.[33]

The missionaries did not envision relying on Dakota kinship practices to attract their members, nor did they want mixed-blood fur traders (like Renville) to be the main congregants in their church. First, the missionaries described mixed-bloods as lazy and morally lax. Stephen Riggs complained that as "a class the Dakota half breeds are not over stocked with energy, and spend a good deal of time in smoking." Second, the missionaries believed that mixed-blood Dakotas were easily influenced and would learn only the worst of Euro-American culture from "designing persons" (white traders) who violated the Sabbath, drank alcohol, and participated in "illegal" marriages. According to Thomas Williamson, interaction with the white traders also would "increase the aversion to labour which is natural to savages." Finally, the traders "desired not to make ... [the Dakotas] agriculturalists" so that the men could hunt furs. This potentially affected church membership, as hunting took members away from church meetings and schools for extended periods.[34]

The Board, however, warned the missionaries to keep their negative opinions about the fur traders to themselves. Just as the mission community needed to placate government officials, the missionaries needed to appear to be getting along with the traders. Thus, missionary letters, which often contained long paragraphs complaining about the fur traders, were explicitly highlighted as not for public review. For example, after a lengthy discourse criticizing the fur trade, Gideon Pond wrote that his diatribe was "not intended for the public eye. It is my opinion, and it is also the *unanimous* opinion of this mission that it is *inexpedient* that [it] ... be printed or in any way made public." If this did happen, the fur traders could "hinder ... or obstruct the operations of the missions."[35]

Despite his status as a mixed-blood member of the fur-trade community, Joseph Renville initially did nothing to hinder or obstruct the mission. Indeed, while Samuel Pond generally found the traders to be "neither elevating nor improving," he made an exception for Renville because of his support of the Lac qui Parle mission. Although Pond and the other missionaries gratefully received Renville's help, they wanted the trader to play a supportive role in the mission. That is, he was not to challenge policy, make suggestions, or question the missionaries' authority and decisions.[36]

Conflicts over Strict Admission Standards

Renville, however, was not content to play the role of subordinate. In 1837, he asked Thomas Williamson to admit some of his relatives to the Lac qui Parle church. After examining the potential converts, Williamson decided that he could not receive the trader's relatives "because they gave to us no satisfactory evidence of a change of heart." Renville's family allegedly "wept aloud" when they learned that Williamson would not receive them. In retaliation, Renville sent a message to the missionaries, informing them that "I have prepared these persons for admission to the church and if you do not admit them they will never attend your meeting again . . . If you can do without me I can do without you." He followed through with his threat and stayed away from the missionaries for several months. The trader believed that all the help that he had given the missionaries should give him some say in church admissions and affairs.[37]

Despite the fact that the missionaries needed Renville on their side, they were required to follow the strict standards of conversion set by not only their faith but also by the Board in Boston. The Board demanded that Indian converts meet the same strict set of requirements for church membership as Euro-Americans. To become full members of the ABCFM church, Indian converts needed to read and understand the Bible, attend weekly meetings, and experience a "change of heart," or a conversion experience. Once potential members had met these standards, a committee of missionaries tested them on their knowledge of the scriptures, their commitment to Christian morality, and the validity of their conversion experience. Overall, Indians needed to provide "substantial evidence that they are born again . . . to make a profession of religion."[38]

While civilization was not supposed to be the focus of missionary work, the missionaries quickly learned that potential converts also needed to give up numerous "savage" customs prior to acceptance in the mission church. Some of the forbidden practices included "improper marriages," unchastity, Sabbath breaking, playing ball on the Sabbath, and purchasing and drinking alcohol. Many of the Dakotas' everyday activities caused them to break these rules. For example, most Dakotas found the "no travel on Sunday" rule extremely difficult to follow because their subsistence patterns included hunting; certainly, animals would not wait until Monday while church members observed the Sabbath. Moreover, the missionaries worried that because Dakota subsistence patterns were not guided by the days of the week, converts would have difficulty determining which day was Sunday and might mistakenly rest on a Saturday or Monday. Thus, the only way to ensure compliance with the rules was to have converts change their subsistence patterns from hunting to farming and live in permanent homes near the mission. Again, the missionaries' life among the Dakotas brought home the futility of attempting to separate Christianization from civilization programs.[39]

Many members of the mixed-blood community also had knowledge of Catholicism from their French fathers, including Joseph Renville. The missionaries disliked Catholicism almost more than the Dakotas' religion. Throughout their time in Minnesota, the ABCFM missionaries criticized the Catholic religion, the priests who preached Catholicism, and the mixed-blood community who accepted Catholicism, or at least integrated some Catholic rituals into their belief system. Indeed, Mary Riggs reported that Roman Catholic ceremonies "seemed to me less natural than those of the Indians." To become a member of the Lac qui Parle church, converts were required to put aside Catholic beliefs.[40]

The Board also frowned upon the admission of Dakotas involved in polygamous marriages. Some Dakota men practiced sororal polygamy, where a man married two (or more) sisters. There is some dispute among the missionaries as to the prevalence of polygamy among the Dakotas. Thomas Williamson noted that "more than half of the men with whom I am acquainted have two or more wives." Stephen Riggs wrote that polygamy was "quite a common thing." Samuel Pond, however, put the numbers far lower. According to Pond, "polygamy was not general among the Dakotas, a single wife being the rule, and polygamy the exception." He calculated that perhaps "no more than one-twentieth had more than one wife at a time."

Lac qui Parle May 25th 1845

Brother Samuel W Pond

I write now because I have an opportunity of sending a letter by Roi alias Cinkpa and not that I have any thing new or important to communicate We are all in good bodily health but as we are making no perceptible progress in our warfare with the Prince of Darkness but on the contrary seem to be losing ground we have reason to fear that our Spiritual health is not good

This week 4 young men have been dancing to the sun none of them have been baptized but one is a child and two others are grand children of members of our church.

Last sabbath morning the Devil brought along 4 Buffalo near the village and great part of the Indians went in chase of them and succeeded in getting them all. None now in the communion of the church were in the chase but I suppose most if not all

In May 1845, Thomas Williamson reported to Samuel Pond his frustrations with an observance of the sun dance and a hunt on the Sabbath: "None now in the communion of the church were in the chase but I suppose most if not all ate of the meat."

Most Presbyterians of the era, however, believed that even one polygamous marriage was too many. In a letter published in the *Boston Recorder* (a Congregational newspaper), an irate commentator denied that polygamy actually was marriage; instead, he called it a "state of continuous adultery." The writer demanded that potential converts end their polygamous marriages "before they can properly be received as members of the church of Christ."[41]

Although most Indians (and many whites) found it impossible to meet many of the conversion requirements, the Board warned its missionaries not to compromise their standards. Secretary Greene admonished Jedediah Stevens, "Be careful whom you admit to the church. Hasty admissions of persons but very partially instructed . . . is greatly to be deprecated. I fear you were no[t] sufficiently deliberate and cautious." On the surface at least, the missionaries followed strict rules for admission to the church. Tatemina (Round Wind), Renville's brother-in-law, had a dream "in which he saw a man standing before him, dressed after the manner of white men, and holding in his hand a fine musical instrument." Tatemina believed the dream meant that "he was to learn to read and thus be enabled to sing our Sabbath hymns." When he presented himself at the Lac qui Parle church for admission, Stephen Riggs scoffed at his "self-righteous" belief that "he can become a [c]hristian when he pleases" and refused him entry to the church. In addition to rejecting interested converts, the missionaries also suspended members for "transgressions," such as traveling on the Sabbath, drinking alcohol, or failing to attend church meetings.[42]

Subverting Strict Admission Standards

Public stories like Riggs's strong condemnation of Tatemina's conversion and the official lists of suspensions, however, do not tell the entire story of church admissions and retention. During their first five years in Minnesota, several missionaries relaxed admission standards, a fact that they glossed over or hid in their reports. The uncompromising standards set in Boston did not translate well to the Minnesota frontier. For instance, if the missionaries wanted converts at Lac qui Parle, they needed Joseph Renville on their side. After publicizing the mission's strong stance against admitting Renville's relatives, Thomas Williamson quietly admitted them a short time after the trader had angrily left the church. Renville then returned to the meetings and continued to help with translations.[43]

Likewise, the missionaries tended to look the other way when the Renvilles traveled on the Sabbath, left the church for several weeks, and continued to adhere to beliefs that contradicted the missionaries' strict theology. Moreover, despite their claim that the "most prominent traits of . . . [Renville's] character were such as belonged rather to a Dakota than to a white man," the missionaries made him a ruling elder in the church in 1841 and asked the ABCFM to provide compensation for the trader in the later years of his life. Williamson even warned the ABCFM not to have "anything appear in print" that was "in the smallest degree calculated to hurt Mr. R[enville]'s character or feelings." Samuel Pond summarized the importance of Joseph Renville to the Lac qui Parle church: "Mr. Renville considered himself the head of the church formed here and perhaps there was not much arrogance in his assumption."[44]

Because of Renville's importance to the church, the missionaries looked the other way when the Renvilles mixed Protestant, Catholic, and Dakota rituals. Perhaps the best example of their fusion of spiritual beliefs is found in Mary Riggs's description of the burial of Joseph Renville's oldest son. In deference to Dakota beliefs, the Renville family distributed goods to the community and buried the child with some of his possessions, including his cradleboard and bed. They also wrapped the body in white, scarlet, and black. Before they buried the child, the men and women, including the Renville family, wailed over the boy according to Dakota tradition, a practice that the ABCFM missionaries condemned, along with other mourning practices, as "injurious to [their] health." The missionaries believed that "death should be greeted with equanimity" and that mourners should not wail or express excessive emotions. Rather, they should "share images of the happiness of their loved one in heaven, repent of their own sins, and draw closer to God." The Renville family must have understood the missionaries' dislike of wailing and extreme emotion because they stopped their cries when the missionaries arrived to watch the proceedings. However, they began again immediately after the Protestants left.[45]

The Renvilles followed Christian traditions by burying the child instead of placing his body on a scaffold in a tree as Dakota practice dictated. While the missionaries applauded the Renvilles for burying the body, they complained about the presence of certain Catholic rituals, such as placing candles around the coffin during the visitation, which Riggs could only surmise "was to enlighten purgatory." Technically the use of Dakota and Catholic practices should have merited a suspension from the church. While the missionaries certainly disliked what they witnessed, no records show that any of the Renvilles were suspended following the funeral.[46]

All of the missionaries overlooked aspects of the Renvilles' syncretic expression of religion. Thomas Williamson, however, went one step further by openly supporting church admission for Dakota men and women involved in polygamous marriages. This question, more so than quietly admitting the Renville children to the church or overlooking Catholic rituals and traveling on the Sabbath, divided the mission community. The issue of admitting polygamous church members came to a head when Tachanhpetanineya (Left Hand), Joseph Renville's brother-in-law, presented himself and his two wives for admission to the Lac qui Parle church. Although he seemed to be a "true believer," the missionaries, led by Stephen Riggs, refused to admit Tachanhpetanineya. Joseph Renville bitterly protested this policy in support of his relative. He argued that the Bible recognized polygamous relationships in some cases, especially when the marriages had been established before contact with Christian missionaries. Moreover, he complained that the missionaries' policy contradicted their oft-stated teachings on the sanctity of marriage. He argued that Tachanhpetanineya had married the women "in a state of ignorance—that to put one away would subject the woman to difficulties and expose her to temptations, and that he wished to keep the mother for the sake of the children."[47]

Thomas Williamson agreed with Joseph Renville. In the 1830s he tentatively defended polygamous congregants; by the early 1840s, Williamson publicly advocated accepting both men and women from polygamous marriages into the mission churches. Williamson wrote a lengthy article for the *Boston Recorder* criticizing a commentator who had called for those involved in polygamous marriages to be barred from church admission. While he stated that it was "wrong for a man to marry [more than] one wife," he found no passage in the Bible "in which it is expressly forbidden" to keep those involved in polygamous marriage in the church. Like Renville, Williamson believed that Dakotas had entered into these marriages out of "ignorance" and thus should not be punished for something that they did not know was wrong before the missionaries arrived. Samuel Pond also supported Williamson's position on polygamy. He noted that "we have no scriptural warrant for advising the man to put away his wife."[48]

Stephen Riggs, however, was adamantly against admitting men involved in polygamous marriages to the church. When the missionaries reached an impasse, they referred the matter to the Ripley Presbytery in Ohio, the closest governing body of the Presbyterian Church. When the Presbytery ruled that men involved in polygamous marriage were barred from entering the church, Riggs breathed a sigh of relief because "our native church was saved from sanctioning polygamy." While Left Hand was refused admission, his two wives were admitted to the church. Antebellum gender roles influenced this decision. As Stephen Riggs explained, a Dakota "woman is . . . a dependent and inferior being—not a help-meet. These are some of the circumstances which had led us to regard the case of the woman . . . as very different from that of the man." Because Dakota women allegedly had no choice in their marriages, they were not held responsible for polygamy and were allowed to join the church.[49]

As the dispute over polygamy shows, Dakota converts and the ABCFM missionaries struggled to negotiate the boundaries of what it meant to become and remain a Christian. In theory, and often in practice, the missionaries demanded complete adherence to their strict rules of admission and conduct. Dakota converts like Joseph Renville continually tested the boundaries and refused to accept a subordinate role in the church. Some missionaries (like Williamson) were more willing than others (like Riggs) to make these concessions in pursuit of their larger goal of conversion. Even when concessions were made, however, they were frequently downplayed or hidden entirely from the wider evangelical public. Whether publicly expressed or not, contact with Joseph Renville and his family forced all of the missionaries to "reflect upon, renew, revise, or rethink their Christian convictions."[50]

Conflict over the Mission Schools

Conflicts over church membership and policies surfaced in other areas as well. The mission day schools at each station presented a challenge to both converts and missionaries, who disagreed over the focus of the schools. The ABCFM missionaries (following the Board's directives) established day schools to promote conversion to Christianity. As ABCFM secretary Rufus Anderson noted, the object of schools was "first, the conversion of pupils and secondly, the procuring of native Christian helpers." Stephen Riggs agreed with Anderson, noting that the schools served "as a most important and indispensable auxiliary" to preaching the gospel.[51]

Because conversion was their primary goal, almost every aspect of instruction was designed to promote Christianity. The missionaries taught students to read so that they could contemplate the Bible on their own. In their reading lessons, students worked with translated religious texts and listened to teachers read passages from the Bible; they also sang translated hymns. Even if they struggled with reading, the children quickly picked up the hymns in their own language. At the Lac qui Parle school, Stephen Riggs was surprised by his students' "good voices" and "aptness to learn" the songs. He hoped that these hymns would "prepare [the students] to join in the new song before the great white throne above." Likewise, Samuel Pond hoped "songs of Zion" would replace Dakota war songs.[52]

Despite their orders to focus on Christianity in their lessons, in practice the mission schools also promoted "civilized" cultural practices, gender roles, and subsistence patterns. The teachers lectured about the dangers of gift-giving, warfare, and feasting and attempted to change their students' gender roles by teaching the boys "to work in the garden and on the farm; the girls to knit, sew, and attend to the common duties of housekeeping." In the end, the missionaries hoped that the boys would "grow up to revere the laws and institutions of civilized society; the girls, to exert a hallowed influence in the domestic circle as Christian daughters, wives, and mothers." Because the missionaries knew that the Board did not want them to focus on civilizing the Indians, they argued that these secular lessons would lead to quicker conversions. However, the line between religious and secular instruction was ambiguous, which meant the missionaries in the field and the Board in Boston were frequently at odds over what happened in classrooms.[53]

Dakotas and Schools

While the Board and its missionaries argued over the schools' focus, Dakota students and parents offered their own interpretation of what the schools should offer. Many Dakotas simply wanted to learn to read and write. Joseph Hancock, an ABCFM teacher, lamented that the chief of the band "wanted us to... teach their children to *read* and *write*, and *that only*." Abel Stewa-winika, a native teacher employed by the missionaries in the 1840s, echoed the same sentiments. Referring to his efforts to teach his peers, he wrote that "[t]here is one thing . . . I have been doing and continue to do, I mean teaching the book. But . . . plowing, making houses, and letting the women remain at home, I have not yet been able to accomplish."[54]

Some Dakota students even used their reading lessons to bolster their cultural practices instead of undermining them as missionaries intended. For example, the missionaries often refused to honor Dakota requests for gifts. As soon as Dakota students learned to write, they penned notes asking the missionaries to give away some of their possessions. Stephen Riggs complained that "[i]f a man wanted me to give him a shirt he had only to write it on a piece of paper and bring it to me—the shirt would be forthcoming." Williamson also noted that when he gave his students pen and paper, they used it to write "short notes chiefly for the purpose of begging." In this case, Dakota students used a missionary-taught practice—writing—to strengthen a traditional one—gift-giving. This is not what the missionaries intended when they opened their day schools.[55]

For generations, Dakota people had used a sophisticated system of drawings and carvings to communicate, so the concepts brought by the missionaries were not new. But the ability to read and write also provided a more flexible way for Dakota people to correspond. The Mdewakantons, Wahpekutes, Sissetons, and Wahpetons lived in scattered villages throughout Minnesota territory. Marriage and other ties linked their communities, and writing offered a way for separated families to keep in touch. Alexander Huggins, the teacher at Lac qui Parle, reported that a Dakota man wanted "to know the book very much [so] he could write to his brother" who had learned to write earlier that year at the Lake Calhoun school. Once several Dakotas had learned to read and write, Dakota men carried mail between the mission stations. These letters opened up a new way for Dakotas to keep each other informed about everyday affairs, work out disputes, and discuss important issues affecting their communities.[56]

In addition to using the schools for secular ends, many of the students, especially the girls, challenged the utility of adopting Euro-American gender roles. The missionary women reported that most of the Dakota girls "seem to feel that it is of little use for them to learn these things [spinning, weaving, and knitting] while they have neither the raw material, nor houses in which to perform these operations." The Dakota students correctly pointed out the absurdity of carrying heavy spinning wheels or looms between their sugar, ricing, and hunting camps. Even the missionaries conceded this point, commenting that they had "no dwelling in which such things could conveniently be performed, or wheels and looms preserved from the weather." Many Dakota women argued that the lessons taught at the mission schools would not improve their lives but would increase their burdens.[57]

Further discord arose when some of the teachers used corporal punishment on their students, which violated Dakota methods of discipline. Dakota parents rarely spoke harshly to their children or disciplined them with physical force, relying instead on verbal suggestions or illustrations to correct their behavior. Stephen Riggs commented on how the two competing philosophies of discipline created friction. "We find . . . [teaching the children] difficult work," he wrote. "Dakota parents are very sensitive about the way in which their children are taken care of . . . [I]f they are naughty and we correct them, it makes quite a buzz in the community." Missionaries who used corporal punishment frequently found that Dakota parents asked to have their children removed from a classroom because a teacher "has pretty scriptural notions in regard to the use of the rod, which is not quite popular among these native Americans." In one case, for example, the missionaries used corporal punishment to discipline Carrie Ironheart, a Dakota who attended the Lac qui Parle school. When her parents visited the school, they "took her away, alleging as the reason that we whipped her."[58]

In addition to eschewing physical force, Dakota child-rearing methods stressed learning by role-playing and exploration. The missionary teachers, however, attempted to impart knowledge through regimented and disciplined instruction. They held their schools at the same time and place and broke their lessons into discrete tasks that needed to be accomplished in a sequential order. The instructors expected students to arrive on time, remain the entire school session, and perform their given lessons in an orderly and timely fashion. They also taught by rote, which did not allow for exploration or creativity.[59]

The Dakota students rebelled against the missionaries' strict code of classroom conduct. They refused to conform to a schedule or to sit quietly in rows. Mary Riggs commented that she frequently allowed the Dakota students to leave before the end of the day because she could not "make them sit still or refrain from talking and sometimes I am almost confounded by their chattering." Moreover, the children came and went throughout the school day with the blessing of their parents. Samuel Pond lamented the fact that "[i]n pleasant weather the children prefer playing and hunting to attending school and their parents let them have their own way."[60]

This regimented school schedule did not take Dakota subsistence patterns into account. Although families resided in semi-permanent planting villages during the summer months, they moved to different locations during the rest of the year to hunt, fish, and gather rice and sugar. Children could not continue to attend class and move with their families. Thus, parents pulled their children from school when they left to hunt or for a sugar or ricing camp. This practice, of course, affected attendance. In 1836, the missionaries noted that although "[s]chools have been opened at each of the stations . . . the number of pupils [sic] have been exceedingly variable. When Indians are on their hunting excursions, few children are left behind." As a result of irregular attendance, the missionaries complained that as soon as students advanced in reading, they would leave and forget everything they had learned.[61]

Conflict over Dakota Instructors

To deal with the irregular attendance, missionaries asked the Board for permission to hire native teachers who would travel to Dakota villages and teach adults and children how to read and write. This plan would allow the missionaries to reach Dakotas who did not live near a mission station; it also ensured that instruction continued during hunts and harvest time. The missionaries proposed paying these teachers five dollars for each student they taught to read and write. The missionaries justified the expense as a way to promote Christianity. Thomas Williamson informed Secretary Greene that native teachers "would do much to remove the prejudices of their countrymen against the Christian religion and dispose them to hear the gospel when we shall have an opportunity of visiting those villages for the sake of preaching it." The Board initially agreed to pay the native teachers.[62]

Although the ABCFM approved funding for the Dakota teachers, the missionaries' first appointment created conflict. After their mutual anger cooled following the dispute over the war party against the Ojibwe, the missionaries appointed none other than Wambdiokiya to be their first native teacher. He was their best scholar and was well respected in the Dakota community because of his standing as a warrior. As Samuel Pond commented, Wambdiokiya "was a man of uncommon mental abilities." He "was one of the most prominent, intelligent, and warlike members of the Lac qui Parle band." The Board was incensed over the missionaries' choice, focusing on the "warlike" and non-Christian aspects of Pond's description.[63]

Secretary Greene demanded that the missionaries not engage Wambdiokiya and instead appoint a church member as a teacher. Williamson defended his choice. "If we had pious persons otherwise properly quallified [sic] for teachers we should of course choose to employ such," he wrote. "But the members of our church are either females incompetent to teach or persons whom we could not hire to engage in this business." Teaching far-flung Dakotas to read and write, which "would do much to remove the prejudice of their countrymen against the Christian religion," was more important than the fact that Wambdiokiya had not yet converted. Again, as in the realms of warfare, gift-giving, and church membership, directives enacted in Boston did not always translate well to the field. Missionaries like Williamson often found it necessary to bend the rules if they wanted to achieve the goals set forth by the ABCFM.[64]

Conclusion: Conflict and Compromise

Thomas Williamson's disagreement with the Board over native instructors fits into a larger pattern of conflict he faced during his first five years in Minnesota. He differed with his fellow missionaries and with the ABCFM over policies, methods, and how much to compromise with the Dakotas. He worried about not finding enough time to study the Dakota language or to preach. The perennial lack of funding from the ABCFM and conflicted relations with the local Indian agent created tension. Most upsetting for Williamson, however, was his failure to convert large numbers of Dakotas to Christianity.

In a series of private letters to the Pond brothers, which were never meant to be published, Williamson discussed his anguish over missionary work. In February 1840, Williamson informed Gideon Pond that he was "assailed by passions which I have long since thought subdued till I am ready to feel discouraged. Sometimes [I] am tempted to think I ought to leave here." After expressing this sentiment, however, Williamson warned that he wanted his comments to remain private. "I would not write these things except to a [c]hristian brother and but that I hope to be helped by your prayers." In a letter to Samuel Pond a few months later, Williamson again worried that he was not fit for missionary work and wondered if he should resign his post. Once more, he noted that "I do not wish any person to see this letter except yourself and brother."[65]

Both brothers agreed to keep Williamson's confidence. Gideon Pond also counseled him not to resign his post. Williamson needed to remain because "There is enough to do. The *Sioux must hear* the *Gospel* and *somebody must tell it to them*." Williamson thanked the Pond brothers for their advice. After much thought and prayer, he decided to remain. A few months later, Williamson felt more encouraged about his work among the Dakotas and appeared to be somewhat embarrassed about his crisis of faith. He wrote to Samuel, "When I think how much I was discouraged when I last wrote to you I feel ashamed though no[t] half so much as I see I ought to considering how well the Lord has at all times provided for us here."[66]

More so than other missionaries, Williamson articulated the problems he faced living up the Board's high standards and keeping his faith intact when confronting the daily challenges of mission work. Other missionaries, however, assuredly experienced many of the same worries, especially how much to accommodate so-called savage and heathen ways. At times during their first years in Minnesota, all of the missionaries compromised with the Dakotas. For the most part, however, their accommodations were situational and ad hoc rather than comprehensive and pervasive. For example, Stephen Riggs needed Wambdiokiya to end his retaliation against his church, so he staged a feast. The Lac qui Parle missionaries wanted Dakotas to come to their meetings and schools, so they distributed food. The missionaries needed Renville on their side, so they quietly admitted his relatives to the church, looked the other way when they traveled on the Sabbath, and ignored lingering Catholic rituals. The Dakota missionaries had few readers, so they hired a non-Christian war leader as their first native teacher. Sometimes the ABCFM found out about these "transgressions" and admonished the missionaries, but most of the time accommodations were made behind the scenes and intentionally kept quiet.

Certainly, all of the missionaries responded in different ways to the trials of converting the Dakotas. Williamson gained a reputation among the missionaries (and the historical records back this up) of being more willing to accommodate Dakota practices than others. Stephen Riggs commented that Williamson "was a merciful man, and very kindly disposed toward . . . [the Dakotas]. He would give clothing to the naked and food to the hungry to the fullest extent of his ability." Samuel Pond made a similar observation, noting that if Williamson ever "erred in judgment, [he] would be sure to err on mercy's side." Pond described times when Williamson was asked to judge the conduct of Dakota church members for possible dismissal. Williamson usually gave the errant church members the benefit of the doubt. For example, during one "trial," a church member admitted that he had knowingly traveled on the Sabbath. Because the man had repented afterward, Williamson decided not to discipline him. Pond implied that he would have made a different ruling.[67]

While Thomas Williamson earned the reputation of accommodating the Dakotas, Stephen Riggs appears as relatively unaccommodating and rigid. Even Riggs, however, was not immune to questioning some of his beliefs. Stephen Riggs wrote a letter to David Greene, most of which was reprinted verbatim in the *Missionary Herald*. One part of the letter, however, was not published. In the deleted portion Riggs described a Dakota dance that he had attended. He noted that after he became accustomed to the dance, "it does not appear worse than many customs that obtain among more enlightened people." The Board did not want the evangelical public to read a positive evaluation of "savage" dances and exercised their authority to edit the report.[68]

Throughout their interaction with the Dakotas, Riggs (and others) quietly questioned the utility of some of the Board's strict policies. This does not mean, however, that the missionaries abandoned their original ideas about the necessity of converting the Dakotas to Christianity. They never became cultural relativists; they still called the Dakotas heathen savages who needed to adopt Christianity and, by extension, civilized ways. Moreover, even Williamson continued to support conversion through preaching alone. He adhered to the belief that teaching "Christianity [was] superior to Civilization." Although the missionaries might quietly challenge some of the ABCFM's strict guidelines, they never questioned its overall mission. Indeed, in their minds any accommodations were meant to promote conversion, not undermine it. By the standards of their faith, however, conversion remained an all-or-nothing affair.[69]

The fact that the missionaries were forced to confront, think about, and potentially revise such sticky theological and cultural issues is a tribute to Dakotas like Wambdiokiya and Joseph Renville. Both men, and countless other Dakotas, challenged the missionaries at every turn. When they arrived in Minnesota, the ABCFM missionaries were not prepared for the strong mindset of the Dakotas, who refused to play passive and subordinate roles. During their first five years of interaction with the Dakotas, the missionaries filled their correspondence with examples of Dakota resistance; of course, this resistance is defined strictly from the missionaries' point of view, is discussed in very negative terms, and is included to illustrate the mission's overall success or failure. This theme of resistance (and others) continued during the next decade of missionary work (1840–50).

CHAPTER 4

"Leagued together to drive all the missionaries out of their country"

Increasing Opposition and Conflict, 1840-50

The 1840s was a time of increasing opposition and conflict for the men and women of the Dakota mission. The Treaty of 1837, which ceded Dakota territory east of the Mississippi to the U.S. government, was extremely unpopular among the Dakotas, and they directed most of their anger over the treaty at the ABCFM missionaries. Ironically, at the same time Dakota protests reached an all-time high, the ABCFM was able (with the government's help) to send more teachers, laborers, and ministers to Minnesota. Government aid, however, was a double-edged sword, as it solidified the Dakotas' belief that the missionaries were merely a mouthpiece for the government. It also created tension with the ABCFM, which did not want the government to usurp its control over the location of its stations. The reality of raising large families in the field also led to disillusionment among the missionary women. These themes—Dakota opposition to missionary work, the missionaries' conflicted relationship with the federal government, disagreements between members of the Board in Boston and missionaries in the field, and troubles faced by missionary women—were not new. However, these issues intensified during the 1840s and became more problematic.

The decade also illustrates that missionary history cannot be separated from the larger history of the development and settlement of Minnesota. The missionaries wanted to remain isolated from social change, working to proselytize to the Dakotas without outside interference. Although this had never been the reality even prior to the 1840s, change accelerated during this decade. Following the Treaty of 1837, Minnesota's population slowly began to rise. Small settlements—including St. Paul and Minneapolis—were established during the 1840s. In 1849, Minnesota became a territory. The missionaries worried that these new settlements and Minnesota's territorial status would be detrimental to their effort to Christianize the Dakotas.

Other mission stations (both foreign and domestic) had taught the ABCFM that "settlement generally had disastrous consequences for the spiritual and material interests of indigenous peoples." This adage was certainly true for the Dakota mission in the 1840s. The Dakotas would have offered this same evaluation, but for entirely different reasons than their missionary counterparts.[1]

Conflict over the Treaty of 1837

More so than any other event, the Treaty of 1837, which was part of An-drew Jackson's Indian removal policy, defined missionary work among the Dakotas throughout the 1840s and beyond. According to Jackson's policy, the federal government would relocate all tribes living east of the Mississippi River to areas west of the river. The newly vacated lands would be opened for settlement and cultivation, as well as for extraction of resources (such as gold or timber). The Mdewakanton Dakotas, as the only band with villages on the eastern side of the Mississippi River, were the first of the four bands of Dakotas to fall under the guidelines of this aggressive removal policy.[2]

As part of Jackson's policy, twenty-six Mdewakanton Dakotas traveled to Washington, DC, to negotiate and sign a treaty. The resulting Treaty of 1837 ceded to the United States "all their land, east of the Mississippi [R]iver, and all their islands in the said river," totaling approximately 5 million acres. In return, the government would pay the Mdewakantons $1 million in an-nuities and payments over several years. Part of the money from the land cession would be used to purchase medicine, "agricultural implements, me-chanics' tools, cattle, and such other articles as may be useful to them." The government also would hire a physician, farmers, and blacksmiths to aid in the Mdewakantons' civilization.[3]

Missionary Reaction to the Treaty of 1837

Although Jackson and his agents extolled the virtues of the Treaty of 1837, the Dakota missionaries were divided over the document. Only Stephen Riggs focused on the potential benefits of the treaty, believing that it would help the Dakotas. He also hoped that the missionaries would benefit from the new paid positions or receive treaty funds to support their schools. In the end, Riggs was "extremely anxious that the treaty . . . be ratified." If the treaty was not ratified, he worried that the Dakotas would lose "confidence in our government," and this might cause the missionaries to "have to leave their country."[4]

For various reasons, Riggs's colleagues did not support the Treaty of 1837. Many of the missionaries especially criticized the annuities established by the treaty. Samuel Pond, for example, believed that annuities would make the Mdewakantons lazy and dependent on government handouts. He commented that "[t]he pay which they receive for the land" could enable them to "better their condition and live comfortably or to spend their time in idleness and dissipation. I fear they will choose the latter." Likewise, Thomas Williamson said that treaty annuities would "do them more harm than good." Mary Riggs bluntly stated that annuities would "be a curse."[5]

Several missionaries also expressed concern that the treaty would increase the availability of alcohol, despite government claims to the contrary. Williamson wrote that once the lands east of the Mississippi were sold to the United States, whiskey would flow in "like a flood and soldiers as well as Indians will be drunk." Williamson also feared that the Mdewakantons would have to travel to Fort Snelling to retrieve their annuities, which would bring them into contact with "strong drink." The missionaries staunchly supported temperance and established Indian temperance societies at each station. Free-flowing whiskey would undermine their efforts to eradicate the sin of intemperance among the Dakotas.[6]

Mary Riggs—alone among the missionaries and in opposition to her husband's relatively positive view of the treaty—offered a stinging critique of Jacksonian Indian policy. In letters to her family, she called the government guilty "of treacherous cruelty in reference to the aborigines of our land." Her main criticism was the role that "unscrupulous" traders played in many treaty negotiations, including those associated with the Treaty of 1837. She accused the traders of driving the Indians into debt and then stealing money from land sales to pay those debts. Following the sale of the Dakotas' land, Mary Riggs complained that the traders "receive[d] far the largest share of the money." She called the traders' actions "wrong." She also scolded government agents for signing the treaty on the Sabbath, which showed that they were not true Christians. For all of these transgressions, Mary Riggs informed her father that surely "God hates [such] a wicked nation as the United States."[7]

Because of the problematic nature of the Treaty of 1837, Mary Riggs was concerned that the Dakotas would fail to distinguish between "wicked" federal Indian policy and what she saw as the benevolent designs of the missionaries. Nevertheless, she decided that the Dakotas "are so discriminating that they will perceive the different motives which actuate us in our labors if we daily live as disciples of Jesus, reflect his image, and walk in his steps."[8]

Dakota Reaction to the Treaty of 1837

Despite Riggs's hopes, the Dakotas perceived the missionaries and government agents as working together to deprive them of their land, money, and autonomy. The Dakotas had many reasons to believe that the missionaries supported federal Indian policy and the 1837 treaty. First and foremost, although the missionaries (except for Stephen Riggs) expressed misgivings about the treaty, they never voiced their concerns publicly. Mary Riggs sent her stinging critique of federal Indian policy only to her family members. Thomas Williamson and the Pond brothers offered their critiques in private letters. Because the missionaries failed to publicly criticize the treaty, the Dakotas had no reason to question the missionaries' support of government actions.

Moreover, the missionaries openly took money from the Treaty of 1837 to fund their mission. Immediately after the treaty was ratified, the Indian agent distributed treaty funds to the ABCFM to help defray the cost of their mission day schools. Although the Indian agent did not appropriate educational funds to the ABCFM after the first year, the Mdewakantons continued to believe that the ABCFM used their treaty money to finance mission schools. The Dakota missionaries also received appointments as federal farmers and teachers, and Williamson was hired as a government physician to the Mdewakantons, positions funded by treaty monies.[9]

In response, Dakota protests erupted at all of the ABCFM's mission stations, growing in intensity and continuing throughout the 1840s. Certainly, Dakota opposition to missionary programs and actions was not new; during the first five years of the Dakota mission many Dakotas had criticized and challenged some of the ABCFM's policies and actions. However, these early protests had been localized and had arisen mainly in response to ad hoc situations specific to the mission station and people involved. Following the Treaty of 1837, however, the protests spread across Minnesota and continued for over a decade. The conflict over the treaty eventually included the Sissetons, Wahpetons, and Wahpekutes, even though they had not been directly involved in the Treaty of 1837.[10]

A League of Opposition

The protests at stations near the Sissetons, Wahpetons, and Wahpekutes did not occur spontaneously; they were cultivated by Mdewakanton representatives who made every effort to form a "league . . . against missions and schools" by sending messengers to villages located near ABCFM stations. These messengers spread the word about the missionaries' role in the Treaty of 1837. In 1840, for example, Thomas Williamson noted that Mdewakanton messengers had arrived to use "all their influence with the Indians here [at Lac qui Parle] to have us removed." The council at Lac qui Parle "had three meetings in the night and one that morning for deliberation on important matters." After the meeting, the majority of Lac qui Parle Wahpetons chose to support the Mdewakantons in their dispute with the government and missionaries. Thomas Williamson reported that several representatives came "to tell us the result . . . [T]hey told us they had deteirmined [sic] to stop . . . our school and religious meetings."[11]

The Wahpetons had many reasons to join the Mdewakantons in challenging the ABCFM missionaries. Familial ties between Dakota villages dictated that the Lac qui Parle Wahpetons support the Mdewakantons. Thomas Williamson explained that many of the Wahpetons "were related by blood and marriages to the Mdewakantonwan," which led them to manifest "a less friendly feeling toward us and our school." The Mdewakantons also told the Wahpetons that the Treaty of 1837 affected their band. Although it was not technically true, the Mdewakantons informed the council members that the missionaries used monies from the 1837 treaty to fund the Lac qui Parle school. According to Williamson, "[s]ome ill disposed persons" told the Wahpetons that "we were paid for teaching the Warpetonwan here out of the money due the Mdewakantonwan for lands sold to the U.S." In other words, the Mdewakanton Dakota accused the ABCFM missionaries of misappropriating their treaty monies to fund all of their mission schools, even those outside of the treaty's boundaries. Though the charge was not true, confusion and anger over the education clause increased animosity against the ABCFM missionaries at all stations. Finally, Wahpeton villagers worried about the precedent set by the treaty. In future treaty negotiations, the

Mdewakantons warned that the Wahpetons would suffer a similar fate. According to Stephen Riggs, the Wahpetons believed that "[i]f they ever made a treaty, and sold land to the government," the missionaries would "bring in large bills against them."[12]

The success of the Mdewakanton emissaries in bringing the Lac qui Parle Wahpetons into their dispute with the ABCFM missionaries and government officials motivated them to seek alliances with other Wahpeton, Wahpekute, and Sisseton villages. In 1843, Williamson reported that "Tatepose has sent word" about the missionaries' role in the controversy over the Treaty of 1837 "as far as he could and that was his principal business when he was up [here] and they held those consultations last spring." Stephen Riggs also mentioned that "[o]ccasionally some one would come up from below and tell about the fight that was going on there *against* the Treaty appropriation for Education."[13]

Evidence of this widespread and united opposition is found in the letters and reports written by the ABCFM missionaries over a ten-year period. In 1844, Stephen Riggs, from his post at Lac qui Parle, reported that the Mdewakantons "have been making efforts to form a league among themselves against missions and schools. The Warpekute, Warpetonwan and Sisitonwan bands . . . have been imbibing too much of the same feeling; and some . . . have become open opposers." In 1846, Thomas Williamson complained that some of the "principal men" at Lac qui Parle "forcibly stopp[ed] our school &c. last winter." This occurred after "[s]ome of the Medwakantonwas requested the Indians here to break up the school." At Traverse des Sioux, Robert Hopkins noted that "[a]bout a month ago, the Indians of this place met together in council and decided to stop entirely attendance at Meeting for the worship of God, and also coming to school." Stephen Riggs wrote in his memoir *Tah-Koo Wah-Kan* that throughout the 1840s, a "strong organized opposition grew" among all Dakotas "on the Mississippi and lower Minnesota."[14]

Boycotting Mission Schools

The first target of the anti-mission coalition was the mission schools. Indeed, the ABCFM schools at every station had trouble attracting students for nearly a decade following the Treaty of 1837. According to Stephen Riggs, "the provision for education made by the treaty of 1837 effectually blocked all efforts at teaching among those lower Sioux." Jedediah Stevens abandoned his plan to construct a boarding school for the Mdewakantons because the "Indians of this Band the year past have apparently been far less disposed to receive instruction, or have their children instructed." Stephen Riggs summarized the problems the missionaries faced at the schools: "so far as book education is concerned, those lower bands are in a far less hopeful case now, to all appearance, than they were . . . years ago . . . In their educational interests they have been thrown back a generation." In 1843, Cordelia Pond lamented that her heart "was often pained and discouraged to see how little desire they have to receive instruction."[15]

The missionaries directly linked these boycotts to the Treaty of 1837. Stephen Riggs reported that "[t]he correspondence which has taken place between the Government and the mission in regard to schools has stirred . . . [opposition] up anew and appears greatly to have increased it." Like Riggs, Samuel Pond linked fallout from the treaty with the rise of opposition to the schools. "It was not until after the sale of their lands in 1837," he commented, "that they manifested any decided hostility to our schools." Even the Dakotas' Indian agent admitted that the treaty hurt the missionaries' educational efforts. Agent Amos Bruce commented that Mdewakantons objected to the ABCFM schools in hopes that "the money intended for education, and other useful purposes, would be paid to them in specie."[16]

Destroying Mission Property

In addition to boycotting the schools, the Dakotas destroyed mission property. Although all mission reports between 1840 and 1849 included references to the destruction of mission property (especially livestock), two years—1844 and 1849—are representative of the type of frustration the missionaries faced. In 1844, the missionaries reported that the Dakotas "committed serious depredations on the cattle belonging to the mission." In that year, the Traverse des Sioux and Lac qui Parle stations lost more than $300 worth of cattle. At Lac qui Parle, the Wahpetons killed nearly two-thirds of the mission stock. The missionaries summarized their 1844 losses to the commissioner of Indian affairs: "[W]ithin a year, they have destroyed three oxen and nine head of cattle, besides pigs, sheep, and poultry—taking full two-thirds of our entire domestic animals." Matters had not improved five years later. In 1849, Moses Adams reported that the Dakotas "killed one of our best cows." At Lac qui Parle, the Wahpetons destroyed three-fourths of the missionaries' stock. By the end of the 1840s, Thomas Williamson noted that he had so much difficulty keeping a team of any kind that he had to hitch up the family's milk cow to haul firewood.[17]

Traditional Forms of Social Control

Although the anti-mission Dakotas directed most of their ire toward the schools, churches, and property, Dakotas who continued to attend schools and meetings also faced repercussions. Dakotas who opposed the missionaries and the Treaty of 1837 used traditional forms of social control, including ridicule, ostracism, and the forming of *tiyotipis*—a policing society meant to quiet dissent and to carry out the laws and customs of the village—to convince these Dakotas to sever their ties with the ABCFM mission.

Ridicule was one of the main methods used to keep Dakotas from attending the mission churches and schools. Charles Eastman, a Dakota, reported that "there is one thing above all else which a Sioux cannot bear—that is the ridicule of his fellow warriors." Samuel Pond made the same observation, noting that "popular odium was not . . . a light thing for an Indian to bear, for he could not isolate himself but must continuously live with those who upbraided and despised him."[18]

ABCFM ministers reported dozens of incidents of anti-mission Dakotas ridiculing students who attended the mission schools. Robert Hopkins, for example, noted that at his mission "most of the young men manage to ridicule those who try" to learn to read. Those who attended church faced similar obstacles. Hopkins complained that everyone who attended meetings faced disdain. In an 1848 summary report to the ABCFM, the missionaries wrote, "In order to prevent those who desire it from attending the public worship of God, threats are sometimes used and occasionally executed, but more generally scoffs and ridicule are made use of, and as their language is peculiarly adapted to such a purpose such means are very effectual."[19]

The experiences of three Lac qui Parle converts illustrate the power of such ridicule. In 1842, Abel Itewawininhanyan became a member of the Lac qui Parle church. Soon after his conversion, he wrote a letter to the missionaries describing his treatment. "You have given us the Bible, and now there are forty-six of us who have joined the church," he wrote. "But the Indians think it is bad and say bad things to us." Two female converts described similar treatment. Gideon Pond noted that after hearing a noise during a Sabbath meeting, one woman immediately left "lest she should be seen at our meeting." Another female convert "was present at the same time who dare not come openly but frequently steals her way to our place of worship on the Sab[bath] . . . but she evidently suffers much mentally lest they discover her." The missionaries lamented the fact that Itewawininhanyan and the women were "deterred from . . . [conversion] by fear of ridicule and opposition" and by threats that they would lose standing in their villages.[20]

Communities also used ostracism to challenge the missionaries' programs. Dakotas who attended the mission churches and schools occasionally were "thrust . . . out of society" and not allowed to participate in hunts, religious ceremonies, or council meetings. For example, at Traverse des Sioux, "the Indians . . . met together in council and decided to stop entirely attendance at Meeting for the worship of God, and also coming to school . . . If any who belong[ed] to the Sacred Dance should come for such a purpose, they were to be neglected at their sacred feasts." Joseph Napesniduta ignored this decree and converted to Christianity. As a result, Thomas Williamson recalled that "principal men of the village . . . inquired of him if it were true . . . that he had abandoned the religion and customs of their fathers, and embraced the religion of the white men." When Napesniduta replied that he had joined the mission church, "[t]hey then told him if he would return to their customs and worship as they did, they would attend to him in his sickness as they did to each other, and furnish him with good medicine." If he did not, Napesniduta would have to rely on the missionaries' inferior medicine to cure him if he became ill.[21]

Despite the effective use of ridicule and ostracism, some Dakota men and women continued to associate with the missionaries. In such cases, villages located near ABCFM stations turned to another traditional means of social control, the *tiyotipi* (soldier's lodge), to end association with the missionaries. According to ethnohistorian Catherine Price, the *tiyotipi* originated to maintain control on communal hunts. Before the hunt, the village council appointed *akicita* (soldiers, warriors, or enforcers of decisions) to the *tiyotipi*. Once the hunt began, these soldiers had extensive powers to punish a person if, for example, he went ahead of the hunting party and frightened the game. When the hunt ended, the *tiyotipi* was disbanded. Over time, the *tiyotipi* evolved and also was used to quiet dissent and to carry out the laws and customs of the village. According to Michel Renville, the son of Joseph Renville, *akicita* were empowered to enforce the council's decisions by destroying "property, cutting up blankets or tents, breaking guns, or killing horses." Once order had been restored to the community, the *tiyotipi* was disbanded.[22]

Throughout the 1840s, Dakotas formed these soldiers' lodges to prevent men, women, and children from associating with the ABCFM missionaries. The Lac qui Parle mission had the most visible and active *tiyotipi*, which is not surprising given that Lac qui Parle had the largest number of Dakotas interested in Christianity. Nancy McClure, of Dakota and English descent, summarized the techniques used by the soldiers to keep her, and others, away from the Lac qui Parle mission. McClure, who lived with the Riggs family, recalled that one Sunday, when she and several other Dakota children tried to go to church, "twenty or thirty 'medicine' Indians, all armed, were at the building and calling out that they would take away the blankets from all who entered and destroy them." Although she was "as proud [of her blanket] as the grandest lady in the land can be to-day of her seal-skin" she, along with some of her friends, continued to attend church after losing their blankets to the soldiers. The soldiers kept up their harassment after she entered the church. McClure recalled that "the men outside began to shoot at the church bell as a target [and] . . . cracked it so that it would not ring." Stephen Riggs was so "affected that he cried" in front of the small congregation.[23]

Although Nancy McClure attended services that Sunday, the actions of the soldiers generally kept the Dakotas away from the missions. In a letter to her sister, Mary Riggs said that the Lac qui Parle council "decreed to 'akicita kte' that is mob every person man woman or child who should attend meeting or school at the mission. The school was suspended for a short time in consequence of this decree." At other mission stations on the Mississippi and lower Minnesota, the soldiers targeted the schools and churches and "kept them for months together from re-assembling." In 1851 Robert Hopkins reported, "Two years ago it was decreed in a council of these Indians at which all the principal men were present, that no one should attend preaching or school. If a child should do so it was to be whipped, an older person should have his [or her] clothes cut to pieces. These policies were effective, and . . . [w]e have not had any Indian scholar since."[24]

Consequences of Dakota Resistance

The widespread opposition to the ABCFM schools, churches, and property throughout the 1840s arose out of the ABCFM's complicated and conflicted relationship with the federal government. Although concerns about this relationship surfaced during the missionaries' first five years in Minnesota, the Dakotas' reaction to the Treaty of 1837 confirmed that whether they liked it or not, the missionaries' fate was inextricably linked to unpopular government actions and policies. The Dakotas had no choice but to see the missionaries as fully supporting the Treaty of 1837, as they never publicly denounced the document. Moreover, the missionaries' repeated requests for funds in the wake of the treaty certainly showed that they hoped to benefit from the Dakotas' loss of lands.

The Dakotas refused to act passively or subordinately when faced with challenges to their sovereignty and lands, and their reaction to the Treaty of 1837 was consistent with past behavior. During the first five years of the ABCFM mission, Dakotas such as Joseph Renville, Wambdiokiya, and countless others challenged the missionaries' policies and actions. If the missionaries proved to be particularly recalcitrant, Dakotas boycotted the churches and schools and even destroyed mission property. These same methods—although more coordinated and intense—were used in response to the Treaty of 1837. Throughout the 1840s, the Mdewakanton Dakotas organized a loose coalition dedicated to undermining the ABCFM's mission stations. They forced schools to close and caused church membership to decline. Thomas Williamson lamented that in the mid-1840s, "only two adults have been received on profession of faith & only 8 children of natives have been baptized." Williamson even worried that Lac qui Parle "shall cease to be occupied as a missionary station."[25]

The Dakotas' united resistance during the 1840s left the missionaries with few members in their churches and few prospects for new converts. Of course, the measure of a mission's success was the number of men and women who joined the church. Because of the lack of success in the 1840s, the Dakota mission seemed to be moving backward, not forward. The missionaries (quietly) questioned whether they had the ability and faith needed to persevere against these unforeseen and unwelcome obstacles.

Conflict over the Location of Mission Stations and Government Positions

ABCFM corresponding secretary David Greene also worried about the Dakota missions' lack of success in the 1840s. Instead of fingering the Treaty of 1837 as the source of these problems, however, Greene focused on the location of the ABCFM's stations. He believed that the current mission stations were too close to growing white settlements that followed in the wake of the Treaty of 1837. Greene informed Samuel Pond that white settlements "distract the attention and agitate the minds of wild Indians, and render them unsteady." He made the same point to Thomas Williamson, arguing that "As a general thing there can be little doubt that the more remote missionary stations are from white settlements the fairer will be the prospect of conferring [any] benefits on those for whom we labour."[26]

Because of the deleterious effects the new settlers would have on their missions, Greene counseled that all ABCFM stations should be located far from white settlements. Greene informed the Ponds that they should "become permanently established in a more favourable location more out of the way of white influence and more in steady contact with the Indians." In practice, this meant that the brothers should move at least fifty to one hundred miles from their current Lake Harriet station. In theory, all Dakota missionaries agreed with Greene that stations should be located away from white influence. Thomas Williamson feared that the "most favourable time for bringing the gospel to bear on this people" was fading away because "the white population is rapidly approaching." Williamson believed that the "Whites in this region" would serve as poor role models for the Indians because they were "licentious" and "entirely neglect the means of grace making the Lord's day a day of amusement or worldly business." This would have a "pernicious influence on all the Indians."[27]

Although the Ponds agreed with Williamson's statement, they also needed to consider the wishes of the Indian agent. The agent wanted them to remain near Fort Snelling and even promised to build them a house and a school. In addition, the Pond brothers worked as paid farmers for the government and feared losing these positions if they went against the agent's wishes. For these reasons, the Ponds chose to follow the agent's orders over those of the Board. In 1843, Samuel and Gideon opened a new station at Oak Grove (present-day Bloomington, nine miles from Fort Snelling). In 1847, Gideon remained at Oak Grove, while Samuel moved to Prairieville (present-day Shakopee, twenty miles from Fort Snelling). Later, another station—Red Wing—also was opened in the region.[28]

The Pond brothers were not the only ABCFM missionaries to accede to government requests. In 1846, Thomas Williamson, who fully supported the ABCFM's policy of locating stations far from white settlements, was asked by the Dakotas' agent, Amos Bruce, to move from Lac qui Parle to Kaposia (formerly a Methodist mission) near Fort Snelling. Agent Bruce told Williamson that one of the leaders of the village had requested a school. If he moved to Kaposia and started the school, Bruce promised to employ Williamson as a physician to the Mdewakantons for $240 a year. Like the Ponds, Williamson acquiesced to Bruce's orders and relocated to Kaposia; he immediately received the physician's appointment.[29]

During the rest of the 1840s, the ABCFM built most of their stations near Fort Snelling. In return, the Ponds and Williamson received government salaries for their work among the Dakotas. Moreover, the government allowed the ABCFM mission to expand by paying for additional workers to join the Dakota mission. In 1848, the agent appointed Moses Titus, Gideon Pond's nephew, to serve as a government farmer at Oak Grove. In 1849, the government paid John Aiton to teach at Red Wing; S. M. Cook filled the same position at Kaposia. Although the Board did not initially support the government's desire to have stations so close to settlements, the cash-strapped organization assuredly benefited from these "free" positions. Aiton, for example, did not need the entire $500 he received from his government salary and (reluctantly, as it later turned out) gave the rest to the ABCFM. Likewise, Gideon Pond had "no need to draw on the treasury of the Board any more than what is already allowed me" due to government funding. These federal salaries freed ABCFM funds to hire still more workers for the Dakota mission. Throughout the late 1830s and the 1840s, the Board sent Stephen and Mary Riggs, Robert Hopkins, Moses Adams (a relative of Riggs), Jonas and Eli Pettijohn, Joseph Hancock, and Joshua Potter (formerly of the Choctaw mission). Several young female teachers also received appointments, including Sarah Rankin and Marjorie Cunningham.[30]

Although the government positions allowed the ABCFM to increase its workforce among the Dakotas, they remained a double-edged sword. Because some of the workers' salaries were paid from treaty funds, the Dakota opposition saw this as further proof that the missionaries were stealing their treaty money. The long-standing debate over civilization and Christianization also intensified once most of the ABCFM workers were tied in some way to federal funds. The Indian agents continued to stress that civilization should take precedence over Christianization; of course, the ABCFM missionaries persisted in reversing the order. Finally, while relatively lucrative, the government positions interfered with missionary work. According to Gideon Pond, the tasks required by his farming position were "varied and laborious." The $600 he earned came at a price; he built storehouses for the Indians and shelter for their cattle, herded and fed their cattle, cut hay, and plowed their cornfields. Because of this work, Pond had less time to preach. Throughout the 1840s, missionaries like Pond struggled to reconcile their loyalty to the Board and their evangelical Christianity with their growing ties to government officials.[31]

While the Dakota missionaries generally acceded to government requests, they also exerted their independence by launching one new station far from any of the new settlements. Traverse des Sioux was located about sixty miles southwest of Fort Snelling on the Minnesota River. Like Lac qui Parle, Traverse des Sioux was a trading post operated by the American Fur Company. It was run by an independent trader named Louis Provencalle, or Le Bland. Unlike Lac qui Parle, however, where the missionaries had the support of Joseph Renville, Louis Provencalle and the Dakotas near Traverse des Sioux did not want the ABCFM to establish a station there. Provencalle allegedly said that "he [did] not want missionaries and if he did he should prefer a Catholic." The ABCFM ignored the trader's remark and in 1843 sent Stephen Riggs and his family to Traverse des Sioux.[32]

Riggs should have taken the warning seriously. When he arrived at the station, he reported that a young boy "pulled a gun out of the forward end of the canoe and . . . fired at us. Fortunately, the shots were received chiefly by the side of our canoe [with] only one of them . . . inflicting a small flesh wound." Although Traverse des Sioux would undoubtedly be "a hard place to work," Riggs vowed to remain. Two years later, conditions had not improved. Indeed, many of the Traverse des Sioux Dakotas had joined the "league" of anti-treaty Dakotas who opposed mission churches and schools across lower Minnesota. In 1845, Riggs reported that "there is very little of a favorable character to report . . . among the Indians at Traverse des Sioux . . . [and] heathenism is strengthening itself."[33]

Despite Dakota opposition and federal interference, the ABCFM increased its presence among the Dakotas throughout the 1840s. By 1850, the ABCFM operated six missions to the Dakotas—at Lac qui Parle, Traverse des Sioux, Prairieville, Oak Grove, Kaposia, and Red Wing. These new mission stations encompassed all four bands of Eastern Dakota. The Board employed six male missionaries and three male and eleven female assistant missionaries as well as several native teachers. Although the ABCFM lauded this expansion, each of the stations was problematic in some way. The stations near Fort Snelling were too near white settlements, government interference, and alcohol. Indeed, Stephen Riggs complained that St. Paul was nothing but "grog-shops" in the 1840s. Traverse des Sioux, while further removed, was filled with opposition to the missionaries' presence from its beginning; it also proved to be a thoroughfare for alcohol despite its location. Table 2 provides a summary of the expanding ABCFM missions during the 1840s.[34]

Table 2. Summary of ABCFM Stations, 1834–50

Station	Year Established/ Ended	Missionary in Charge	Location
Lake Harriet/ Lake Calhoun	1834–43	Gideon and Samuel Pond	Present-day Minneapolis
Lac qui Parle	1835	Thomas Williamson (1835–46) Stephen Riggs (1837–43; 1846–54)	150 miles from Fort Snelling
Traverse des Sioux	1843	Stephen Riggs (1843–46) Robert Hopkins (1846–51)	Near St. Peter, 60 miles from Fort Snelling
Oak Grove	1843	Gideon and Samuel Pond	Present-day Bloomington
Kaposia	1846	Thomas Williamson	Present-day South St. Paul
Prairieville	1847	Samuel Pond	Present-day Shakopee
Red Wing	1848	John Aiton Joseph Hancock	70 miles below the Falls of St. Anthony

Increasing Conflicts for Missionary Women

The 1840s was a watershed decade for the Dakota mission in general, as tensions grew exponentially among the Dakotas, missionaries, government officials, and the Board. This decade also was extremely important for women of the Dakota mission. During these years conflicts faced by women, which had been brewing since the mid-1830s, came to a head. Women increasingly found it impossible to reconcile independent missionary work with domestic chores and their growing families. As a result, they experienced self-doubt and depression, and even questioned their own moral character and abilities as their dreams of heroic missionary work faded away.

The evangelical press, however, rarely mentioned the conflicts missionary women experienced as they struggled to navigate conflicting priorities. Instead, the literature lauded missionary women as "noble" and praised them for their "heroic devotion and Christian fortitude." As illustrated by letters written by the women of the Dakota mission, however, life in the field bore little resemblance to the heroic stories that filled antebellum missionary literature. Women faced difficult relocations, never-ending domestic chores, and constant worries about how to raise their children in a "heathen" environment.[35]

Relocations

Missionary women suffered more than their husbands from the frequent movement between stations during the 1840s because they had to reestablish their households. Mary Riggs's experience with several relocations in the 1840s serves as an example of the traumatic nature of these moves for the women. In 1843, the Board ordered Stephen Riggs to move to Traverse des Sioux. Mary Riggs, however, did not want to leave Lac qui Parle because she lived in a comfortable home after sharing quarters for several years, had an established garden, and knew the area. She also had contact with several other mission families. Traverse des Sioux was isolated, hostile, and undeveloped. Her opinion ultimately did not matter, however, and her family moved to the new station. After relocating to Traverse des Sioux, Mary Riggs wrote that she had "many cares and duties pressing heavily upon [her] during the past summer" because of her family's move to "a new and uncultivated field of labor."[36]

Even after she had re-established her home, Mary Riggs was isolated and homesick at her new station. To stave off her loneliness, Mary Riggs planted flowers around her home. In a letter to her mother, Riggs explained the importance of her flowers. "Perhaps you will wonder why I should bestow any of my precious time upon flowers when their cultivation is attended with so many difficulties. The principal reason is, that I find my mind needs some such cheering relaxation. In leaving my childhood's home for this Indian land, you know my dear mother, I left almost [every]thing held dear, and gave up almost every innocent pleasure I once enjoyed . . . I feel that I have grown old beyond my years."[37]

After her initial displeasure with the move, Riggs grew to love the home and garden that she had painstakingly re-created at Traverse des Sioux. Riggs also felt tied to Traverse des Sioux because her brother was buried near the station. For nearly a decade, Riggs had begged family members to visit her in Minnesota. Just after relocating to Traverse des Sioux, her brother Joseph arrived from Massachusetts. Tragically, he drowned a short time later and was buried beneath a "beautiful scrub oak" close to her cabin.

When the Board ordered her husband back to Lac qui Parle in 1846, she again did not want to leave. Stephen Riggs, however, quickly accepted, stating that it was his "duty" to move. Mary Riggs was unable to "see the necessity of such a change." In a rare show of anger and defiance against her husband, Mary Riggs lamented the subservient role that forced her to meekly accept the move. "Oh how I loved those low rude log cabins at Traverse" and the oak that was the "resting place of that loved one." Although she conceded that she had to accept the move "for Christ's sake," she could not help being angry that she was forced to leave "because the wife must be in subjection, as Paul says." She described the move as a "trial" that a missionary wife must endure.[38]

Domestic Chores

Even without the additional burden of moves, all of the missionary women noted that domestic chores increasingly filled their days and took a physical and emotional toll. Sabrina Stevens, a missionary who labored just north of the Dakota missions among the Ojibwe, commiserated to her friend Cordelia Pond about the amount of domestic work she performed. Stevens noted that missionary women had "a field of labor within your own doors which will occupy all your time and energies." Pond and the other Dakota missionary women agreed with her statement. Mary Riggs wrote that "a multitude of little duties and cares have filled up even the fragments of time." She was often tired, overworked, and overwhelmed but knew that that was "the lot of a missionary wife."[39]

The women's days were filled with a constant cycle of sweeping, cleaning, and washing. Mary Riggs called her daily chores "one monotonous round of duties." As a result of her domestic labors, she believed that "both the temporal and spiritual suffer in consequence, and that I am becoming slothful, stupid, and melancholy." While all tasks were monotonous, laundry seemed to be universally the most hated. Mary Riggs found washing to be "hard" as she "had not been accustomed to do a day's washing." Likewise, Marjorie Cunningham, a teacher, frequently commented in her diary about how much she hated helping with the wash. "Wash day! Oh dear I would that it never comes[!]" Several of the missionary women hired Dakota women to perform this chore, but they complained that the Indian workers demanded exorbitant pay and required extensive supervision. Therefore, most missionary women "performed all the work of her house with her own hands."[40]

Unrelenting domestic chores severely restricted the hours that most women could spend doing missionary work. Although they still taught in the schools and organized sewing circles, by the 1840s married women with children averaged about an hour a day working with the Dakotas. In 1840, Mary Riggs reported that she "spent from eight until nine in teaching reading to our Dakota little girls . . . and Mrs. Hopkins has taught them to sew the hour following." In 1841, Riggs was "too busy and ill" to teach in the winter. In some cases the short time that the women reported working with the Dakotas could have been influenced by Dakota opposition to the schools; they simply may not have had many students to teach. Even if students had flocked to the schools, however, the women could not have devoted as much time as they would have liked to missionary work.[41]

Missionary Children

Much of the women's increased domestic burden stemmed from the arrival of children. The average missionary woman delivered a child every two years. Mary Riggs delivered her first child shortly after her arrival at Lac qui Parle in 1837 and had her last (eighth) child at the age of forty-six in 1859.

Gideon and Agnes Pond, about 1854.

Cordelia Pond (married to Samuel) had four children before her death in 1852, while Sarah Pond (Gideon) had seven children prior to her death in 1853. Agnes Hopkins had three children born at Traverse des Sioux; she was widowed in 1851 when her husband, Robert Hopkins, drowned in the Minnesota River. Later, Agnes Hopkins married Gideon Pond. The blended family consisted of her three children and his seven, along with six more they had together, for a total of sixteen children.[42]

These large families severely circumscribed the time that missionary women could spend teaching, studying, or writing letters. In 1840, Mary Riggs complained that she could not finish her letter home because she had a "little daughter, not three months old." Although "she is not a troublesome babe . . . she has repeatedly interrupted me while I have been writing this letter." With the arrival of each child, Riggs's life became increasingly circumscribed by her home. By 1848, with the birth of her fifth child, Riggs complained to her mother she felt "oppressed with care and labor and know not how or where to obtain the assistance I think I need . . . My mind as well as body suffer." After the arrival of her sixth, her husband noted that his wife was overwhelmed with work. Because their family was so large, Riggs reported that all of Mary's time was consumed with "trying to teach, clothe, and feed [the children]."[43]

While any mother of the era could relate to the amount of time devoted to childcare, missionary women also dealt with unique issues that set them apart from other antebellum mothers. Unlike their sisters in Massachusetts or Ohio, missionary women worried about raising their children in a "heathen and savage" environment. The women's main goal was to "train [their children] for heaven," and they fretted about achieving this objective living near Indians. All of the missionary mothers worried that their children might be in "danger of becoming little Indians in their tastes, feelings, and habits" because of their proximity to the Dakota.[44]

While most of their fears did not come to fruition, the women witnessed their sons and daughters mimicking several Dakota gender roles. Their daughters observed Dakota women "packing" (carrying goods) on their backs. To her dismay, Mary Riggs found her daughter Isabella had a fondness for packing. She complained, "if she has a piece of cloth or paper or picks up a pair of scissors, as if by instinct she places them on her neck behind and then tries to fasten them with a pocket handkerchief . . . and parades around the room with evident satisfaction . . . [H]er favorite pack is the . . . chair cushion." Likewise, Lydia Huggins's seven-year-old daughter "delights to pack her little sister of two, holding her by a blanket as do the Indians." According to Euro-American gender roles, women did not carry heavy burdens. Because Dakota women carried their tents and belongings between camps, missionaries often called Dakota women "slaves" to their husbands and used packing to illustrate the degraded position of Dakota women. Missionary women were horrified to see their daughters imitating what they considered to be a demeaning practice.[45]

Missionary boys attempted to hunt like the Dakota boys. For his birthday, Alfred Riggs received "a very small bow and arrow, from an Indian man, who is a frequent visitor." While Alfred was thrilled with the gift, his mother did "not feel desirous that he should prize a bow or gun as do these sons of the prairie." Instead of becoming a hunter (a "savage" occupation), Riggs's prayer was "that he may early become a lamb of the Good Shepherd's fold." Against their mother's wishes, Alfred and his brother Thomas attempted to accompany the Dakota boys on hunting expeditions. Because of his mother's dislike of hunting, however, the brothers complained that they did not get enough practice. Thomas Riggs remembered that "when it came to hunting, at first the Indian boys had all the advantages. They knew the places to go and the best blinds and they usually brought in more ducks than I did."[46]

Parents also worried that their children did not receive an adequate formal education in the mission field. Gideon Pond, for example, complained that his children needed teachers who would focus their time on the missionary children, not on Dakota students. Although Robert Hopkins attempted to teach both Dakota and mission children, Pond felt that he could not devote enough time to the mission students. Because of Hopkins's divided focus, Pond reported that his son Edward was "fast becoming a *blockhead* and yet I think he is naturally quite a fine boy—he only needs training. Sarah is a romp and still in favorable circumstance I think might become a fine girl[.] Georg[e]—poor fellow! [His] prospects are dreary but he don't [*sic*] know it." Likewise, Mary Riggs was anxious because her daughters Isabella (age nine) and Martha (seven) could not write and Anna Jane (four) could not read. She worried because her oldest son, Alfred, had been able to master these skills earlier than his sisters "for the simple reason that more time was spent in teaching him."[47]

Because they lacked time to teach their children, missionary mothers tried to convince other women to come to Minnesota. Mary Riggs wrote many letters begging her younger sister Henrietta to come to Minnesota to teach her nieces and nephews. If Henrietta came to Minnesota, Riggs "should feel that our children would not be so much in danger of growing up like heathen." While Henrietta died before coming to Minnesota, other young, single women appointed by the Board to teach the Dakotas instead spent much of their time instructing missionary children. In 1843, Julia Kephart, from Ripley, Ohio, joined the Lac qui Parle mission. While she taught some Dakota children, she spent most of her time instructing the Riggs children. In 1846, Jane Williamson's main duty was to teach Alfred Riggs and her nephews John and Andrew Williamson. In 1849, Mr. Adams taught Alfred geography and English grammar, while Miss Cunningham instructed the Riggs girls.[48]

Some parents sent their children back east to be raised by relatives or friends. These parents believed that "there are many things which they need to learn to fit them for usefulness which they cannot well learn here.

Though it will be painful to part with them, regard to their welfare probably requires" sending them east. Separated from the mission, children could attend schools with other white students and churches where services were not held in Dakota. Sons and daughters learned useful trades and skills under the tutelage of their eastern guardians. Most important, parents no longer needed to worry about the effect of the Dakotas on their children's development.[49]

While Stephen and Mary Riggs opted to keep their children in Minnesota, several other families sent their children east. In 1838, Thomas Williamson sent his daughter to live with their friends in Ohio. Although it was "painful" for his wife Sarah, Gideon Pond also left his daughter Ruth in Connecticut with relatives. While Pond assured his wife that Ruth loved living in Connecticut, he admitted that "it is something of a trial to part with *children* but I think it is right to do so in this case." Alexander Huggins's oldest daughters lived in Ohio for seven years. Huggins kept his son with him in Minnesota but worried that the boy would not "be joined to the Savior by a true and living faith" because he had not accompanied his sisters.[50]

Women's Unrealized Expectations

Life in the field for the women of the Dakota mission bore little resemblance to the heroic or romantic stories that filled antebellum missionary literature. Indeed, Mary Riggs privately commented to her brother that "there is no romance in our circumstances." For obvious reasons, the mission press did not highlight the resentment that sprang from endless domestic chores and the struggles women faced raising children among the Indians. Missionary hagiographies certainly did not focus on children who were sent to live with relatives or friends to isolate them from the Dakotas and provide them with an adequate education.[51]

After reading these hagiographies, some of the missionary women had participated in arranged marriages so that they could work as missionaries. While these women rarely criticized their husbands and surely loved their children, the reality of raising a family and taking care of their home did not allow them to devote their lives to converting the Dakotas. When discussing her marriage to Stephen Riggs with her brother Alfred, Mary Riggs noted that while she was happy with the marriage, "many of my bright visions have never been realized and others have been much changed both

Cordelia Pond to Agnes Hopkins, May 29, 1844.

in outline and finishing." Other missionary women also let their disillusionment and doubt creep into their letters. In 1843, Cordelia Pond noted that she was "accomplishing little good" among the Dakotas. In 1844, Pond expressed the same sentiment to fellow missionary Agnes Hopkins. "Our prospects of usefulness here appear very dark at present," she wrote. "[I]t seems as though we were wasting our time and spending our lives in vain by remaining here." Pond, however, was aware that she needed to edit her words. She concluded her letter stating that "perhaps I ought not to write this. I would not discourage any one." For good or ill, Pond hoped to keep future generations from knowing the conflicted and unfulfilling nature of missionary work for women.[52]

After the 1840s the women of the Dakota mission largely fade from the written record in terms of their contact with the Dakotas and missionary work in general. They still interacted with Dakotas and had strong opinions about federal Indian policy and Minnesota's settlement, but their trajectory had changed. Overall, they no longer filled their letters with issues related to missionary work or the Dakotas; instead their correspondence focused extensively on family affairs and their children. By the end of the 1840s, life in the field had changed the women's view of missionary work, their place within the ABCFM, and their belief in their own ability to convert the Dakotas.

Moving Forward after a Decade of Growing Opposition

The 1840s was a difficult decade for the men and women of the Dakota mission. At both a personal and an institutional level, they seemed to be farther from their goal of converting a large number of Dakota to Christianity than they had in the 1830s. In 1849, Samuel Pond summarized this general disillusionment. He informed Secretary Treat that "Our hopes and expectations of seeing many of this people soon brought into the fold of the great Shepherd are not so sanguine as the[y] once were . . . Our want of success causes us great and increasing anxiety." Even Stephen Riggs, perhaps the most confident of all ABCFM workers, described missionary work in the 1840s as "emphatically one of trial and difficulty." Samuel Pond concluded that, unfortunately, "the greater part of this people love darkness rather than light . . . [T]hey manifest no desire to hear the Gospel and many of them seem unwilling that any should listen to it."[53]

Despite these dire evaluations of the Dakota mission, no missionaries officially abandoned their posts in Minnesota during the 1840s. Most continued to believe that they were "planting the seeds" of Christianity that could bloom at any time. Moreover, it is possible that the missionaries remained in Minnesota because they hoped, despite all evidence to the contrary, that further governmental presence in Minnesota might help (or at least not hinder) their efforts to convert the Dakotas. Despite their negative evaluation of the new settlements that followed the Treaty of 1837, the missionaries also hoped to use Minnesota's new territorial status to further their work. In 1849, Gideon Pond served for one year as a member of the lower house in the new territorial government. During that time, he attempted to get several aspects of the ABCFM's agenda passed into law. He proposed two pieces of legislation: one "giving civil rights equally to all" and the other "prohibiting Sabbath violation." According to his brother Samuel, "in these efforts he was in a measure successful and the initiatory steps taken by that legislature formed a substantial foundation for future action." In that same year Thomas Williamson and Joshua Potter appealed to the new territorial governor to finally resolve issues from the Treaty of 1837 that had impeded the ABCFM's work for close to a decade. Thus, as Robert Hopkins summarized it in a letter to the Board, the missionaries left the 1840s with "hope mingling with fear."[54]

CHAPTER 5

"I cannot feel satisfied with the result of my labors for these heathen"

Missionaries, Dakotas, and the Treaties of 1851, 1850-54

In 1854, Samuel Pond sent a resignation letter to Selah Treat, the new corresponding secretary of the ABCFM—one that he never would have envisioned writing in 1834. After much thought and prayer, Pond resigned from the Dakota mission, concluding that his efforts to convert the Dakotas had failed. Reading stories about successful missions in the *Missionary Herald* helped to convince Pond to end his affiliation with the ABCFM. "I read . . . [the *Missionary Herald*] with some such mingled feelings of satisfaction and chagrin as a soldier might be supposed to experience while hearing the account of a battle in which the main army to which he was attached was victorious," he explained, "while that particular detachment to which he belonged was defeated." When he compared his work with the Dakotas to more successful missions (or at least portrayed as flourishing by the evangelical press), he concluded, "I cannot feel satisfied with the result of my labors for these heathen." Samuel Pond was not the only Dakota missionary disillusioned with his work. By 1854, all of the missionaries, except for Thomas Williamson and Stephen Riggs, had resigned their posts.[1]

Historians have attributed these resignations entirely to the 1851 Treaties of Traverse des Sioux and Mendota, which affected all four bands of Dakotas and resulted in the loss of their lands in Minnesota and the establishment of an impermanent reservation on the Minnesota River. An examination of the missionaries' private correspondence, however, shows that the treaties of 1851 played a relatively minor role in their decisions to leave the ABCFM. Rather, different combinations of problems that had arisen over the past two decades of work finally came together and pushed the missionary men to tender their resignations. The treaties were only the most recent in a series of long-standing conflicts that had informed missionary work since 1835 and led several missionaries to question the Dakota mission's viability long before 1851.[2]

The missionaries' troubles during the 1850s, however, paled in comparison with those of the Dakotas. In 1851, government negotiators used heavy-handed tactics to push through the Treaties of Traverse des Sioux and Mendota, which cost the Dakota all of their remaining land in Minnesota. Most Dakotas did not support these unpopular treaties and resisted their implementation. Many refused to move to the impermanent reservation on the Minnesota River, or if they agreed to relocate, quickly left and only returned to collect their annuities. Moreover, following the treaties, Dakotas continued to resist missionary (and government) efforts to convert and civilize them. Indeed, throughout the entire treaty and post-treaty period, missionary letters and reports portray the Dakotas as strong, resilient, and willing to challenge unpopular missionary programs and government orders. Unlike modern historians, however, the ABCFM missionaries did not laud these examples of resistance; rather, they saw Dakota opposition to Christianity and civilization as misguided, uninformed, and even dangerous to their survival as a people. When faced with this resistance, many of the missionaries—like the Pond brothers—increasingly saw conversion as an impossible task. In sum, Dakota opposition forced the missionaries to "assess why they were among them" and to rethink their role as missionaries, which was something that they had never questioned prior to arriving in Minnesota.[3]

Dakota Resistance to the ABCFM

Evidence that the Dakota mission might fail continued to accumulate even prior to the 1851 Treaties of Traverse des Sioux and Mendota. Indeed, the missionaries faced unremitting opposition at all their stations in the early 1850s. Most of this opposition stemmed from the Treaty of 1837, even though the document had been ratified over a decade earlier. Thomas Williamson summarized the complicated treaty provision that continued to plague the Dakota mission. According to the Treaty of 1837, the government was to spend $5,000 per year on the Mdewakantons' education. In most years, however, no "more than half of this sum [was] expended" and in "many years no part of it." As a result, by the early 1850s, the amount accumulated exceeded $50,000.[4]

The Mdewakantons wanted the $50,000 released to them immediately and not held for civilization programs. By 1850, however, the government still refused to distribute these funds and even authorized a small release of the money to pay two ABCFM teachers. Williamson recalled the immediate outcry after the dispersal. "As soon as it was known that the teachers had been thus appointed," he wrote, most of the villagers refused to attend school. Again, as in the 1840s, anger over the ABCFM's use of treaty monies spread to all mission sites. Williamson reported that the village council near Oak Grove "resolved that if any of their people attended the . . . meetings of the missionaries they should be stripped of their clothes, whipped and deprived of their share in the annuities." Samuel Pond also complained that the missionaries could not "maintain a school without having a . . . quarrel with the Indians." Once again, the Dakotas' tactics were effective. At Oak Grove, Dakota protests forced Gideon Pond to shut his mission school. In 1850, the schools at Traverse des Sioux and Prairieville also remained closed.[5]

While Dakota protests centered on the mission schools, opposition also carried over to ABCFM churches. The missionaries reported that religious meetings at all ABCFM stations remained largely unattended in the early 1850s. As a result, few Dakota men and women professed their faith. Because of the low attendance and lack of converts, Samuel Pond lamented the sorry state of religious education: "The aspect of things here is quite discouraging even at our most favored station," he complained. "We have very little opportunity to preach the Gospel. The Indians will not hear us."[6]

In 1851, just prior to the opening of treaty negotiations, Gideon Pond summarized the Dakotas' lack of interest in education and Christianity: "[W]ith few exceptions," he wrote, "the Dakotas do not want missionaries, *will not* hear the truth, and *will not* suffer their children to be taught to read." Robert Hopkins agreed, stating that the debacle over 1837 treaty funds had neutralized their "general influence, and caused many to feel that we are deceivers . . . [This] almost entirely [prevented] attendance on the means of grace" and served as "an effectual barrier to schools." In light of the long-standing protests against the Treaty of 1837, the missionaries obviously worried about the effects a new treaty would have on their work.[7]

The Treaties of Traverse des Sioux and Mendota (1851)

Against the backdrop of continued Dakota protests resulting from the 1837 treaty, federal agents arrived in Minnesota to obtain the Dakotas' remaining lands in 1851. When the Dakotas learned about the negotiations, their primary concerns were losing their lands, the size and location of a reservation, and making sure that the new treaty did not repeat the mistakes made in the Treaty of 1837, especially the controversial education fund. Many Dakotas also wanted to ensure that the ABCFM missionaries did not benefit from the sale of their lands. Robert Hopkins explained that prior to the negotiations, "evil reports circulated about us. I suppose a majority believe that we are expecting money [from] . . . the expected treaty . . . All agree that the Missionary shall have nothing, but the fear is that neither the Missionary nor the Gov. will consent to this."[8]

Missionary Evaluations of the Proposed Treaties

Although most Dakotas believed that the missionaries fully supported the government's position, they actually were divided over the desirability of a new treaty. Given Stephen Riggs's support of the Treaty of 1837, it was no surprise that he generally favored a new treaty. More than the other missionaries, Riggs believed that removing the Dakotas to a reservation would allow them to be "operated on [more] effectively" by the missionaries. Moreover, the government could more easily protect private property on a reservation, as that was "one of the most serious obstacles in the way of their civilization." Finally, Riggs hoped that a new treaty would provide money for an education fund, over which "the Indians should have no control." Ideally, he believed the fund should be turned over to the ABCFM missionaries.[9]

Although the other ABCFM missionaries realized that land cessions and removal were inevitable, they disagreed with Riggs that these changes would promote Christianity among the Dakotas. Gideon Pond wrote that "God only knows what will be the result of the contemplated treaty." His brother Samuel echoed the same sentiment, stating that in the past the government had pursued "a hurtful policy toward . . . [the Dakotas]." The Pond brothers continued to worry that treaty annuities would impede the Dakotas' progress toward civilization. Samuel reported that he had waited nearly fifteen years for the annuities from the Treaty of 1837 to expire so that the Dakotas could "resume habits of industry." A new treaty would dash "all our hopes of a change for the better," because further government annuities would keep the Dakotas "from making any efforts to improve their condition."[10]

Robert Hopkins also worried about annuities, but for different reasons than the Pond brothers. Before negotiators arrived, rumors circulated among the Dakotas that the missionaries would use the annuities to fund their stations. Although this is exactly what Riggs wanted, Hopkins informed the Dakotas that he would not use their annuities in this way. Just before negotiations opened, Hopkins invited the Dakotas to travel with him to St. Paul to meet with territorial governor Alexander Ramsey. During this conference, Hopkins promised to "sign a writing in the presence of the Gov. binding myself not [to] receive money for what I have been doing in the country." Even though no Dakotas showed up at the meeting, Hopkins signed the document. Hopkins's efforts, however, failed to convince the Dakotas that he did not covet their monies and land.[11]

The Treaty Provisions

Most of the missionaries were ambivalent about a new treaty. Federal negotiators, however, had no qualms about taking the rest of Dakota lands in Minnesota. In 1851, agents pushed through the Treaties of Traverse des Sioux and Mendota. The Treaty of Traverse des Sioux bound all Sissetons and Wahpetons to sell approximately 21 million acres, including "all their lands in the State of Iowa; and also, all their lands in the Territory of Minnesota." In return for their land, the government promised to establish a permanent reservation on the Upper Minnesota, "extending for ten miles on either side of the river and from the western end of the cession down to the Yellow Medicine River." Although they could remain on their ceded lands for two years before moving to the reservation, the territory would be opened to settlement immediately after the Senate ratified the treaty.[12]

The Sissetons and Wahpetons also would receive $1,665,000, but not in cash. Instead, the government designated $275,000 to remove and settle them on the reservation. Every year thereafter, they would receive $40,000 in cash and $10,000 in goods and provisions. The treaty also included a large civilization component in which the government would spend money from the land cession to establish individual farms, erect mills, and build manual labor schools. The treaty also established a $6,000 annual education fund, as desired by Riggs.[13]

The Treaty of Mendota, negotiated with the Mdewakantons and Wahpekutes, was similar to the Treaty of Traverse des Sioux. Like their northern counterparts, the Mdewakantons and Wahpekutes "relinquish[ed] all their lands . . . in the Territory of Minnesota, [and] in the State of Iowa." In return, they were promised a reservation "of the average width of ten miles on either side of the Minnesota River." They also received monetary compensation for their lands totaling $1,410,000. They would not have access to most of these funds, however, as the money would be used to pay for their removal and resettlement on the reservation, and for their civilization and education.[14]

The Treaty of Mendota differed in several ways from the Treaty of Traverse des Sioux, all of which arose out of the Mdewakantons' experience with the Treaty of 1837. Federal negotiators promised to distribute $30,000 in cash after the treaty was accepted to make up for a portion of the disputed funds from the Treaty of 1837. Agents promised to issue all future annual payments from the fund in cash. The commissioners agreed to make the new treaty "so plain that there [would] be no misunderstandings at all." The Lower Dakotas, however, worried that the treaty would be changed in Washington. As a council member commented, once the Treaty of 1837 had been ratified, "the Indians found out very different from what they had been told, and all were ashamed." The agents promised the Senate would not change the treaty. For these reasons, Thomas Williamson proclaimed that the Dakotas had "won" the long-standing dispute over the Treaty of 1837 and "the enemies of education [had] succeeded."[15]

Despite these minor concessions, the Treaties of Traverse des Sioux and Mendota were acclaimed by government officials and Minnesotans alike. Federal negotiators had added more than 35 million acres to the United States at the cost of $3,075,000 for both treaties. The Dakotas would be removed to a small reservation and prime farms lands opened for sale. For these reasons, Alexander Ramsey, Minnesota's territorial governor, proclaimed that the treaties ushered in "an era full of brilliant promise." A newspaper editor offered an even more hyperbolic evaluation of the treaties, noting that they "let open a great region, black with barbarism, [to] the flood of refulgent civilization." James M. Goodhue, editor of the *Minnesota Pioneer* (the first newspaper in Minnesota), called the treaties "the pillar of fire that lights us into a broad Canaan of fertile lands."[16]

ABCFM Missionaries' Involvement in the Treaty Negotiations

Unlike the government agents and the Minnesota press, the ABCFM missionaries had gone into negotiations extremely ambivalent about new treaties. Despite their concerns, many of the missionaries played prominent roles in both treaty councils. At Traverse des Sioux, Stephen Riggs and

Thomas Williamson opened the day with "religious exercises." The missionaries also took the federal delegation on a tour of their mission station and school at Traverse des Sioux, hoping this would convince officials to earmark forthcoming treaty monies to fund all the ABCFM schools. Riggs and Gideon Pond also served as official translators; Riggs translated the final draft of the Treaty of Traverse des Sioux into Dakota, while Gideon Pond fulfilled the same role at Mendota. Thomas Williamson worked as the government physician at the Traverse des Sioux council.[17]

Several ABCFM missionaries also labored behind the scenes as quasi-government agents to convince Dakotas to accept the treaties. William LeDuc, who moved to Minnesota in 1850, noted that the ABCFM missionaries "who have been among them, and understand their language, have been unceasing to effect this [Traverse des Sioux] treaty." He especially singled out Stephen Riggs as tirelessly working to convince the Upper Dakotas to cede their lands to the government. According to LeDuc, Riggs spent "all hours of the day and night" explaining to the "different bands the provisions of the treaty," answering objections, and trying to persuade the "stubborn warriors" to accept the terms of the treaty. Alexander Ramsey summarized the role that ABCFM missionaries (especially Riggs) played in the treaties. "The missionaries in this region have been useful auxiliaries to the government, and, in a thousand ways, of incalculable service to the Indian."[18]

ABCFM Missionaries and the Immediate Aftermath of the 1851 Treaties

Because some missionaries played prominent roles in the treaty negotiations, the Dakotas perceived all of the ABCFM missionaries as fully supporting the new treaties. Thus, when government agents broke promises made at Traverse des Sioux and Mendota—including the loss of the permanent reservation, the controversial traders' paper, and the failure to stop settlers from settling in Indian lands—the missionaries stood in the crossroads between furious Dakotas and unpopular government policies and actions. The Dakota missionaries made things worse by failing to speak out against these wrongs, or, if they did so, they offered support based on their own agenda and religious convictions, not because they supported the Dakotas' interpretation of events. At times, as with the controversial traders' paper, Riggs failed to support the Dakotas at all.

The Loss of the Permanent Reservation

The ABCFM missionaries, like the Dakotas, were blindsided by the loss of the permanent reservation. During the ratification process, the Senate struck the reservation clause out of both treaties. Without consulting the Dakotas, senators inserted a new amendment that gave the president the power to decide where the Dakotas lived and how long they could remain. In other words, the Senate took away the Dakotas' reservation without providing other permanent lands in return. According to treaty protocol, the Dakotas were supposed to accept or reject the amended versions of the treaties; however, this did not happen. Governor Ramsey (who was charged with gaining the Dakotas' consent) kept the affair quiet until he gathered the needed Dakota signatures and sent the treaties back to Washington. The Senate ratified the two treaties, without the reservation and without the majority of the Dakotas' consent, on February 24, 1853.[19]

Following ratification of the treaties, the decision of where to relocate the Dakotas fell to President Millard Fillmore. Fillmore eventually decided that the Dakotas could move to the same reservation that had been stricken from the treaties, but he only guaranteed their tenure for five years. After that time, they would have to move, but no lands were set aside for their relocation. To add insult to injury, the Dakotas did not know when those five years began. If the time was counted from when the treaties were first signed, the Dakotas might only have three years before they could be forced to move to an unknown location. Despite the impermanent nature of the reservation, Robert Murphy, the Dakotas' agent at the time, began to survey and lay out the lands. The reservation would be divided into two agencies; the Sisseton and Wahpeton would reside on the Upper Agency, while the Mdewakanton and Wahpekutes would move to the Lower Agency.[20]

The Dakotas strongly protested the loss of their permanent reservation. Even the commissioner of Indian affairs acknowledged (in an understatement) that "[s]triking out the provisions allowing them a large reserve on the Minnesota [R]iver ... d[id] not meet their approbation." The changes to the treaties, as well as the underhanded method Ramsey used to gain consent for the amendment, caused the Dakotas "deep dissatisfaction" and threw "daily more and more obstacles in the way of their removal."[21]

The ABCFM missionaries also believed that the Senate had done an injustice to the Dakotas. During a trip back east, Stephen Riggs met with

President Fillmore to discuss the Dakotas' reaction to the loss of their permanent reservation. Although the newspapers in St. Paul portrayed the Dakotas as "very well satisfied" with their situation, Riggs warned the president that he "need not believe a word of it." Riggs told the president that "Wabashaw is reported to have said, 'There is one thing more which our great father can do, that is, gather us all together on the prairie and surround us with soldiers and shoot us down.'"[22]

Although Riggs protested against the loss of the reservation, he did so for different reasons than the Dakotas. The Dakotas accused the government of lying, breaking signed agreements, and stealing lands that had been promised to them. While Stephen Riggs admitted that the Senate had done "a great wrong . . . to this people," his condemnation of the government's decision rested on the belief that the loss of a permanent reservation would irreparably harm the Dakotas' chances of becoming civilized Christians. According to Riggs, the Dakotas needed a permanent reservation "to give the Indians a motive to industry." Thomas Williamson echoed Riggs's point of view. The "knowledge that the country is not theirs," he bluntly stated, "will impede their improvement."[23]

The Traders' Paper

While the missionaries merely commented on the loss of the reservation, they were intimately involved with the so-called traders' paper controversy among the Upper Dakotas. During the signing of the Treaty of Traverse des Sioux, council members were asked to initial what they believed to be a third copy of the treaty. In reality, the document was not a copy of the treaty, but a paper that bound the Upper Dakotas to give about $400,000 to mixed-blood Dakotas and several other interests (especially traders). The ABCFM also would receive $800 for cattle killed by the Dakotas. After these interests had been paid, the Upper Dakotas would receive only about 7 cents an acre for their land. Because of the underhanded way in which the commissioners and traders had obtained the Dakotas' signatures, historian Roy Meyer referred to the traders' paper (and by extension the entire 1851 treaty process) as a "monstrous conspiracy." According to Meyer, the traders' paper did more than any other federal action to create a legacy of bitterness and anger among the Dakota people.[24]

The Sissetons and Wahpetons immediately protested the traders' paper.

They asserted that the paper had been "obtained through fraud, misrepresentation, and deceit—they never having been fully explained and interpreted." Worse, the Dakotas charged that Ramsey had forced them to pay the traders and other interests by withholding their annuities and imprisoning several men. Samuel Pond agreed with the Dakotas that they had been cheated; he noted that it was his "private opinion" that many of the traders "got a little too much of . . . [the Dakota's treaty monies]." Although Pond kept his comments private, other men, including a trader named Madison Sweetser, agreed to help the Upper Dakotas present their charges to the government. As a result of Sweetser's petitions, as well as the negative publicity generated by the affair, the Senate decided to investigate the controversy.[25]

During the inquiry, the commission asked dozens of men to publicly comment on the situation, including Thomas Williamson and Stephen Riggs. Both missionaries had been present for the signing of the traders' paper; indeed, their signatures appear at the end of the document as witnesses. Although Riggs and Williamson agreed that they had witnessed the document, they differed over whether the paper had been translated and, if it had been accurately translated, whether the Dakotas understood what they were signing. Thomas Williamson offered incendiary testimony against the government agents. He claimed that he had witnessed the Traverse des Sioux treaty signing and believed, like the Dakotas, that they were signing multiple copies of the same document, not a traders' paper. At least one government official believed Williamson: "I cannot doubt for a moment the truthfulness of the Indians' statement when they say that they were deceived and defrauded . . . when a gentleman of the intelligence of the rev. Mr. Williamson, a man speaking the Sioux and understanding it well, being present all the time, assisting in making the treaty, should have been so far blinded as not to have heard a word in relation to the agreement, but supposed it a copy of the treaty."[26]

Stephen Riggs's testimony, however, differed from that of his colleague. Although he admitted that he had never interpreted the traders' paper to the Dakotas (although he had translated the final treaty), he was sure that they understood it. Like Williamson, Riggs's character was extolled, but to prove that the Dakotas had not been deceived. Alexander Ramsey wrote the commissioner of Indian affairs that "[y]ou will also see that the Rev. Mr. Riggs who witnessed the distribution of indebtedness, by the Indians, among the traders—a most excellent interpreter, and a man of most unexceptional character, witnesses this paper—a most significant fact." In the end, the Senate believed Riggs's testimony over Williamson's and cleared Ramsey and all other officials of wrongdoing.[27]

Despite Williamson's testimony, which backed up the Dakotas' claims of fraud, the missionaries' involvement in the treaty process and its aftermath further decreased many Dakotas' already low opinion of the ABCFM. Indeed, the Dakotas attributed a series of bad events that befell the missionaries after 1851 to their involvement in the treaty process and the traders' paper. For example, in 1854 the Riggs's home at Lac qui Parle burned down. Riggs reported that some of the Dakotas called this misfortune a judgment "from God upon us because we helped the traders rob them of their money." After hearing this charge, Riggs brushed off their criticism, noting that it concerned him "very little what they say or think about me."[28]

The Arrival of Settlers

At the same time the Dakotas protested the loss of their reservation and the traders' paper, they were assaulted on another front: settlers moved onto their recently ceded lands in record numbers. In the 1850s the white population of Minnesota rose by 2,831 percent, the highest percentage increase in the nation at the time. Immediately after the treaties were signed, Taoyateduta (Little Crow) reported that "the white settlers came in and showered their houses all over our country." The ABCFM missionaries also commented on the flood of settlers. According to Stephen Riggs, "No sooner was it known that the Senate had ratified the treaties made with the Dakotas in the summer of 1851, than multitudes flocked to the west side of the Mississippi." Near the ABCFM's Red Wing Mission, Joseph Hancock witnessed the arrival of "troops of claim hunters" and marveled at their dishonesty in staking out claims. Because the land had not yet been surveyed in 1852, each settler paced off his own 160-acre claim. Hancock called some of the settlers' strides "astonishing" in their length. Indeed, one farmer discovered he had walked off enough land for about three claims once the lands were finally surveyed. In this unorganized land grab, some settlers ended up fighting over conflicting claims. Fortunately, Hancock noted, "no lives were lost and none . . . seriously injured."[29]

As in the 1840s, the missionaries were ambivalent about the growing white population. On the one hand, they applauded the construction of civilized buildings and farms. The arrival of white settlers also meant that for the first time since the opening of the Dakota mission the missionaries (especially those located near Fort Snelling) preached to full congregations of new settlers. Even before the treaties were signed, Thomas Williamson noted that Presbyterian churches for white settlers were organized at Stillwater and St. Paul.[30]

Conversely, the ABCFM missionaries worried that their attempts to Christianize and civilize the Dakotas would be undermined as less-than-pious settlers set a bad example for the Dakotas. The missionaries were concerned that unconverted whites might drink, travel on the Sabbath, or model other immoral behavior. The new governor of Minnesota Territory, Willis Arnold Gorman (1853–57), is a prime example of the type of settler the missionaries deplored. Gorman, as an Irish Catholic, already had that strike against him in the eyes of the Protestant missionaries. In 1853, he allegedly "took an Indian concubine" and "compelled the Indians to council with him on the Sabbath." As a result of the governor's actions, Stephen Riggs called Gorman a "shameful character." Williamson likewise found Gorman to be "a disgrace to mankind."[31]

Many of the settlers also exhibited immoral behavior in their relations with the Dakotas. The missionaries reported on the volatile situation that followed the 1851 treaties. In 1853, Joseph Hancock stated that Mdewakantons who resided near the Red Wing Mission had been forced to leave their village after their "houses . . . were all burned by the white settlers." The new press in Minnesota did nothing to ease these tensions, and in some cases even promoted violence against the Dakotas. Thomas Williamson noted that the "tone of our Press is calculated to make matters worse by comparing the Sioux to Wolves and Panthers and it is reported that Gov. Gorman has told some who complained to him to shoot the Indians if they find them stealing."[32]

ABCFM Missionaries Leave the Dakota Mission

All of the missionaries realized that Dakota opposition to the treaties would make their work more challenging. Each of the missionaries agonized over whether he should remain at the Dakota mission. When faced with the changing situation in Minnesota, Samuel and Gideon Pond, Alexander Huggins, Jonas Pettijohn, Joseph Hancock, and Moses Adams decided to resign their positions as ABCFM missionaries to the Dakotas. By 1854, only Stephen Riggs and Thomas Williamson remained.[33]

The ABCFM's publications, including the *Missionary Herald* and *Annual Reports,* attempted to minimize the mass defection from the Dakota mission. Until this point, the mission press had portrayed the Dakota mission as troubled, but promised that success was attainable with hard work, commitment, and faith. The large number of resignations was harder to explain but did not come as a surprise to those with firsthand knowledge of the missionaries' personalities and the mission's conflicted history. An analysis of why Riggs and Williamson remained, and the others left, summarizes key themes of the ABCFM's struggle to convert the Dakotas to Christianity.

Why Riggs and Williamson Remained at the Dakota Mission

Stephen Riggs and Thomas Williamson, alone among all the missionaries, continued their affiliation with the ABCFM's Dakota mission. Following the 1851 treaties, the Williamson family relocated to what became known as the upper reserve (home of the Sisseton and Wahpeton), where they ministered to the Wahpetons at a new station called Pajutazee (Yellow Medicine). In 1854, after his family's home at Lac qui Parle burned down, Riggs joined Williamson on the upper reserve and established a second station (first called New Hope, and later, Hazelwood) about three miles from Pajutazee.[34]

It is not surprising that Stephen Riggs, of all the missionaries, remained affiliated with the ABCFM. From the time of his arrival at Lac qui Parle in 1837, Riggs rarely questioned his faith or his duty to the Dakotas in his writings. In fact, Riggs appears to be wholeheartedly committed to his cause, self-righteous, and, in some cases, intractable. He generally was unwilling to accommodate Dakota cultural practices or lessen his admission standards in any way, as seen by his responses to polygamy and warfare, for example. More than other missionaries, Riggs supported government initiatives and treaties, worked as a government translator during treaty negotiations, and upheld the government's position in the traders' dispute.

Thomas Williamson, on the other hand, seemed one of the least likely of the missionaries to remain. He frequently agonized over the success of his missionary work and the negative effect of government programs on the Dakotas. Compared with Riggs, he was more willing to compromise with the

Thomas Williamson, third from left, with women of the mission and Dakota members of the church in front of the Williamson home at Pajutazee mission, August 1862. (Adrian John Ebell)

Dakotas over issues of church admission, polygamy, and cultural practices like gift-giving. For Williamson, missionary work, on many different levels, was a constant struggle. Even Riggs, looking back on their forty-year collaboration, admitted that "there were abundant . . . differences of judgment" and that both men "freely criticized each other's work."[35]

Given their divergent personalities and missionary philosophy, it is not surprising that the two men offered different reasons for their decision to remain with the Dakotas. Even after decades of Dakota opposition and resistance to his proselytizing and schools, Riggs still believed that *all* Dakotas would eventually accept Christianity. Williamson, on the other hand, admitted defeat among the Lower Dakotas, especially the Mdewakanton. However, he still believed that the Upper Dakotas (the Sisseton and Wahpeton) had the potential for change. "Among these Mdewakantonwan we can seldom get a hearing except from the few," he explained. "And this is the chief reason why I wish to go among the Upper Indians." He hoped to have more influence among the Upper Indians because they "have less intercourse with white people" and "Roman Catholic traders." Riggs followed along to the Upper Dakotas not because he admitted defeat among any of

Hazelwood mission, about 1860.

the Dakotas but for reasons of expediency; after Riggs's home burned, the ABCFM suggested that he rebuild near Williamson to consolidate their efforts.[36]

Regardless of their differences, the two men continued to believe, despite evidence to the contrary, that the federal government would aid their cause on the upper reserve. While Williamson and Riggs criticized parts of the Treaty of Traverse des Sioux, they described the "treaty with the Upper Indians [as] . . . a good one for both them and the government." They praised the treaty for confining the Dakotas to a reservation, as the Sisseton and Wahpeton would then have no choice but to commence farming and attend the mission churches and schools.[37]

However, Congress took away the permanent reservation, an action Williamson called a "calamity" and Riggs termed "a great wrong." Both Williamson and Riggs hoped that the government would allow the Dakotas to remain on the impermanent reserve. In fact, with the help of ABCFM secretary Selah Treat in Boston, the men began a public campaign to convince government agents to honor the original reservation boundaries. In this Riggs and Williamson deviated from their long-standing policy of remaining quiet about federal Indian policy. They began by writing memorials on the subject to Congress, the Indian agent, and the governor. After their writing campaign, both men felt relatively certain that the Dakotas would be allowed to remain on the reserve and begin farming and living settled lives. Riggs informed Secretary Treat that he believed "it is the present intention of the government" to let the Dakotas occupy their reservation "for many years to come."[38]

Once the Dakotas were settled on their reserve, Riggs and Williamson hoped to benefit from the treaties' education funds. The Treaties of Traverse des Sioux and Mendota each set aside $6,000 for education. Both missionaries asked the Indian agent to give $6,000 to their organization. Williamson, however, asked that the entire $6,000 come from the Upper Dakotas, whereas Riggs wanted $3,000 from each of the Lower and Upper Dakotas. In whatever combination, both missionaries planned to use the money to construct and run Dakota boarding schools. Williamson also suggested using some of the money to pay white families (including those of the missionaries) to raise Dakota children.[39]

Riggs and Williamson also vowed to continue their work among the Dakotas in part to keep treaty monies away from Catholic priests. Both men feared that if the ABCFM abandoned the field, Catholic priests would move in and undo the Protestant seeds they had so painstakingly planted. Thomas Williamson warned "that the Romanists are now making a strong and united effort to get hold of the entire school fund of the Dakotas." They saw evidence everywhere of this supposed Catholic plot to take over the mission field. Riggs complained that some mixed-blood Dakotas had signed a petition demanding that the education money be given to the Roman Catholics instead of to the Protestant missionaries. Riggs and Williamson worried that the new territorial government officials supported a Catholic agenda. Stephen Riggs again targeted Governor Gorman, calling him a "swearing swaggering Catholic" who did not know "the a.b.c. of Indian character." Because of Gorman's "predilections for Catholicism and rank democracy," Riggs feared "but little good can be expected of him."[40]

Like Riggs and Williamson, the Board members in Boston did not want "immoral" Catholics to take over the Dakota mission. The Board strongly supported the men's arguments for relocating to Pajutazee and Hazelwood. In a letter to Gideon Pond before his resignation, Selah Treat expressed optimism that the Dakotas would convert to Christianity. "[I]n looking over the entire field of our failed effort we have learned that an unprosperous mission may at an early day undergo a complete change," he wrote. "The attitude of my mind then is this. We must wait a little longer. The time has not come for discouragement." He offered a similar explanation to Stephen Riggs in giving him permission to relocate to the reservation. "Some of your number take a dark view of the field, and not without reason. But I look ahead." Perhaps the new reservation, an infusion of education funds, and the support of two fully devoted missionaries would precipitate the long-awaited conversions.[41]

Reasons for Leaving the Dakota Mission

Because Treat supported Riggs and Williamson, he did not publicize the real reasons for the resignations of John Aiton, Jonas Pettijohn, Alexander Huggins, Joseph Hancock, Moses Adams, and the Pond brothers. In fact, the mission press was noticeably quiet about the resignations. One article simply mentioned that these missionaries left because they had "other responsibilities . . . demanding time and attention." The same article explained that Gideon Pond would have remained with the ABCFM, but "the circumstances of his family did not admit of it." A memorial written for Gideon Pond stated that "Mr. Pond elected to remain and labor among the white people" after the treaties of 1851. The article made sure to mention, however, that "Mr. Pond never lost his interest in the Dakotas, nor did they cease to love him."[42]

Historians have perpetuated the ABCFM's long-standing practice of obscuring the complexity and conflicted nature of the Dakota mission. Most secondary sources attribute the missionaries' resignations to the Treaties of Traverse des Sioux and Mendota. However, the missionaries' writings show that the treaties of 1851 played a relatively minor role in the resignations. Rather, different combinations of problems that had arisen over close to two decades of work finally came together and pushed each of the missionary men to tender his resignation.

John Aiton (1848–50)

The first missionary to resign his post actually left prior to the treaties of 1851. John Aiton said that he needed more money to "discharge the duties which . . . [he and his wife] owe to their parents." It was ironic that Aiton complained about financial considerations, as he was better paid than most of the ABCFM missionaries. He received $500 per year as a government teacher at Red Wing; the same year, the Board paid one of its assistants a salary of $250. Although he made more money than his peers, Aiton believed that the ABCFM should supplement his government salary. Aiton complained that "the Mission will not allow me a specific salary, as Dr. Williamson gave me reasonably to expect that they would do so" when he was recruited to come to the Dakota mission. Moreover, Aiton did not want to pay the difference between his larger salary and the Board's salary back to the ABCFM, even though this was their policy.[43]

When the Board refused to increase his salary, Aiton asked Secretary Treat if he could purchase land. Treat responded that the Board was "not in favor of having our missionaries encumbered with much land, or many secular cares, except where it is absolutely necessary." All of Aiton's complaints about money and land irritated his fellow missionaries, who had been living frugally for almost two decades. Thomas Williamson grumbled that Aiton's "talents for acquiring language and preaching appear to me considerable under par . . . and the management of secular matters as much above par." Robert Hopkins bluntly stated that "Bro. Aiton wanted a more lucrative business, and retired to seek it." Aiton tried to defend himself, stating that Thomas Williamson had misled him from the beginning about his salary. When the controversy over funds escalated, Aiton shot back that "*if the mission will bear half the blame, I will the other half.* But if not, not." It appears that the rest of the missionaries never acknowledged blame, as the Board accepted Aiton's resignation without further comment. After leaving the ABCFM, Aiton became a colporteur for the American Tract Society. In the spring of 1852, he purchased land in West St. Paul, Dakota County.[44]

Robert Hopkins (1843–51)

Robert Hopkins never had the chance to resign from the ABCFM mission, as he drowned in the Minnesota River on July 4, 1851. However, evidence indicates that had he lived, he would have been among those who left after 1851. His correspondence during the year before his death was negative about the Dakota mission's prospects. Hopkins wrote that despite their combined efforts, the missionaries had produced "no visible results." He claimed that "[t]he people are wholly indifferent, if not averse, to the calls of the Gospel; and we can succeed in but a few instances in inducing them to hear it." Those who listened to the missionaries only did so in "the hope of being more prepared in secular concerns." Turning to even harsher words, he called the "depravity among this people . . . terrible," declaring that it made him "sick and I feel the desire sometimes to 'Fly away and be at rest.'" In the end, his troubles converting the Dakotas made it "impossible" for him to "answer the expectations the churches entertained of missionaries." Given his negative evaluations of the Dakota mission, as well as his professed belief that he could no longer meet the expectations of the evangelic public, it is likely that Hopkins would have left the ABCFM Dakota mission.[45]

Jonas Pettijohn (1846–52)

Prior to the negotiations at Traverse des Sioux, Jonas Pettijohn worked as a government farmer at the Lac qui Parle mission. In resigning his affiliation with the ABCFM, Pettijohn cited the Board's policy on slavery; he refused "to remain in church fellowship with Slaveholders." While in theory the Board did not support slavery, the organization had become mired in the issue of Cherokee and Choctaw converts who owned slaves. Pettijohn was not alone in demanding that the Board categorically denounce slavery. The rest of the Dakota missionaries also spoke out strongly against slavery and urged the Board to sever all ties with slaveholders.[46]

Although all of the missionaries supported Pettijohn's position on slavery, Stephen Riggs attributed the farmer's resignation to less noble sentiments. He stated that Pettijohn "had taken pre-emption fever and had left the mission and gone to the Traverse and made a claim." Immediately after his resignation, Pettijohn purchased a claim in LeSueur County, Minnesota.[47]

Alexander Huggins (1835–52)

Like Jonas Pettijohn, Alexander Huggins cited both religious and material reasons for leaving his service with the Board. Huggins believed the Dakotas could not be converted. The missionaries had failed to convert the Dakotas in the past, and the post-treaty situation assured that they would continue to fail in the future. In 1852, Huggins wrote that "when I first entered on the work as an assistant Missionary I expected to labor in it as long as I should live[.] But now the Indians have sold their country and will soon be removed from this place[.] And I shall probably never feel it to be my duty to follow them."[48]

Alexander Huggins also worried that his eight children "may not be pre-pared to be useful" after living near the Dakotas for most of their lives. He fretted about the moral implications of growing up near "savage" Indians; he also felt that his children had not received an adequate education in the mission setting. Huggins wanted his children to attend seminaries and col-leges back east, and he needed more money to pay for their education than his small farmer's salary from the Board provided. Thus, he left the ABCFM so that he could "provide for his family." Like Jonas Pettijohn, he bought a claim in LeSueur County, Minnesota, immediately after the Board accepted his resignation.[49]

Joseph Hancock (1848–54)

Like the other missionaries, Joseph Hancock offered several reasons for his decision to leave the ABCFM. Hancock cited the Dakotas' long history of refusing to accept Christianity, which predated the treaties of 1851. He in-formed the corresponding secretary that "[t]he Dakotas. . . manifest no sincere desire to have us continue with them as religious teachers." He also noted that he could "think of nothing that has transpired during the year which may be considered favorable to our success." Moreover, Hancock cau-tioned the Board not to take action if Dakotas asked that a missionary be sent to their village. Hancock explained that such requests were likely for "tem-poral advantages" rather than spiritual guidance. For example, Hancock told the ACBFM that a chief from Red Wing "wanted us to go to their new coun-try with them and teach their children to read and write, and 'that only.'"[50]

While Riggs and Williamson argued that the government's treaty funds would aid their mission, Hancock took a more cynical view. In 1854, the gov-ernment refused to fund the mission school at Red Wing; as a result "there is no prospect of teachers being wanted for such schools for one year at least." He did not want to "wait longer in uncertainty" for the government to fulfill its treaty responsibilities. Given the Dakotas' resistance to the missionaries' proselytizing, as well as government ineptitude, Hancock believed that his talents would be better put to use preaching to the newly arrived settlers. In 1854, following his resignation, Hancock accepted a position with the American Home Mission Society and began to preach to white settlers in Minnesota. In January 1855, he organized the First Presbyterian Church of

Red Wing and served as its pastor for seven years. During the remainder of his life, he remained affiliated with that church.[51]

Moses Adams (1848–53)

While some of these missionaries were blunt about the prospects of the Dakota mission, none of the resignations was acrimonious. The same cannot be said of Moses Adams. Adams was upset with the Board and his fellow missionaries about many issues and continued to write angry letters to the corresponding secretary long after he was officially released from the Dakota mission.

Adams's first reason for leaving had nothing to do with his fellow missionaries or Board policy; his wife was ill. He worried that Lac qui Parle was "more than 200 miles from . . . any professed physician except the Great Physician of souls, who is *very near.*" His wife had a "complicated disease," which required better medical care. This did not create conflict with his peers; all of the missionaries (both male and female) understood that missionary life was difficult for women.[52]

In addition to his wife's illness, however, Adams cited more controversial reasons. Like several other Dakota missionaries, he did not think that the Board was doing enough to denounce slavery. More important, Adams was displeased with Thomas Williamson's stance on polygamy. Adams wrote dozens of letters to the corresponding secretary deriding Williamson for suggesting that men involved in polygamous marriages could theoretically be admitted to the church. Adams called polygamy a "licentious and vile sin" and stated that the "social relations of the Dakotas are rotten to the core with this vice." Although Adams reluctantly admitted that no men involved in polygamous relations had been admitted to the church, he stated that it was no thanks to Williamson. In the winter of 1841–42, Adams noted that a Dakota man with two wives applied to become a church member. According to Adams, Williamson and Joseph Renville had voted in favor of his admission, Huggins had abstained, and Riggs had opposed. Because of this, Adams believed that Williamson could not be trusted to keep men involved in polygamous relationships out of the church.[53]

Secretary Treat wrote back, asking Adams if "the Dr. ever admitted a polygamist to the church?" Treat answered his own question: "I presume not. And is the fact that he entertains this theoretical opinion honestly a reason for your leaving the Board . . . ?" Adams responded that "while it is true no polygamist has yet been received to the communion of the church in this Mission no credit is due to Dr. W. for it was prevented in spite of his vote and influence." After more letters between the secretary and Adams, Williamson felt compelled to defend himself. He promised that he was "no friend of polygamy" but maintained that "there is [not] any scriptural warrant for requiring a man . . . to put one of . . . [his wives] away." He had publicly held this view since the 1830s.[54]

As a result of the fight over polygamy, it is no surprise that Williamson and Adams did not see eye to eye. Williamson wrote that Adams "has so good an opinion of himself and is so given to saying and writing hard things of others it is very doubtful whether a sufficient number of associates . . . could be found to act harmoniously with him." This is one of the few times Williamson ever spoke harshly against a fellow missionary. He was not the only one to complain about Adams. Even though Stephen Riggs sided with Adams over the issue of polygamy, he also found Adams to be impossible to work with. At Lac qui Parle, Riggs complained that Adams "dislike[d] being controlled or even guided by those who have been longer in the field."[55]

It was a long-standing Board policy not to publicize internal conflicts between missionaries. Treat noted that "it is always painful to see Christian brethren at variance" and worked to quiet Adams as quickly as possible. To this end, Treat informed Williamson that "[i]t is very clear that Mr. Adams had better be out of the mission for he will only make trouble for it." Treat wrote the same message to Adams. "[I]t is painfully evident that you cannot be expected to labor pleasantly and harmoniously with the Dakota Mission, in future years. Hence, the Com. have voted that the connection of yourself and Mrs. Adams with the Board be dissolved." After his acrimonious dismissal from the Board, Adams ministered to settlers in Nicollet County from 1853 to 1860. As he settled into home mission work, he purchased a land claim for his family near Traverse des Sioux. He later worked as an agent for the American Bible Society in Minnesota and was appointed Indian agent to the Sisseton under President Grant.[56]

Gideon Pond (1835–52)

While other missionaries' reasons for leaving the Dakota mission provide insight into the mission's conflicted history, perhaps the most telling resignation came from Gideon Pond. He resigned from the Board, he wrote, because he believed that the Dakota mission had failed and would continue to fail. Despite the missionaries' best efforts, he believed that the Dakotas had not, and would not, become Christians. Unlike Williamson and Riggs, Pond concluded that given the past relationship between the Dakotas and ABCFM missionaries, there was "no reason whatever to suppose that a change of location or increased annuities will change the character of the Indians for the better." He resigned from the Dakota mission and suggested that the Board close all of its stations because he saw *"no bright spot in the future."*[57]

Pond also offered a scathing critique of government policy toward the Dakotas. He stated that "The course which our Government pursues with them is such that I cannot conceive [sic] how they could manage worse, and manage at all." Pond criticized the current treaties but also argued that federal policy had never worked to promote the Dakotas' Christianization. "The whole course of the government from first to last in their management with the Dakotas, I firmly believed makes directly against their Christianization and civilization ... We can't depend on the Govt. to help us. If we accomplish any thing it must be *in spite* of the government."[58]

At the same time he criticized federal Indian policy, he took the Board (and his colleagues) to task for covering up the extensive conflicts the Dakota mission faced. In the post-treaty era, Pond tried to set the record straight and discourage further investment in the Dakota mission. In his private resignation letter to the Board, he cited numerous examples of misleading reports submitted by the Dakota missionaries; in turn, these reports had been further edited for publication in the *Missionary Herald.* He cited an article lauding some *"very poor devoted Dakota christians [sic]* at Lac qui Parle" for giving "$25 to the Bible Society." In reality, Pond claimed that two-thirds of the money had been donated by the missionaries themselves and a few white traders, rather than pious Dakota Christians.[59]

Pond also accused other missionaries of covering up the failure of *Dakota Tawaxitku Kin,* or the *Dakota Friend,* a newspaper Pond edited that was published in both Dakota and English from November 1850 until August 1852. Stephen Riggs, for one, had touted the publication's success to the Board. According to Riggs, Dakotas received the *Dakota Friend* "with enthusiasm, and ... they waited for the subsequent numbers with impatience." Riggs also boasted that Dakotas had purchased many subscriptions to the newspaper. However, Pond reported that most of the copies at Lac qui Parle were purchased by whites the first year, and he predicted only four Dakotas would subscribe the second year of its publication. The numbers were even worse at other mission stations, which had no subscribers. Given the lack of Dakota readership, Pond wanted to halt production of the newspaper, as it was expensive and time-consuming to publish without any discernible results.[60]

While Pond criticized his colleagues and the Board for misleading the public about the Dakota mission, he did not let himself off the hook. He stated that "I have *never* felt free to make such statements as I desired to make because they would not entirely harmonize with those of others in the mission whom I am willing to allow are my superiors. I have endeavored to avoid saying any thing to embarrass the mission and have consequently not often written to you." Obviously, other members of the mission had painted their work in more positive terms. However, after the treaties of 1851, Pond decided that he could not continue to hide the reality of mission work. Indeed, he felt that "we ought not to attempt to conceal, that with very few exceptions, the Dakotas do not want missionaries, *will not* hear the truth, and *will not* suffer their children to be taught to read." After leaving the mission, Gideon Pond purchased a land claim in present-day Bloomington, Minnesota, and joined the Home Mission Society.[61]

Samuel Pond (1835–54)

While Gideon's brother, Samuel, did not accuse the Board and his fellow missionaries of misleading the public, he did share his sibling's view that the Dakota mission had not and would not succeed. Samuel Pond explained the reasons for his resignation to Secretary Treat. "I no longer hope as I did formerly to see a general and decided improvement among the adult Dakotas," he wrote. "There may be some change for the better soon but at present the prospect is dark and discouraging." He summarized the status of the Dakota mission in 1852 in dismal terms: "I saw very few Dakotas who seemed to give evidence of piety. A few at Oak Grove, a few at Lac qui Parle, and that was all." Moreover, unlike Riggs and Williamson, who hoped government funds would strengthen the Dakota mission, Pond predicted that the treaty would only make things worse; indeed, after 1851, he wrote that "the state of matters among [the Dakotas] is truly discouraging." Overall, he predicted that the treaty would be a disaster, and would only "render them more indolent and reckless." Following his resignation, Pond, like many of the other missionaries, switched to the home mission field. He also purchased land in Shakopee, Minnesota.[62]

Reasons for Leaving: Conflicts, Disappointments, and Deception

When examined in light of the Dakota mission's troubled history, the missionaries' resignations become more understandable. Their reasons for leaving the ABCFM reflected issues that had been discussed, debated, and sometimes hidden for many years. For instance, the missionaries had long-standing conflicts with their governing Board. From 1835 on, the Dakota missionaries clashed with the Board over inadequate salaries and the need for further investment in their missions. Over the years, it became more difficult to live on such small salaries, especially when missionary parents needed money to send their older children to school. The mission press touted the image of the selfless missionary who was above material and secular cares. By 1851, many of the missionaries found it impossible to live up to this self-sacrificing ideal when faced with the reality of raising and educating large families.

While conflict over funds was not new, the missionaries further divided with the ABCFM over its handling of slavery in the early 1850s. Although they lived on the Minnesota frontier, the missionaries were not isolated from the larger events of the antebellum period. They especially followed the national debate concerning slavery. They received anti-slavery publications through the mail, and relatives in the East filled their letters with anti-slavery news. It is not surprising that the Dakota missionaries adamantly opposed slavery, as it violated their strong moral code and interpretation of Christianity. Indeed, the Board selected its missionaries based on these characteristics. Unfortunately, the same qualities that made a good missionary were turned against the Board when its ambiguous position on slavery violated some of the missionaries' strict moral values.

While slavery was a national concern at the time, some issues unique to the Dakota mission also divided the missionaries from each other. Living near the Dakotas forced the missionaries to consider their own religious positions on several issues. For instance, Adams was upset over Williamson's position on polygamy. While Adams's anger was extreme, all of the missionaries struggled with how much to accommodate "savage ways" in their quest to obtain converts. Should they hand out food to attract converts? Should they look the other way when the Renvilles traveled on the Sabbath? Should they continue to teach Dakotas to read and write even when their religious message was ignored? Many saw accommodation as a slippery slope; if polygamous church members were admitted, what would come next? While Adams, like Jedediah Stevens before him, alienated his fellow missionaries, he brought up issues that boiled below the surface for all the Dakota missionaries as well as Board members back east.

Even with accommodations and more than twenty years of effort, most Dakotas had not, and would not, convert to Christianity. The resignation letters stressed this fact above all others; most Dakotas had openly rejected the missionaries' message. By the 1850s, most mission schools were closed, and only a handful of Dakotas had converted. Even those who had been accepted into the mission church, like Joseph Renville and his family, rarely followed the strict conversion guidelines established by the Board. If Dakotas had not flocked to the mission under better circumstances, it was highly unlikely that they would join in worsening conditions.

The strained relationship between the missionaries and Dakotas worsened because of the ABCFM's close (albeit conflicted) relationship with the local Indian agent and federal Indian policy. With reason, the Dakotas saw the government agents and the ABCFM missionaries as one and the same. Indeed, even when the missionaries disagreed with government policies (which they frequently did), they chose to keep their comments to themselves. They also criticized government programs for different reasons than the Dakotas. Finally, they took paid government positions and publicly asked that treaty funds be diverted to the Dakota mission. The Dakotas' history of directing their anger over reviled government policies (such as the Treaty of 1837) at the ABCFM missionaries did not bode well for the post-treaty period.

Given this background, the Treaties of Traverse des Sioux and Mendota were the proverbial straw that broke the camel's back. In the context of the Dakotas' failure to convert to Christianity and their reaction to previous government programs, most of the missionaries believed that the treaties of 1851 would bring nothing but trouble to their already troubled stations. Samuel Pond articulated this line of thinking: "While other missionaries hoped the treaty of 1851 would be of great benefit to the Indians, we, taught by past experience, believed the results of the treaty would be evil, and only evil."

Gideon Pond expressed a similar view. "I thought all along that a treaty with these Indians could not render matters worse with us but now I see that I did not know," he explained. "We can't depend on the Govt. to help us. If we accomplish anything it must be *in spite* of the government." Following the treaties, the resigning missionaries called government policy toward the Indians "[h]urtful" and "[s]hameful."[63]

While the missionaries criticized government policies and the treaties, they also quietly purchased lands that had been taken from the Dakotas. Of course, this is exactly what the Dakotas had accused the missionaries of wanting in the first place. Most of the missionaries did not comment on their hypocrisy in their letters; they simply registered their claims without fanfare and began preaching to the newly arrived settlers. At least one missionary, however, had difficulty reconciling his land purchase with his initial idealism about missionary work. Samuel Pond informed his sister that "I am richer than I ever expected to be but it does not greatly increase my joy." He called the "claims business" "unpleasant" and vowed that it gave him such trouble that he was "heartily sick of it." Such sentiments, however, assuredly did not appease the Dakotas. They must have seen the duplicity of missionaries who criticized the treaties with one hand, and with the other quietly bought land ceded by those same treaties.[64]

The missionaries' purchase of lands was never mentioned in the mission's publications. While the *Missionary Herald* noted that many of the missionaries switched to home mission work, its articles never mentioned where they lived. Increasingly, several of the missionaries were uncomfortable with the edited version of the Dakota mission that was presented to the public. Gideon Pond called the Board, and other Dakota missionaries, to task for presenting a less than realistic account of the prospects of the Dakota mission. He wanted the truth to be told, even if the truth reflected poorly on the Dakota mission and the ABCFM in general.

After the Treaties: Continued Deception and Challenges

The Board pointedly ignored Gideon Pond's call to tell the truth about the Dakota mission. Indeed, Secretary Treat, Thomas Williamson, and Stephen Riggs publicly stated that although the prospects of the Dakota mission looked grim, the seeds of Christianity planted over the last twenty years could bloom at any time. Following the resignations, Secretary Treat filled his letters with references to the fact that the Dakota mission could still be successful. In response to Alexander Huggins's negative points about the mission's prospects, Treat commented that while "[s]ome members of your mission appear to take a discouraging view of the prospects of the Dakotas . . . I have been inclined to hope that the darkest hour had passed." He noted that other ABCFM missions had taught the Board that "*Unpros-perous missions may at an early day undergo a complete change.*" Indeed, the "[d]arkest hour comes just before the dawn."[65]

In 1852–53, Williamson wrote several long letters providing evidence that Treat's theory was correct; seeds he had planted in the 1830s and 1840s finally seemed to be flowering despite the troubling events in Minnesota. One of his letters, written in 1853, was printed as an article almost verbatim in the *Missionary Herald*. Entitled "Encouragement," the article informed evangelical readers that Williamson "had some things to cheer him in his labors. Though he had but few hearers on the Sabbath . . . the Word had not been preached altogether in vain." Wambdiokiya (Eagle Help) finally "wished to be baptized and thus unite [himself] with the people of the Living God." Of course, those who followed events at the Dakota mission would have heard about Wambdiokiya and his long history with the Lac qui Parle mission. Despite the warrior's conflicted relationship with the mission, Williamson touted the fact that after the treaties, Wambdiokiya "was more serious and diligent in his attending of public worship than formerly and he manifested more gratitude for my going to his dwelling to give religious instruction to himself and family." Indeed, Williamson placed all of his hopes for the Dakota mission on the warrior's shoulders. "If he is truly converted as I hope and no other good should ever result from our coming hither we should and I trust would feel that all our losses and sufferings are nothing in comparison with the value of his soul." Williamson did not know it at the time, but Wambdiokiya would never join the mission church.[66]

Williamson and Secretary Treat must have realized at some level that success stories like Wambdiokiya's were misleading. Indeed, Treat's behind-the-scene actions show just that. At the same time *Missionary Herald* readers were reading "Encouragement," Treat was invited to give a talk on "the success of Indian missions" at Troy, New York. The purpose of this talk was to "show that Indian missions had been much more successful than was commonly supposed." In preparation for his talk, he sent questionnaires to all the Board's Indian missions asking for success stories. But he excluded the

Dakota mission from his survey. When Riggs asked Treat why, the secretary bluntly replied that "I did not send it to your brethren, as you have so little to report."[67]

Treat's brusque evaluation summarizes key themes surrounding the beleaguered mission's challenges. From 1835 until the mid-1850s, the Dakota mission was defined by conflicts among the missionaries, the ABCFM, the U.S. government, and the Dakotas. While various combinations of these conflicts surfaced throughout the first decades of missionary labor in Minnesota, the treaties of 1837 and 1851 gave notice that conflict with the government would increasingly overshadow the others in importance. Even as tension with the government grew, however, both the Dakota missionaries and the Board continued to hide the extent of these divisions from the evangelical public.

In addition to downplaying tension in the field, the missionaries attempted to conceal the fact that interaction with Dakotas, and the missionary experience in general, changed them in subtle but profound ways. In the field, interaction with the Dakotas led the missionaries to make compromises and accommodations they could not have envisioned making before they left for Minnesota. Some accepted these accommodations as necessary evils, while others fought them to the bitter end. The missionaries also questioned, clarified, and sometimes refined their own religious and cultural beliefs. Dakota comments even led several missionaries to view some of their own actions as hypocritical. Most important, life with the Dakotas forced missionaries to question their own skills and roles as missionaries. The culmination of these questions, challenges, and conflicts was the resignation of all but two missionaries following the treaties of 1851.

Despite its diminished size, the Dakota mission did not end after 1851. It continued to limp along until war broke out in 1862. Stephen Riggs, Thomas Williamson, and their children (some of whom became missionaries in their own right) would continue to face the same challenges that had defined missionary work among the Dakota since 1835.

CHAPTER 6

"We have opposition from Indians and from white men"

Conflicts Intensify, 1854-61

By 1854, Stephen Riggs and Thomas Williamson were the only missionaries remaining from the original ABCFM Dakota mission. Despite their professed optimism following the resignations of their brethren, they continued to face conflict at their new stations on the upper reserve. The missionaries' challenges increasingly involved not only the Dakota but also white government officials and other Minnesotans. As Stephen Riggs wrote in 1854, "We have opposition from Indians and from white men." Since their arrival in Minnesota, the ABCFM missionaries had disagreed with government agents about teaching methods, derided the character of Indian agents and governors, and questioned the United States' treaties. These long-standing arguments intensified as government agents took over civilization programs, played a larger role in Indian affairs, and negotiated yet another treaty. More than ever, missionaries saw the "government partnership [as an] encumbrance."[1]

In the mid-1850s and early 1860s, the missionaries began to openly question several aspects of the government's treatment of the Dakotas. They published articles in the local and national media critical of federal Indian policy and wrote letters to the secretary of the interior, the commissioner of Indian affairs, the Indian agent, and the governor promoting their vision of reform. The missionaries' criticism of federal actions, however, stemmed from their evangelical beliefs and did not reflect the Dakotas' interpretation of federal treaties and Indian policy.

The ABCFM missionaries (especially Stephen Riggs) also earned the enmity of the growing Minnesota population for their changing views of the Dakota language. Decades in the field had led the missionaries to question and occasionally change their definitions of Christian and civilized behavior—both for themselves and the Dakotas. This pattern continued into the 1860s; in fact, the missionaries' changing view of the Dakota language is perhaps the best example of how interaction with the Dakotas forced the missionaries to confront, and reevaluate, several of their preconceived notions. By the 1860s, both Riggs and Williamson deemed Dakota a "civilized" language, which, by extension, meant that Dakota speakers should be eligible for state citizenship. Riggs began a public campaign for citizenship for civilized, Dakota-speaking men. Minnesota's white population felt differently. Most believed that Dakota was not a civilized language and that Indians could never be the equals of whites; political and social separation, not integration, should be the goal.

In sum, the decade prior to the Dakota War of 1862 once again reflected a continuation and intensification of themes that had informed ABCFM relations with the Dakotas since the mission's beginning in the 1830s. Throughout this decade, Riggs and Williamson attempted to navigate the increasingly complex social and political situation in Minnesota. At various times they failed miserably, angering and alienating the Dakotas, government officials, and settlers. Riggs commented on these challenges: "This is indeed a hard 'life-battle' we have among the Dakotas," he stated. "Difficulties disappear on one hand only to appear again in another quarter."[2]

Increasing ABCFM Conflicts with the Dakotas

Conflict over the Sawmill

The Dakotas would have had little sympathy for Riggs's difficulties. Indeed, several of Riggs's problems were of his own making. His long-standing intractability was worsened by reservation life. An incident involving his mission sawmill illustrates how a preexisting controversy was intensified in the post-treaty era. In 1854, Riggs received funding from the ABCFM to construct a "small circular mill" at his new station on the upper reservation. He planned to use the mill to cut boards to construct a mission home, a small boarding school, and a church. He also wanted Dakota men to use boards to build permanent, single-family homes. In short, the sawmill was to be used to promote civilization and Christianity.[3]

Instead of encouraging the Dakotas' conversion, however, the sawmill met with "considerable opposition." Riggs had barely opened the mill when nearby Dakotas "became alarmed and raised the old song about the timber."

Dakota communities always had criticized the missionaries for taking grass, timber, and land without permission or compensation. The missionaries' appropriation of resources, however, was more detrimental in the post-treaty period. Even Riggs admitted that the reservation had little timber. He noted that the new upper reserve was "so destitute of woods that it affords no game larger than racoon [sic] and they have fears that they will not be able to obtain timber enough for fuel and fencing." To keep the missionaries from taking their scarce timber, Dakotas marked "the trees around a five acre lot and then came and told [Riggs] that [he] must be confined within that." Riggs refused to "submit to their dictation" and "paid no attention whatever to their decree." He was extremely upset that Paul, one of his few converts, sided with "this narrow minded childish policy."[4]

The conflict intensified when Riggs made the Dakotas pay to use the sawmill. To convince the Dakotas to allow the ABCFM to construct the mill, Secretary Treat allegedly promised that the missionaries would cut all of the Dakotas' wood for free. Once the sawmill was in operation, however, Riggs charged the Dakotas for lumber, claiming that Treat had not made this promise; later, Treat confirmed that he had not said the mill's services would be free. Riggs continued to charge for mill services even when faced with repeated complaints.[5]

The situation further escalated when Riggs used the mill to cut boards for church pews. Many Dakotas protested against using precious reservation resources to promote Christianity. More galling, however, was Riggs's demand that the church pews be constructed of maple. Maple trees played a central role in the Dakotas' subsistence patterns, as they were tapped to make sugar. Although Riggs was fully aware that the Dakotas "very much forbid [him to use] their sugar trees," he asked Paul and Joseph (two church members) to cut maples. At first, Paul refused and proposed a compromise. He suggested that the congregation "could sit very well on basswood seats." Riggs flatly refused, retorting that "God told his people to build his tabernacle" with cedar, as it was "the most precious kind of wood." Paul interpreted Riggs's statement literally and immediately said that he would gather cedar for the benches. Riggs, however, demanded that the seats be constructed with maple because that wood was most dear to the Dakotas. The existing letters do not tell if Riggs backed down, but the missionary's past actions and personality make it likely that his small congregation sat on maple benches.[6]

When the two sides reached an impasse over the mill, the Dakotas asked the government to intervene. They called Andrew Robertson, a government farmer, to a council. At the meeting, the Dakotas presented their case against Riggs. They demanded that he stop stealing their timber and then charging them to cut it into boards. Riggs defended himself, stating that he had lost money on the boards, money which came "out of my children's mouths." The farmer sided with Riggs, calling the Dakotas "unreasonable." After the farmer's ruling, the Dakotas promised to "continue to agitate it." They took their complaint to the governor and called other Dakota villages to their assistance. According to Riggs, "The people at the Rapids called to their assistance Running Walker and his village. They were further strengthened by the presence of Little Crow . . . In their various councils they declared over and over again that no one should pay for sawing." They also boycotted the mill. Despite these protests, Riggs continued to call the Dakotas' complaints "unreasonable and ignorant" and promised that their actions did not "for a moment disconcert me." Although Riggs publicly refused to compromise over the issue, he eventually dismantled the sawmill.[7]

Conflict over Boarding Programs

Tensions also increased with the Dakotas over two expanded ABCFM programs designed to separate Dakota children from their families and communities. In the mid-1850s, the missionaries received authorization and funding from the ABCFM to construct a boarding school at the Hazelwood mission. The Hazelwood boarding school, like its late-nineteenth-century counterparts, was designed to isolate students from their families, community, and religion by confining them to the school at all times. In this way, problems associated with the mission day schools—such as irregular attendance—would be addressed. The boarders also would quickly learn to read and write, which in turn would aid in their eventual conversion.[8]

In addition to opening a boarding school, Thomas Williamson attempted to expand an existing ABCFM program for Dakota children. Since the opening of the mission, families had taken Dakota children into their homes to raise them in a "civilized" and Christian environment. Williamson wanted to extend the ABCFM's small program and asked the Indian agent to use part of the education funds from the treaties of 1851 to place Dakota children "in pious families where [they] will be well cared for." In 1858, Joseph Brown, the Dakotas' agent from 1857 to 1861, supported this plan and asked the commissioner of Indian affairs to give $75 to each white family who agreed to take a Dakota child into their home. Brown argued that the money would be well spent because "[t]he further Indian children can be removed from the influence of their parents or the prejudices of their people the more effectual will be their civilization, and the more thoroughly they will be weaned from all savage habits and propensities."[9]

The ABCFM also contributed money to this project. In 1861, Stephen Riggs requested that the ABCFM give two Minnesota settlers $25 each for taking two Dakota boys into their families. In a letter asking for the funds, Riggs stressed the settlers' piety. According to Riggs, the two families needed supplementary funds to help raise the two boys because they had spent their own money constructing a church near their homesteads. In addition to providing stipends to settlers, the ABCFM increased the sum available to missionaries for raising Dakota children in their own families. Both Riggs and Williamson, as well as the mission teachers, had at least two or more boarders in their families at all times. Williamson, for example, took a Dakota boy into his home, even though he already had several other board-ers, "to prevent the boy from falling into the hands of the Romanists." Even retired missionaries participated in this program. Jonas Pettijohn, who had left the mission after the treaties of 1851, boarded a Dakota boy in his family. Gideon Pond also placed a Dakota girl with one of his church elders.[10]

Dakota boys and girls who lived in the boarding school or with white settlers or mission families found it difficult, if not impossible, to visit fam-ily members or to take part in the religious and cultural activities of their villages. For this reason, some children who were raised with white families lost ties with their own kin and communities, just as the missionaries and government officials had intended. Jane Williamson, an ABCFM teacher, told the story of two "very young Dakota children," called Susan and David, who were placed with a white family to "see what environment would do for the Indian." During their time with the settlers, Susan and David had no contact with their parents or other relatives or with Dakota cultural prac-tices. The missionaries reported that from a young age Susan spoke English and no Dakota, knew how to read the New Testament, and had committed to memory a number of hymns. Even more promising, at least according to Susan's white family and the ABCFM missionaries, was that "Little Susan, though a Sioux Indian, was dreadfully afraid of Indians having always lived with the white people."[11]

The missionaries' story about Susan does not say how the little girl came to live with this family, how her Dakota relatives felt about the situation, or if she truly was afraid of her own relatives. While these questions were certainly important to the girl's Dakota kin, they did not interest the missionaries or their antebellum evangelical readers. Susan's story, like all mission stories, was carefully crafted to prove that separating children from their families produced civilized and Christianized Dakotas. The morality of taking children from their families was never questioned, nor did the missionaries worry about how this affected Susan or her family. What mattered to the missionaries was the girl's conversion and salvation.

Hazelwood

In order to promote conversion on a larger scale, Riggs next extended the concept of separation to the community level. In 1854, he decided to create an entirely separate village composed of civilized Christian Dakota families. To this end, Riggs founded the Hazelwood mission on the upper reserve. Families living at Hazelwood would devote themselves to the mission church and farming. Overall, the Dakotas' agent supported Riggs's project and designated part of the funds from the Treaty of Traverse des Sioux to construct permanent houses and to purchase farming implements and seeds. Approximately twenty-five Dakota families moved to Hazelwood and settled in the newly built homes. Riggs proudly declared that Hazelwood was composed of men who "had cut off their hair and exchanged the dress of the Dakotas for that of the white man." Riggs called Hazelwood an oasis in the middle of "seven thousand shiftless savages." The *St. Paul Financial Advertiser* went a step further, extolling Hazelwood as a bastion of civilization in "the very Hades of Indian barbarism."[12]

Because of the unique nature of this community, Riggs wanted the Hazelwood residents to officially become their own band, separate from other "uncivilized" Dakotas. To achieve this goal, a group of Dakota men living at Hazelwood wrote a constitution in 1856 and formed the Hazelwood Republic. The constitution, originally written in Dakota, provides a window into mid-nineteenth-century conceptions of civilization. In the constitution, members of the Republic promised (among other things) to put their faith in one God, to adopt white man's dress and system of labor, to support education, to conform to the habits of white people, to protect private property, and to obey the laws of the U.S. government. The constitution also established a system of government, with a president, a council, a secretary, and three judges. Seventeen Dakota men signed the constitution. At Riggs's urging, the men presented both Dakota and English versions of the constitution to the Indian agent and asked to be declared a separate band. The agent agreed, officially creating the Hazelwood Republic.[13]

Dakota Responses

Many Dakotas resisted the missionaries' expanded and more aggressive civilization and Christianization programs, as they had done for nearly twenty-five years. At first the Dakotas used a method that had worked against the missionaries in the past: they boycotted the mission schools. In 1855, for example, during the controversy over the sawmill, Dakotas on the upper reserve boycotted the ABCFM day school. Riggs reported that the Dakotas withdrew their children from the school "as a consequence of the fuss got up about sawing boards." Once again, this boycott was successful. According to Riggs, "So few have attended our Dakota school that I stopped it two weeks ago." Riggs seemed to reach a breaking point after he closed his school, petulantly calling the parents "unreasonable and ignorant." The boycott even carried over to the Pajutazee day school, where Williamson reported that it was "painfully manifest to us that the Dakotahs are less disposed to send their children to school than they were a year or two ago." In 1855, the Pajutazee day school had an average attendance of only thirteen students.[14]

Dakota parents also boycotted the new Hazelwood boarding school. In 1858, Riggs reported that only four students—two girls and two boys— lived at the boarding school. When students finally enrolled in the school, many only remained a short time before returning to their villages. For example, two girls—Anna and Mary—both left the school after a month because they preferred to live with their relatives. The missionaries complained that two other girls, who had been enrolled in the school by their Euro-American fathers, were "stolen" away by their mothers and brought home to their Dakota communities. Although a few students remained for several years, most of the boarders returned to their communities in a year or less. As students left the school, Riggs confessed that "the difficulties of getting scholars and keeping them have proved more than I anticipated." Overall, the boycotts of mission day and boarding schools were successful.

Riggs and Williamson complained that "there is a lamentable want of interest in all educational efforts among the Dakotas."[15]

Dakotas also continued to use ridicule to challenge missionary programs and those Dakotas who chose to associate with the ABCFM. Members of the Hazelwood Republic especially faced ridicule for joining the community. In 1860, Joseph Brown reported that the "farmer" Indians of Hazelwood were ridiculed every time they walked to their fields. They were called many pejorative names, including "the fools in pantaloons," "Dutchmen" (after German settlers living around the reservation), "white-washed Indians," "cut-hairs," "breeches men," "farmers," and "men who had made themselves into women." When a man cut his hair, Riggs reported that his wife cried "whenever she looked at the shorn head of her husband." According to Riggs, those Indians who cut their hair and began to farm endured a "trial of mockings" from their friends and relatives. Likewise, Williamson reported that Dakotas near his mission station refused to attend meetings "for fear of being laughed at and persecuted."[16]

While boycotts of mission schools and ridicule effectively challenged missionary efforts, Dakotas increasingly turned to more violent forms of protest as tension rose on the Minnesota frontier. This represented both a continuation and an intensification of the Dakotas' long tradition of protesting missionary actions. At first, violence was confined to the destruction of property. In 1855, for instance, a group of Sissetons and Wahpetons killed more than ten of the missionaries' cattle, many of them "without any attempt at concealment." The missionaries demanded that the Dakotas reimburse them for their lost property. The Dakotas refused and "openly declared that they would pay for none of them." After the refusal, the missionaries took several measures to obtain compensation for their cattle. They met with the Dakotas' agent and asked that he deduct money from the Upper Dakotas' next annuity payment to pay for their cattle. They also wrote a memorial to the commissioner of Indian affairs demanding reimbursement. Finally, they petitioned the Minnesota territorial legislature to pass a law protecting mission property. After all of these efforts, the agent agreed to reimburse the missionaries using Dakota funds. The fact that the missionaries received some of the Dakotas' annuities literally added fuel to the fire; the Dakotas did not stop targeting mission property and, in 1860, set Williamson's stables and wagon house on fire.[17]

Dakotas who allied with the missionaries also had their property destroyed. The missionaries reported that several Hazelwood farmers' crops were ruined and their livestock killed. In 1860, Joseph Brown noted, "Oxen and other property belonging to [farmer Dakotas] have been taken and killed or destroyed to deter the improvement Indians from wearing the dress and following the customs of the Whites." A few months later, Brown reported that one "farmer Indian" had his oxen and horse "killed the past winter by the anti-improvement Indians." Other Dakotas who farmed at Hazelwood reported thefts of their crops. In 1856, for example, several Dakotas took potatoes from Henok, a member of the Hazelwood Republic. Food also was taken from his two sisters and brother Eli.[18]

By the late 1850s, conditions had deteriorated to such an extent that violence was directed at people as well as property. On both the lower and upper reserves, the missionaries reported stabbings and shootings. In 1859, the agent recounted that two Mdewakanton men from the lower reserve who changed their dress were shot and at least one was killed. A similar attack occurred "among the Sisseton and Wahpeton against those who adopted the dress of the white man." Williamson confirmed that both incidents happened and added further details about the events on the upper reservation. According to Williamson, shortly after a Hazelwood man cut his hair and changed his dress, he "was violently assaulted by a half dozen of the opposite party who came to his tent in the night." The man "narrowly escaped with his life, not yet having recovered from his wounds."[19]

Riggs described another incident of violence against a convert on the upper reserve in 1859. One of the Yellow Medicine church members was stabbed on the way to Sabbath school. The affair, Riggs commented, "was not at all favorable to our Sabbath services . . . Men still carry their guns loaded." By 1860, commissioner of Indian affairs William Cullen reported that the struggle "between the improvement Indians and those who refused to relinquish their tribal customs and habits has been so severe . . . that it was deemed advisable to station a company of United States troops at Yellow Medicine" to protect the farmers.[20]

ABCFM Conflicts with the Federal Government

The arrival of troops was just one government action that contributed to the deteriorating situation on the Minnesota frontier throughout the late 1850s. Indeed, Riggs and Williamson increasingly, and publicly, blamed federal policies for the trouble at their stations. There certainly was much to criticize. During the late 1850s and into the 1860s, the government failed to properly implement the 1851 treaties, drew the missionaries into the Inkpaduta–Spirit Lake crisis, negotiated yet another unpopular treaty, and administered aggressive civilization programs. The missionaries denounced each of these actions, although for their own reasons, which differed from those of the Dakota. John Williamson, the son of Thomas Williamson, summarized his view of government actions during the late 1850s: "These Employees of Gov't have a vast influence for good or evil among the Indians . . . this influence has been too much employed on the side of evil."[21]

Government Failure to Carry Out Treaty Obligations, 1855–58

The government's failure to honor the terms of the 1851 treaties contributed to John Williamson's negative evaluation of federal Indian policy. During negotiations at the Treaties of Traverse des Sioux and Mendota, negotiators had promised that payments would be made regularly and on time. Despite these assurances, government agents failed to properly disperse the treaties' education and civilization funds. In 1855, Thomas Williamson complained that the "failure of our government to fulfil [sic] several of the treaty stipulations causes a vast amount of suffering . . . and we missionaries as well as other American citizens come in for a share of the ill will and distrust thus generated towards the officers of our Government."[22]

The missionaries linked the lack of payments to protests against their missions. According to Thomas Williamson, the government's failure to expend the education fund "will probably for many years frustrate every attempt to establish schools among them. It will also doubtless impede our operations among these Indians." Williamson noted that he had a small school and only a half congregation on the Sabbath. He claimed that "this is chiefly owing to . . . Our government's withholding the educational funds." In the end, Williamson described the government's failure to expend the education fund as "an immense log across a road that had long impeded our way."[23]

In addition to failing to disperse education funds, the Indian agent also neglected to provide the Dakotas with cattle and agricultural implements as required by the treaties of 1851. The missionaries worried that this negligence would create starvation and desperation. Riggs was usually one of the first to complain to the agent about the loss of his cattle. However, because the government failed to honor its treaty obligations, Riggs charged that "some of the government functionaries [were] more to blame for ... what they stole from our Indians" than those Dakotas who killed his cattle. The missionaries (and the Dakotas) demanded that the government disperse the promised funds to avert starvation on the reservation.[24]

When the agent still failed to provide food and seeds, Thomas Williamson openly undermined the government's civilization efforts. As a physician, Williamson had tracked disease and death among the Dakotas for decades, and he continued to do so on the reservation. After the government failed to disperse their "flour and pork," Williamson noted that many reservation Dakotas "died in the consequence." After witnessing these deaths, Williamson visited the nearby village and told the young men "to hunt deer." Due to the shortage of game on the reservation, Williamson was in essence suggesting that the men leave the reservation to hunt. This was not the first time Williamson had encouraged hunting. In 1846, when the Dakotas' crops had failed, he asked the Indian agent to send the Dakotas ammunition so they could hunt; the agent rejected Williamson's request. Encouraging the Dakotas to hunt directly contradicted the government's focus on agriculture. However, life in the field had taught Williamson that some flexibility was necessary; keeping the Dakotas alive certainly was more important than rigidly adhering to standards of "civilization." Moreover, Williamson clearly saw hunting as a legitimate subsistence pattern, especially in times of need. The agent did not agree.[25]

The Spirit Lake Massacre, 1857–58

In 1857, the Spirit Lake Massacre (as it was called by settlers and government officials) led to further divisions among federal officials, missionaries, Dakotas, and the growing number of settlers on the Minnesota frontier. The crisis began on the Iowa-Minnesota border. After a long winter of disputes over property and resources with several white pioneers, a small band of Wahpekutes led by Inkpaduta killed some forty settlers and took four women captive. Upon learning of the violence on the frontier, federal troops were sent to punish the band and gain release of the four captives. The soldiers failed to achieve both objectives and merely buried the dead. The aftermath of the crisis reverberated across the Minnesota frontier for months after the initial events. Ironically, the missionaries at first benefited from the Spirit Lake Massacre through their relationship with Christian Dakotas. On their own, two Wahpeton men from Lac qui Parle rescued one of the captives, Margaret Ann Marble, and brought her to the Hazelwood mission. For their efforts, the government agent awarded each man $500. Although the two men had acted on their own initiative, Riggs immediately took credit for their actions. He claimed that the men had risked their lives to save the woman because they "had received instruction from the missionaries" and their mother was a member of the ABCFM church.[26]

Several weeks later, three other mission-affiliated men were sent by the Dakotas' agent, Charles Flandrau (1856–57), to rescue the remaining women captives. The group succeeded in obtaining the release of one of the captives; however, the other two women had been killed. For their "courage and tact," the three men "received high commendation." Once again, the missionaries took credit for the men's success. An article in the *Missionary Herald* informed readers that "[i]ntelligent white men, who are conversant with the facts, speak of the rescue of these women as one of the fruits of missionary self-denial." According to the ABCFM's celebrationist rhetoric, these men clearly had "learned humanity from our missionaries."[27]

As events progressed, however, Riggs and Williamson became increasingly critical of government actions and tried to distance themselves from the affair. The divide began when Agent Flandrau attempted to organize one last expedition of mission-affiliated Dakotas to capture Inkpaduta and to punish other members of his band. When Christian Dakotas refused to go, the commissioner of Indian affairs declared that he would withhold all Dakota annuities until "an effort should be made to punish Inkpadoota [*sic*]." The ABCFM missionaries, like many Dakotas, strongly protested the decision to withhold annuities for all because of the actions of a few. Thomas Williamson called Flandrau's decision "very unjust and cruel" and complained that it "created not a little dissatisfaction." The situation became even more tense as "1000–1500 Dakotas from the prairies arrived on the scene" at Yellow Medicine demanding their annuities. The missionaries believed that the annuities should be dispersed and declared that failure to do so "will work immense evil to the nation." The government brought further troops to the reservation to keep the peace.[28]

Government officials and the growing number of settlers on the Minnesota frontier disliked the missionaries' criticism of the annuity withholding. Throughout the Spirit Lake crisis, the missionaries clearly distinguished between Christian Dakotas, who should be praised and rewarded, and Dakotas associated with Inkpaduta, who should be punished. Most settlers, however, saw all Indians as the same; an Indian was an Indian, even if he had the outer trappings of civilization. As such, Riggs reported that following the Spirit Lake Massacre the "white people [had] become very much prejudiced against the whole Dakota nation." In this tense atmosphere, many of the settlers began to "talk loudly of having the reserve taken off." Because of their defense of Christian Dakotas, however limited, Riggs commented that "this Spirit Lake massacre is doing immense damage to our operations"; clearly settlers and government officials, as well as many Dakotas, were unhappy with the missionaries' role in the crisis. Increasingly, Riggs and Williamson stood between competing sides, ultimately pleasing no one.[29]

Treaty of 1858

The ABCFM missionaries also found themselves caught between government officials, settlers, and Dakotas with the new treaty ratified in 1858. Following the events at Spirit Lake, calls for further land cessions reached a crescendo. In 1857, Agent Flandrau recommended opening part of the Dakotas' impermanent reservation along the Minnesota River to further white settlement. Government official William Cullen agreed with Flandrau, writing that the Dakotas' reservation was "much larger than they can under any possibility require" and should be released for purchase. The new treaty would blatantly and unapologetically open Dakota lands for further white settlement.[30]

Continuing their long-standing criticism of potential treaties, Williamson and Riggs argued that the reservation lands should not be decreased. As usual, their reasoning directly related to their overall mission; that is, shrinking the Dakotas' land base would work against Christianization and civilization. The Dakotas would have less wood which would keep them from building fences and constructing permanent homes. Moreover, the missionaries pointed out the contradiction inherent in asking the Dakotas to become settled farmers at the same time the government continuously moved them away from land they had improved. Indeed, the missionaries noted that rumors of a new treaty had already affected their civilization efforts. "By reason of the uncertainty of the future," they complained, "many became unwilling to put forth those endeavors for the improvement of their condition."[31]

Although Riggs and Williamson clearly did not support a new treaty, at first they voiced their concerns only to the ABCFM officials in Boston. As rumors grew, however, the missionaries began to publicly challenge the wisdom of another land cession. The Dakotas played a role in convincing the missionaries to speak out against the proposed treaty. When it became clear that negotiations were imminent, a small group of Sisseton and Wahpeton men approached Riggs and asked him to write a letter protesting a new treaty. Riggs agreed, and the resulting memorial was published in several newspapers throughout Minnesota. Although the article was written from the Dakotas' point of view, most people assuredly knew the author's identity. This article, as well as other publications and comments made by the missionaries, created a perception among government officials and settlers that the ABCFM missionaries supported the Dakotas' position at the expense of white settlers.[32]

The missionaries' limited efforts, however, did not stop a new land cession. According to the terms of the 1858 treaty (actually two documents, one for the Upper and another for the Lower Sioux), the Dakotas ceded the northern area of their reservation; in total, they lost 550,000 acres from the upper reserve and 4,500 acres from the lower reserve. For this land, the Dakotas received 30 cents an acre—approximately one-twentieth of what the reservation land was then worth. Moreover, most of these reduced proceeds went directly to the traders, just as had occurred following the treaties of 1851. While the Senate confirmed the Dakotas' title to the southern portion of the reservation, they divided these remaining lands into eighty-acre lots for each family.[33]

As with the other treaties, the Dakotas were not pleased. Wamditanka (Big Eagle), a Mdewakanton man, summarized the problems associated with the treaty of 1858. It "caused great dissatisfaction among the Sioux," because they were moved "to the south side of the river, where there was but very little game, and many of our people . . . were induced to give up the old life and go to work like white men, which was very distasteful to many."[34]

Like Wamditanka, Riggs and Williamson criticized the new treaty. Their complaints, however, diverged both from the Dakotas' objections and even from their own pre-treaty comments. After reading the treaty, Riggs and Williamson did not comment on the land loss, the low payment, or the role that traders played in the negotiations. They also did not mention how the treaty would influence civilization efforts. Rather, they focused on two provisions that materially affected their mission stations. They worried that the government could arbitrarily close their stations and exclude the ABCFM from the reservation. They also grumbled that, "In no part of the treaty is any provision made for securing to the Board the improvements at the missionary stations." Riggs and Williamson had Secretary Treat write to the commissioner of Indian affairs, asking him to address these "two omissions in the treaty" by giving a "quarter section" of land to the ABCFM to protect their investment and legitimize their presence on the reservation. Treat never heard back from the commissioner.[35]

In the aftermath of the 1858 treaty, the missionaries continued their long-standing history of agreeing with the Dakotas that federal treaties left much to be desired, but disagreeing over the substance of their complaints. Even these limited challenges, however, separated the Protestants from most Minnesotans, who supported the land cession without reservation.

New Government Civilization Programs, 1859–61

The missionaries also criticized the government's new, aggressive civilization program, but again for different reasons than the Dakotas. Following the treaty of 1858, the Dakotas' agent began to spend civilization monies. Since 1835, the ABCFM missionaries had been the foremost agents of civilization and religious instruction to Dakota communities. At the end of the 1850s, however, "[t]he Government came in now and encouraged agriculture and the change of dress in the men." While government officials credited the missionaries with sowing "the first seeds of civilization," they made it clear that the "philanthropic system engrafted in the treaties of Traverse des Sioux and Mendota" would complete the Dakotas' transformation into civilized farmers. While the ABCFM missionaries had begun the battle "against their Indian prejudices," the government would "lead on to victory."[36]

Beginning in 1858, William J. Cullen, superintendent of Indian affairs for the northern superintendency, established several programs to civilize the Dakotas. He disbursed $12,000 to dress Dakota men in pantaloons and to set them up on individual farms. Cullen then encouraged these newly "civilized" men to move with their families to a separate community. Cullen saw civilized communities as "the foundation stones upon which the structure of Indian improvement . . . must stand." On the upper reservation, Cullen encouraged Sisseton and Wahpeton men to join the ABCFM's Hazelwood Republic. The Mdewakanton and Wahpekute, however, did not have a similar community. In 1860, Cullen established a federally funded civilized village on the lower reservation to rectify this situation. Joseph Brown, the Dakotas' agent, described the salient features of this new community. Similar to the Hazelwood Republic, families "associated themselves together, elected a judge and council, thr[ew] off their tribal relations, and, in their articles of association, bound themselves to discard the clothing and habits of Indians, and to refrain from the use of spirituous liquors of whatever kind." By 1861, twelve Mdewakanton and Wahpekute families had joined the government farming village, which was headed by Joseph Napesniduta, Joseph Renville's nephew from Lac qui Parle.[37]

Although these government programs were modeled on their own efforts, the missionaries strongly criticized the government's methods. They believed—as they had since the 1830s—that religious conversion must precede civilization. As always, the "Bible was the great civilizer." Without the firm foundation of a true conversion, the missionaries warned that the agents would never achieve their long-term goals because they would "only be building upon the sand." Handing out clothing and cutting the men's hair only convinced the Dakotas to become "white men *externally*." The missionaries offered evidence that the agent's actions did not lead to religious conversion. Despite the vast expenditure of funds, "few of those who have changed their dress," they pointed out, "attend worship with us more than formerly."[38]

Riggs and Williamson took their critique one step further and charged that the agents' new programs undermined the ABCFM's teachings. For instance, the missionaries reported that Superintendent Cullen asked Taoyateduta (Little Crow) to cut his hair and put on pantaloons. Taoyateduta refused, informing the agent that the missionaries had taught him that he needed to change his religion before he could be considered a white man. Because he did not want to "give up his Medicine sack, Gourd shell, and armor" and "wished when he died to go to the same place where his fathers are," he refused to comply with the superintendent's request. Cullen, however, directly contradicted the missionaries' teachings. He told Taoyateduta that "he might retain all th[e]se and worship what, and how, he pleased, if he would only have his hair cut and put on a hat and Pantaloons." Taoyateduta's situation was not an isolated incident. In a letter to the ABCFM, Williamson complained that "Superintendent Cullen tells them to worship what and as they please if they will only go to work and dress as white men."[39]

The missionaries also criticized government programs, such as the farming program, for failing to promote civilization. After withholding funds for several years, the Indian agent finally distributed farming implements, seeds, and individual plots of land to Dakota men. Once a man accepted these items, the government agents counted him as part of the civilized faction. In reality, however, many men took the agents' tools and simply gave them to the women, who continued their traditional roles as farmers.[40]

The Dakotas' failure to follow Euro-American farming practices extended to other issues as well. Williamson noted that many of the Dakotas who "ha[d] adopted Cullen's views" would "one day dress and work like white men, and the next day put on Breech Cloth, leggings and blanket, engage in conjuring over the sick and take part in the sacred feasts, and dances." These examples served as evidence to the missionaries that government programs promoted syncretic (more pejoratively called "superficial" by the missionaries) cultural practices. In the end, Riggs observed that the government could have done "a greater amount of good, with less evil to the Indian . . . in some other way, and at far less expense."[41]

Although the missionaries called government programs superficial, Dakotas interpreted them as a well-funded and aggressive attack on their culture and religion. As such, the opposition that the ABCFM missionaries faced at their stations was increasingly impossible to separate from resistance to government programs. As Williamson complained, "we missionaries . . . come in for a share of the ill will and distrust thus generated toward the officers of our government."[42]

While the Dakotas had a long history of successfully closing mission schools and churches, they were much less effective in demanding concessions from government agents. Indeed, the destruction of property and violence against "farmer" Dakotas only increased the agents' resolve to restore order on the reservation. Prior to the treaties of 1851, Dakota boycotts, ridicule, ostracism, and violence had effectively curtailed the ABCFM missionaries. Throughout the 1850s, the Dakotas used the same methods. Unlike the missionaries, however, the United States had the resources and resolve to not back down.

ABCFM Conflicts over the Dakota Language and Citizenship

In the midst of this growing conflict, the missionaries added fuel to the fire by declaring Dakota to be a civilized language and beginning a public campaign for state citizenship for "civilized" Dakota-speaking men. Riggs's fight for citizenship for Hazelwood members illustrates that his thinking about issues of civilization and race had diverged from that of other Minnesotans. While many Minnesotans perceived Riggs as joining the Dakota camp, however, Riggs never asked Dakotas to contribute to the debate over what constituted a "civilized" language, nor did he ask them if they wanted state citizenship. Indeed, throughout his correspondence, Dakotas are portrayed as passive, with Riggs as the instigator.

A Language of Power and Beauty

Even though Riggs described the Dakotas as passive, they undoubtedly influenced the missionaries' changed view of the Dakota language. By the late 1850s, Dakota had become, in the missionaries' estimation, a "civilized" language, equal to English. Riggs explained how his view of Dakota had changed over the years. "There had been times when the Dakota language seemed to be barren and meaningless. The words for Salvation and Life, and even Death and Sin, did not mean what they did in English. It was not to me a heart-language. But this passed away. A Dakota word began to thrill as an English word. Christ came into their language." Riggs now characterized the Dakota language as full of "power and beauty."[43]

The missionaries' belief that Dakota was a civilized and powerful language led to a clash with government officials in the late 1850s. Government policy stated that all Dakota students must be taught in English. The missionaries initially attempted to follow government policy and taught in English at the Hazelwood boarding school. However, Williamson described teaching in English as "the most burdensome, embarrassing, thankless and profitless part of our work." The missionaries decided to ignore government policy and instruct their students in Dakota. Williamson explained that while the "the teachers employed by Government are required to teach English instead of Dakota," we thought that "it would be much better to teach them to read their own language which they understand." After switching to Dakota, Williamson reported that there was "a very decided improvement since we determined that the Scholars must all be taught to read their mother tongue first." Many of the problems teaching his students arose because of "the difficulty of interesting children in learning to read what they cannot understand."[44]

The missionaries challenged government policy by continuing to teach in Dakota at all mission schools. They took this opposition one step further by suggesting that the commissioner of Indian affairs order all government teachers to instruct students in Dakota. Stephen Riggs informed the commissioner that teaching in English did not work. Instead, Riggs asked the commissioner to "put into operation a system of village schools to be taught in their own language." The commissioner flatly rejected Riggs's suggestion and continued to require that all government teachers hold classes in English. After the commissioner's decision, Secretary Treat urged Riggs and Williamson to stop openly challenging the government's directives.[45]

The Citizenship Campaign

Stephen Riggs did not listen to Secretary Treat's admonishment, and he began an open and long-running crusade to have Dakota-speaking members of the Hazelwood Republic declared citizens of Minnesota. Riggs believed that by virtue of becoming "civilized," members of the Hazelwood community had earned "the blessings and privileges" of law. Indeed, citizenship should be used as an inducement to convince other Dakota men "to change [their] habits." Because of the importance of citizenship as both a motivator and a reward, Riggs informed Minnesota legislators that if they did not grant "them the rights of citizenship . . . we press them back into barbarism."[46]

Riggs began his citizenship campaign in 1857, just after the formation of the Hazelwood Republic and in the middle of the Inkpaduta crisis. He traveled to St. Paul and spent five days attempting to convince the framers of the state constitution to grant full citizenship to all civilized Indians. At first, Riggs was hopeful that the authors of the constitution would "make a new dictionary meaning of the word *white* so that it shall include all mixed bloods of Indian descent and civilized Indians." Mary Riggs, however, was not confident in her husband's effort. She wrote her son Alfred that she did not "feel at all sanguine that he will succeed, nor that success would secure very great blessings." However, she tried hard "not to damp his enthusiasm."[47]

Mary Riggs was correct. Riggs's proposal was very unpopular, as there was "a great deal of prejudice against Indians." A letter from a reader printed in the *St. Paul Advertiser* called Hazelwood a "futile scheme of sectarian proselytism," which taught "material civilization" rather than the "inculcation of abstract religious ideas." When faced with the public outcry against Dakotas, missionaries, and Hazelwood, even one of Riggs's initial supporters turned against him, arguing that it would be too easy to "manufacture votes" by dressing up a "wild Indian" in white clothing, having him vote, and then stripping him of his pantaloons and returning him to his tribe.[48]

When the Minnesota state constitution went into effect in 1857, suffrage was based on a combination of both race and one's state of civilization. The vote was given to four classes of men: white citizens of the United States; foreign-born white men who declared their intention of becoming U.S. citizens (they did not have to speak English); civilized mixed-blood Indians; and full-blood Indians who proved in front of a district court that they had adopted the language, customs, and habits of civilization. On this basis, several Hazelwood members were granted citizenship. Altogether, seventeen men had signed the Hazelwood constitution. Of the seventeen, eight were of mixed blood. According to the 1857 state constitution, therefore, those eight were granted citizenship.[49]

While Riggs viewed the citizenship of eight Hazelwood men as a step forward, he desired outright citizenship for all the Hazelwood members regardless of "blood." In late 1859 through early 1860, Riggs attempted to convince newly elected Minnesota governor Alexander Ramsey to support citizenship for all civilized Indians. Before he approached Governor Ramsey, however, Riggs researched the issue of "citizenizing Indians" in other states. He watched events in Massachusetts, for example, as he believed that if one state enfranchised Indians, it would set a precedent that could be applied in Minnesota. In 1849, and again in 1859, the Massachusetts legislature commissioned investigations of "the number and circumstances of Indians and Indian descendants of the state." These findings would be used to support or reject the enfranchisement of Indians. Although Riggs did not know it, in 1859 the report eventually argued that Indians were unable to "exercise the rights and duties of citizen[ship]." Riggs also learned that Connecticut and New York had denied citizenship to Indians. When he failed to find state precedents, Riggs wondered if "some scheme [could be] set on foot to have our people made citizens of the United States."[50]

Despite these setbacks, Riggs had Secretary Treat write to Ramsey. Treat informed Ramsey that Massachusetts was close to offering citizenship to Indians. The governor, however, refused to support expanding Indian citizenship. He wrote, "Unfortunately in a frontier country where the number of wild or uncivilized Indian is large as here . . . it provokes such a prejudice . . . as to delay proper action, even in the case of those Indians who may entitle themselves to an advancement to all the rights of citizenship."[51]

After failing to make headway with Governor Ramsey, in 1861 Riggs pushed for the Minnesota state legislature to pass a bill declaring all civilized Indians state citizens. While Riggs admitted that "there were many other subjects which white people generally would regard as far more important," he was cautiously optimistic that the bill would pass. He made every effort to bring his cause before the legislature: he prepared petitions from the Hazelwood Indians and missionaries, listed potential precedents from other states, and even wrote a draft bill. Riggs then entreated Gideon Pond, who had once served in the territorial legislature, to present the bill to the representatives. Despite his efforts, the legislature refused to consider the subject.[52]

In 1861, Riggs finally took his citizenship crusade to court. According to the state constitution, full-blood Dakotas who proved that they had adopted the "language, customs, and habits of civilization" could petition for citizenship. As a test case, Riggs brought to the district court in Mankato the nine full-blood Hazelwood members who had been denied state citizenship by the 1857 state constitution. In the courtroom, he intended to prove that they had met the accepted criteria for citizenship.

As he prepared his case, Riggs realized that the Dakota language was the main obstacle in the way of the men's citizenship. Only one of the nine spoke English; the rest only spoke Dakota. Riggs continued to believe, however, that Dakota "was not a barbarous language" and was equal to English. As the trial began, Riggs expressed his belief that because "there [was] no specific language of civilization," it was his "purpose to bring the Dakota language under that category." To make his point, he presented to the judge the Minnesota state constitution, which he had translated into Dakota. For Riggs, the translation proved that the Dakota language could adequately express abstract concepts, such as the rights of citizenship, just as well as English. Of course, the Dakota defendants further had composed and signed the constitution of the Hazelwood Republic, which was also written in Dakota.[53]

Although the judge acknowledged that the Dakota men "presented quite a neat appearance," he only granted citizenship to the one Dakota defendant who spoke English, denying citizenship to the other eight. The judge based his decision on the fact that "Sioux was a barbarous language." Despite the translation of the Minnesota constitution into Dakota and the Hazelwood

MINNESOTA MAKOCE

EN

WOOPE ITANCAN KIN.

MINNESOTA MAKOCE kin en wicaxta unyakonpi, Wakantanka wopida unkekiciyapi, woihduha wakan qa ikceka unhapi kin heon; qa wowaxte kin he ohinniyan kta, unkiyepi qa unkicincapi kin hena en unkiçihdusutapi kta uncinpi, heon etanhan Woope Itancan kin de unkagapi qa unhdusutapi.

TOKAHEYA.

WIHDUHAPI WOWAPI.

Oehde 1. Oyate kin ixnana woope ikceka kaga okihipi, qa hena tanyan unpi qa owotanna oranyanpi kta e heon Wokiconze kagapi ece; qa tohan econpi kta iyecece cinhan Wokiconze kin he piyapi qa yutecapi kta ixnana okihipi.

Oehde 2. Makoce kin de en tuwedan reyata iyeyapi kte xni, qa tona wicaxta wicayawapi token wihduhapi qa wicoran econpi ece kin wicakipi kte xni, makoce kin en woope yuhapi kin eciyatanhan xni, qa wicaxta om akiniskokeca kin on yacopi xni kinhan. Makoce kin de en Waxicun sapa iyecen wayaka wicayuhapi kte xni, qa tuwe tawaṭenye xni wowidake yapi kte xni; tuka

Acc.

Riggs's translation of the new Minnesota constitution, printed in 1858.

constitution, the judge found that Dakota was not a "language of literature, by which these people could gain a knowledge of our system of government." Indeed, without understanding English, the judge argued that the Dakotas could never take part in the "elective franchise," which required "a knowledge of a civilized language." In the end, according to historian William D. Green, the judge ruled that "'civilized' meant 'white,' and 'white' meant speaking English." The men of the Hazelwood Republic "were only nearly civilized."[54]

Race, Language, and Civilization

Riggs's fight for citizenship illustrates how far his definition of "race" had diverged from most Minnesotans of the time. By the 1860s, according to anthropologist Bruce White, "Minnesota had become 'white,' a region with a reinvented past that did not include Indian people ... Race had become all important." Riggs rejected an interpretation of race that focused on the superiority of Euro-Americans. Instead, he stressed the unity of mankind and the importance of culture and religion over blood. Indeed, Riggs believed that the Indians' race could be "changed" once Indians adopted civilized ways and Christianity.[55]

The missionaries consistently argued that one's state of civilization was more important than blood, and the fight for citizenship was the most public display of this idea. In 1851, Riggs wrote that he was optimistic that all Dakotas could "become white people" and be "merged in the great American people." In 1857, Riggs again stated his belief that once Dakotas became civilized Christians, they "frequently pass[ed] into the white race" and could be absorbed "in the great American people." Thomas Williamson agreed, arguing that the Indians should be allowed "all those rights which at the origin of our nation we declared belong to all men, and make him, before our laws, equal." In sum, a person's state of civilization was more important than his or her race. Civilized full-blood Indians were equal to whites and mixed-bloods, while uncivilized mixed-bloods could be just as savage as an uncivilized full-blood. Indeed, the missionaries even suggested that the Dakotas could be better than what they termed "degenerate whites," including fur traders, some soldiers, and many settlers. Secretary Treat hoped that the Dakotas "will aim to be better than *many white* men."[56]

While the Dakota missionaries' ideas about race remained consistent from 1835 until the late 1850s, their evaluation of the Dakota language changed during their time in Minnesota. The Dakota missionaries, and antebellum philologists in general, originally believed the Dakota language could not express abstract concepts. The ABCFM instructed its missionaries to learn the Dakota language, but only until Indians learned English. Over the years, however, the missionaries changed their views of the Dakota language. In the 1830s, they learned that Dakota was a difficult and complicated language. In the 1840s and 1850s, they slowly began to think that Dakota could become a civilized language. By the 1860s, they saw Dakota as a fully civilized language, equal to English. Riggs's campaign to have Dakota declared a civilized language by the Mankato court reflects how his evaluation of the Dakota language had changed. Riggs believed that although God had "scattered and separated the one great family of man, by introducing a diversity of languages," the "earth was of one language and speech." By bringing the Bible to the Dakota language, the missionaries had succeeded in "restoring the family of man again." The Mankato judge, and most antebellum Americans, did not agree.[57]

In the end, the fight for Dakota citizenship was Riggs's fight, which he defined in his own terms. While the eight Dakota men who stood before the judge at Mankato were not passive, and must have offered their own commentary on the trial, Riggs never included their thoughts in the dozens of letters he wrote on the subject. He did not record whether the Dakotas offered a definition of what it meant to be a state (or even a federal) citizen. He did not ask them to comment on how they viewed their own language. They were not asked how the Dakotas defined race. Riggs did not record this information because it was not important to him. As an evangelical missionary, Riggs was secure in his belief of what it meant to be white, a Minnesotan, and an American. While Riggs tinkered with the definition of what it meant to be civilized by declaring Dakota to be a civilized language, he still demanded that Dakota men and women change their dress, subsistence patterns, gender roles, and, most important, religion. The Dakota missionaries played a central role in a debate that consumed white antebellum Americans over what constituted "civilization" and the nature of the Indians' race and language. The Dakotas, however, were not asked to comment on that debate.

The Semi-Jubilee: "Trials and Triumphs"

In 1860, in the midst of growing tension on the Minnesota frontier, Riggs and Williamson celebrated the Dakota mission's Semi-Jubilee, marking twenty-five years of labor. To commemorate this anniversary, Stephen Riggs delivered a sermon entitled "Trials and Triumphs." The text of his speech was partially reprinted in the *Journal of Missions*. While Thomas Williamson did not prepare a special sermon for the Semi-Jubilee, he offered comments about the history of the Dakota mission that were published in the *Missionary Herald*. Both men also wrote an extensive report summarizing their quarter century of missionary work with the Dakotas.[58]

Riggs's and Williamson's comments highlighted some of the (albeit small) triumphs of the Dakota mission while continuing to obscure the reality of their work among the Dakotas. Riggs's sermon promised that future conversions were imminent, because the missionaries had toiled for twenty-five years to "lay the foundation." Indeed, he wrote, some of these seeds had already sprung "up and b[ore] fruit, and some of the harvest is already garnered." He noted that in 1860, there were fifty Dakota church members. Although he admitted that this congregation was a small (but respectable) harvest, he hoped more Christians would be added to the fold in the near future.[59]

Riggs also touted the fact that some Dakotas had adopted civilization, which he attributed directly to the influence of Christianity. In his sermon, Riggs noted that initially he was shocked by the Indians' "habits and customs," which offended "taste and good breeding." He experienced "bad smells and bad sights and bad sounds. There are bad words and bad actions. There is gross sensuality as well as devilish wickedness," especially in their "begging dance." Over the years, however, Riggs proclaimed that "labor is becoming more respectable and dancing is going into desuetude." Through endurance on the part of the missionaries, by the "influence of the truths of the gospel," and by the "sale of their land to the United States government," the Dakotas had "learned to be less unreasonable."[60]

Williamson's comments also focused on the successes of the Dakota mission. He argued that in terms of money spent, the Dakota mission actually was one of the ABCFM's most effective, even though it was not generally portrayed as such by the mission press. Williamson calculated that during more than two decades of work in Minnesota, the missionaries had drawn only $40,000 from the Board. Based on this calculation, he argued that "the number of converts among the [Dakotas] is far greater, in proportion to the number of missionaries . . . while the expense is less" than other ABCFM stations. He believed that the Dakota mission "compares favorably with the Northern Armenian [mission], which is generally thought to be the most successful of the Board." In sum, Williamson claimed that "we have more communicants in proportion to the funds expended or the number of preachers employed." In the end, Williamson and Riggs both put a positive spin on the continued resistance and troubles they faced. Indeed, their "trials [were] the means of Triumph. By firm but peaceable resistance—by perseverance—by concession—by patience—by suffering—by faith, God giveth us the Victory."[61]

Unfortunately for the missionaries, their path to victory was increasingly blocked both by their own actions and by events beyond their control. Dakotas living near the two remaining mission stations protested unpopular mission programs such as the sawmill and attempts to divide their families and communities. Increasingly, however, missionary work was hampered by government mismanagement. Government agents failed to expend promised treaty monies and began new and aggressive (but ultimately ineffective) civilization programs. In 1858 yet another treaty further circumscribed the Dakota reservation. While the missionaries protested against many of these programs, they did so from their own point of view, not that of the Dakotas.

While Dakotas saw missionaries as failed allies at best, increasingly Minnesota's white population and Indian agents perceived the missionaries as siding with Indians against their own race. Riggs's failed effort to obtain state citizenship for civilized Dakotas was the main, but not the only, example. ABCFM instructors also refused to teach in English and angered government agents by criticizing government policy, treaties, and failure to distribute annuities. In earlier years, the missionaries hid most of their complaints from government officials and members of the public. By 1860, however, they were increasingly open with their criticism. They published critiques of Indian policy in local newspapers. They also published in national periodicals. Stephen Riggs wrote a lengthy article entitled "The Indian Question" for the *New Englander and Yale Review.* It was highly critical of traders, government programs, and treaties. Finally, Secretary Treat, at the request of the Dakota missionaries, sent letters critical of Indian policy to the governor, the commissioner of Indian affairs, and the secretary of the interior. As the 1860s drew to a close, the Dakota missionaries played a public role in the increasingly tense and violent situation on the frontier. They had the rather unenviable position of standing between two divided sides but pleasing neither. Their position would become even more precarious when war erupted in 1862.[62]

CHAPTER 7

"The Dark Hour"

The ABCFM Missionaries and the Dakota War of 1862

The Dakota people, Minnesota settlers, government agents and officials, and the ABCFM missionaries all saw the Dakota War of 1862 from very different perspectives. Because of these divergent opinions, the missionaries' writings do not tell the entire history of the war, but they do provide unique insight into how one group of evangelical missionaries interpreted the events of 1862 and beyond. Because of their evangelical beliefs and long interaction with the Dakotas, the missionaries interpreted the war differently from most people involved in the conflict, including both Minnesotans and the Dakota. Post-war publications illustrate this divide. According to the evangelical mission press, the Dakota missionaries were the heroes of the war. Minnesota newspapers, however, derided the missionaries for siding with the Dakotas against their own race.

The fact that the mission press and the local press depicted missionary involvement in the war differently should come as no surprise—by the 1860s, the missionaries' thinking about key issues regarding the Dakotas had diverged significantly from that of the general population, and the war only exacerbated their differences. The Dakota missionaries disagreed with most Minnesotans and government officials over the causes of the war, the role of Christian Dakotas in the war, the trials that followed the Dakotas' defeat, and the treatment of Dakotas after the executions at Mankato. Most important, the missionaries interpreted the war as a cosmic battle between Christianity and heathenism. Most Minnesotans, however, defined the conflict in stark racial terms. In all instances, the missionaries attempted to walk the fine line between defending the Dakotas and their ultimate belief that the war was "The Dark Hour" that changed everything.[1]

The war also divided the missionaries. Stephen Riggs, Thomas Williamson, and their families publicly presented a united front in their interpretation of the war and its aftermath. Stephen Riggs, however, diverged from his brethren, and even his family, by working closely with the government. He served as chaplain for the army, played a key role in the trials and hangings, and continued employment with the government while Williamson and others preached in the post-war prisons. Over the years Riggs had supported government treaties and actions to a greater extent than his colleagues, and this pattern continued in the post-war period. In many cases, Riggs attempted to play both sides, even downplaying some of his government work and actions after the fact. The close relationship between Riggs and the government added another layer of complexity to the already complicated relationship among the missionaries, the Dakotas, and the general public. While the missionaries shared the same evangelical background and religious training, they also reacted to events based on their own personalities and histories. There was never one "missionary viewpoint," just as there was never one Dakota perspective.

Conflicts over the Causes of the War

The Dakota War began on August 18, 1862, at the Lower Sioux Agency, about forty miles from Williamson's station at Yellow Medicine. During the six weeks of the conflict, between four hundred and six hundred white settlers and soldiers and around sixty Dakotas died in the fighting, although the number of Dakota casualties grew substantially following the war. Settlers abandoned their homes and fields in more than twenty-three Minnesota counties. Although the military phase of the war ended relatively quickly (on September 23, following the Battle of Wood Lake), the war's legacy influenced the treatment of the Dakotas for years to come. Following the war, settlers and Minnesota officials demanded the immediate exile of all Dakotas from Minnesota, if not their complete extermination as a people. Even if they had not participated in the war, Dakotas were imprisoned, their treaties were abrogated, and they were stripped of their remaining lands in Minnesota. A lengthy conflict between American forces and Dakotas (and other Plains tribes) also continued in the West from the summer of 1863 into the fall of 1865.[2]

While the timeline of the war was relatively clear, the missionaries diverged from the general population over how to interpret many aspects of the war and its aftermath, beginning with what caused the war in the first place. The missionaries attempted to defend some Dakotas while insisting that they never condoned violence. This half-hearted support, however, angered Minnesotans who viewed the conflict in blatantly racial terms.

Non-missionaries and the Causes of the War

Most government officials and settlers did not attempt to understand why the Dakotas had gone to war. They believed the war began because the Dakotas were savages who could not control their passions. Although it is difficult to read the extreme rhetoric used in both published and unpublished sources during and after the war, these comments illustrate the climate in Minnesota at the time, and the missionaries' reaction to the most extreme manifestations of this vitriolic language.

Thomas J. Galbraith, the Dakotas' Indian agent during the war, represents a commonly held viewpoint that the war was caused by the Dakotas' inherent "savagery." "[T]he Indian of the poets and novelists is a pure myth," he explained. "They are bigoted, barbarous, and exceedingly superstitious . . . the young Indian from childhood is taught to regard killing as the highest virtue." Commissioner of Indian affairs William Dole (1861–65) described Dakotas as "savages, far beneath us in moral and intellectual culture." They are "a wild, barbarous, and benighted race."[3]

Settlers also attributed the war to the Dakotas' inherent barbarism. Jacob Nix, a German settler from New Ulm, described a Dakota warrior as "a predator of the bloodthirstiest and most cruel type. The only difference between him and his bestial colleague," he explained, "is that he possesses the body of a human being in which is hidden the brooding beast which is forever planning evil." Stephen Riggs commented that another settler referred to Dakota children as "devils in the process of growth." Because they were devils, the settler reasoned, it could not "be wrong to crush young vipers." Along a similar line, an article in the *St. Paul Pioneer* likened the Dakotas' nature to that of a wolf. "Cultivate him, strive to Christianize him as you will," the author wrote, "and the sight of blood will in an instant call out the savage, wo[l]fish, devilish instinct of the race." According to these settlers, Dakota men—and even children—lacked the basic human qualities of rationality and compassion; indeed, "Dakota" was said to mean "the throat cutters."[4]

Missionaries and the Causes of the War

When confronted with the strong outcry against the Dakotas, the missionaries unequivocally stated that they did not condone violence or killing settlers. Samuel Pond bluntly said that "no one should infer that ... [I] would justify or palliate the atrocious massacre of the whites in 1862." Moses Adams agreed, saying "[w]hatever were the grievances of the Sioux ... there was no justifiable cause for ... the indiscriminate massacre of innocent white settlers." John Williamson called the Dakotas' actions a "dreadful massacre." Stephen Riggs commented that "justice requires that the guilty should be punished—and I have no desire to shield anyone."[5]

While they abhorred the Dakotas' turn to violence and demanded that the guilty be punished, the missionaries also believed that the Indians had valid complaints that drove them to war. According to Stephen Riggs, "this uprising came not without cause." Martha Riggs, his daughter, stated, "The Indians have not been without excuse for their evil deeds." The *Missionary Herald* informed its readers that if the Dakotas "had sinned, [they] have also, most certainly, been sorely sinned against." While some of the causes of the war were "superficial and born of the occasion," others were "deep-rooted and had been long-working."[6]

In the months before the war, the missionaries described a growing crisis over annuities. Riggs and Williamson blamed Thomas Galbraith, the Dakotas' new and inexperienced Indian agent, for precipitating the crisis. Galbraith angered the Dakotas by handing out goods instead of cash annuities, as mandated by the Treaties of Traverse des Sioux and Mendota. According to Riggs, the goods were worth about $2.50 per person, whereas each Dakota man could have made $50 to $100 by hunting during the time they waited for this insignificant distribution. Riggs called this "a terrible mistake of the government at Washington."[7]

The missionaries also criticized the government for a delay in the payment of annuities. Although the distribution traditionally occurred in June, the money had not arrived by early August. The tension was compounded by the fact that the Sissetons' crops had been destroyed by drought and cutworms, which meant that no reserve was available to feed the large group as they waited for their annuities. On August 4, 1862, a group of frustrated Sissetons and Wahpetons broke into the warehouse to get food, and a detachment of Minnesota militia was called to restore order. Although war did not break out at this time, the agent's handling of the annuity situation clearly angered the Dakotas.[8]

Traders made the annuity crisis worse by refusing to give credit to the Dakotas. According to Wicahpewastewin (Good Star Woman), one of the traders told the hungry Dakotas to "go ahead and eat grass but don't come around here asking for food." On August 18, the trader who purportedly made this comment, Andrew Myrick, was found dead with his mouth stuffed with grass. The missionaries believed that withholding the annuities and the traders' refusal to extend credit helped to push the Dakotas to war. As Stephen Riggs bluntly put it, "if the money had been on hand . . . the Sioux war would have been prevented."[9]

The payment of annuities, while an inflammatory issue, was only a "superficial" cause of the war. According to Martha Riggs, problems had been building for years. "Our people have given them intoxicating drinks . . . violated the rights of womanhood among them, robbed them of their dues, and then insulted them! What more would be necessary to cause one nation to rise against another?" Moses Adams wrote of the long-standing tensions on the frontier, "there was much at the time . . . that was exasperating to the Indians and increasingly provoking and vexatious to them."[10]

The missionaries specifically blamed the Treaties of Traverse des Sioux and Mendota (and Jacksonian removal policy in general) for creating tension that finally led to war. Indeed, at least one missionary argued that war might have been averted if the Dakotas had been allowed to "keep their old grounds." While they realized that removal was inevitable given the settlers' desire for the Dakotas' lands, the missionaries criticized government officials for failing to provide a permanent reservation, demanding further land cessions, and implementing a misguided civilization program. Moreover, government officials failed to prevent settlers from moving onto Dakota lands and further depleting already scarce resources; this led to widespread starvation, especially given the lack of annuities. All of these post-treaty challenges simmered until the crisis over annuities lit the fire that ignited the war.[11]

While the missionaries discussed both short- and long-term causes of the war, they also interpreted the events of 1862 through the lens of their evangelical religious beliefs, seeing the conflict as part of the cosmic battle between heathenism and Christianity. The ABCFM missionaries had referenced this cosmic war long before their arrival in Minnesota: they were foot soldiers in the global battle against all non-Christian religions. When the violence ended, the U.S.–Dakota War was merged into this existing narrative. According to the missionaries' interpretation of events, the "heathen" Dakotas went to war to stop the rising tide of Christianity in their communities. Stephen Riggs believed that the war was a "culmination of their hatred of Christianity." The "war Prophets" and "medicine men" were so worried about Christianity that they "hoped to roll back the providential wheels of Almighty God." Thomas Williamson also defined the war as part of the larger conflict between Dakota religion and Christianity. He noted that the outbreak was caused by "the conjurors, or medicine men . . . and they are actuated by hostility to Christianity and civilization, which they look upon as one and the same thing."[12]

The missionaries' interpretation of the war differed from that of most Minnesotans. In the eyes of most settlers and Indian officials, the Dakotas went to war because they were barbaric savages; whites did not assign blame to their own policies or actions. While the ABCFM missionaries abhorred violence and bloodshed, they admitted that the Dakotas had legitimate short- and long-term grievances that had been building over the years, and criticized government policies and the settlers; however, they absolved themselves of any blame for their own civilization and Christianization programs, or for taking Dakota lands and resources to support their missions.

Most important, the missionaries interpreted the war as a sign that Christianity finally was going to triumph over heathenism. Because the missionaries interpreted the war as a battle over Christianity, they explicitly denounced the racial interpretations of the war offered by other Minnesotans. As Thomas Williamson put it, the war "was not of races but of religions," pitting the "many Gods of the Dakotas with the great God of Christians." Thus, the missionaries continued to believe in the prominence of religion over race, as they had from the time they arrived in Minnesota.[13]

Conflicts over the Role of Christian Dakotas in the War

The missionaries further divided with the general public over the role that Christian Dakotas played in the war. Both during and after the war, reports circulated that Christian Dakotas had "exceed[ed] their savage brethren in atrocities." According to Stephen Riggs, most Minnesotans believed that "an Indian [was] an Indian" regardless of his actions. If they had not actually participated in the war, it was "because they lacked opportunity." The missionaries lamented that even before the war, most Minnesotans had failed to distinguish between civilized and uncivilized, Christian and non-Christian, and peaceful and non-peaceful Dakotas. This happened, for example, following the Inkpaduta crisis and during Riggs's fight for citizenship for Dakota-speaking civilized Dakotas. Given the public's long history of seeing all Dakotas as the same, it is not surprising that in the heat of war the distinction was further lost.[14]

In an ironic twist of reasoning, those Minnesotans who did distinguish between Christian and non-Christian Indians argued that Christian Dakotas should receive harsher treatment than those who had not converted. Henry Hastings Sibley, who served as a military commander during the war, explained this line of reasoning. According to Sibley, the missionaries had taught Christian Dakotas about morality, which made these Dakotas "entirely competent to judge of criminality of the proceedings in which they are now implicated and who therefore do not deserve to be judged with leniency."[15]

Although it went against public opinion, the missionaries strongly defended "their Indians" (as they called them) for remaining peaceful and even rescuing whites. During the war, Thomas Williamson was shocked when he heard rumors blaming Christian Dakotas for the rebellion. He called these reports "utterly—it seems to me maliciously—false . . . Nothing could be further from the truth." To set the record straight, Williamson informed evangelical readers that Christian Dakotas "generally, if not universally, abstained from taking part in the massacre." Indeed, they had done "what they could to save lives, not only of those connected with the mission, but of other whites residing among them." In an article published across Minnesota, Martha Riggs issued a similar defense. "It must be remembered," she wrote, "that the *church-members,* as a whole, have had *no hand in it.*" Evangelicals also read about the innocence of Christian Dakotas in the *Missionary Herald.* "[I]t is very gratifying . . . to learn," an article stated, "that the Christian Indians did not willingly participate in this uprising."[16]

In subsequent years, different evaluations have been offered of the Dakotas who rescued white captives. Some Dakota historians and activists resoundingly criticize those members of the so-called peace party who did not fight and who rescued whites. Waziyatawin Angela Wilson, for instance, notes that when the war broke out, "most Dakota people were required to make a conscious choice regarding which side they were willing to stake their lives." She calls those who chose to protect white Minnesotans "the traitors of Dakota people." Other Dakota historians, however, do not share Waziyatawin's perspective. Clifford Canku and Michael Simon, who worked on translations of Dakota letters from prison following the 1862 war, argue that "These Dakota protected their white relatives in accordance with customary Dakota obligations to relatives by marriage." John Peacock attempted to reconcile both positions, finding himself drawn to those who "do not claim to have found the truth, but acknowledge the great variation between what those multiple accounts claim to be true."[17]

The missionaries, as products of antebellum evangelical mission culture, did not value or even consider balanced interpretations. They believed, without question, that Christian Dakota men who rescued captives where heroes, not traitors. Moreover, these men rescued captives not because of Dakota kinship relations but because the missionaries had converted them to Christianity. Summing up these conflicting interpretations, both past and present, Peacock notes that "Dakotas favor stories of their resistance, whereas Whites favor stories of Dakota capitulation." The ABCFM missionaries might have added a third category: they favored stories that focused on the Dakotas' conversion to Christianity and Dakota actions which illustrated the (purported) triumph of their labors.[18]

Rescue of Missionaries

All of the missionaries' letters and publications featured stories about Christian Dakotas who had remained peaceful and risked their lives to save whites. They began these stories with their own rescue. While Riggs and Williamson did not escape together when the war began, their stories followed the same outline. On August 17, Riggs and Williamson were leading Sabbath meetings at their Hazelwood and Pajutazee mission stations, respectively. Initially, they were unaware that anything was wrong, as they were located several days travel north of the Lower Agency where the war broke out. When they learned of the events at the Lower Agency, they brushed off the violence as "only a drinking quarrel" and remained at their respective stations. Once they realized that war had broken out, they continued to remain in their homes; both families were protected by Christian Dakotas who stayed "up all night guarding us while we slept and assisting us when awake in every way in their power."[19]

It was the Christian Dakotas who convinced the Riggs and Williamson families to leave their stations. Both families grabbed a few belongings, woke their children, and fled to safety. Christian Dakotas served as their guides and provided them with food. The missionaries described a terrifying escape filled with fears of attacks by unknown Dakotas; injured settlers; crying children; hunger; and cold, driving rain. At no point in this harrowing journey, however, did the missionaries question the loyalty of "our own Indians," although they "lived in dread of how strange Indians" would treat them. A week later, Williamson, Riggs, and their families reunited and arrived safely at St. Paul. Because of the chaotic situation in Minnesota, the ABCFM did not know whether the missionaries were alive; indeed, a report reached Secretary Treat that Riggs, Williamson, and their families had been killed. As one of their first orders of business when they reached safety, the missionaries wrote Secretary Treat and informed him of their escape and the role that Christian Dakotas played in their rescue.[20]

The missionaries publicized the fact that as a result of the Christian Dakotas' protection and aid, only one man with ties to the ABCFM lost his

The Riggs and Williamson families with others who fled the Upper Agency missions to safety, August 21, 1862. The photo was taken by Adrian Ebell, a young photographer who had traveled to Upper Sioux to take pictures of the distribution of the treaty payment. Riggs is seated directly in front of the woman standing by the wagon wheel.

life during the war. Amos Huggins, a government teacher and the son of Alexander Huggins, was killed near Lac qui Parle. The three men who killed Huggins, however, spared the life of his wife, Sophia, and their two children. After her husband's death, Sophia Huggins and the children were rescued by a man named Spirit Walker and taken to Manitoba. When Stephen Riggs learned about their situation, he sent four Christian Dakotas to bring Sophia Huggins and her children back to Minnesota.[21]

The Counter-revolution

In addition to describing their rescue by Christian Dakotas, the missionaries publicized the role that converts played in the so-called counter-revolution or peace party. According to Riggs, soon after the war began, a counter-revolution headed by Christian Dakotas occurred on both the lower and upper reservation. Members of this group refused to support the war and actively worked to save captives. Scholars Carrie Reber Zeman and Kathryn Zabelle Derounian-Stodola, however, have questioned Riggs's contention that most members of the peace party were Christians. Their research showed that most were Dakotas who had taken up farming but not Christianity.[22]

While Riggs may have overemphasized the number of Christian Dakotas who belonged to the peace party, he was correct that mission-affiliated Dakotas were some of the strongest allies of the whites and some of the most vehement opponents of fighting. Every missionary publication that discussed the U.S.–Dakota War listed the names and actions of Christian Indians who had rescued whites. The missionaries informed the commissioner of Indian affairs that Joseph LaFromboise saved the lives of twenty-two men and forty women and children when he warned them to leave Pajutazee and Hazelwood. Likewise, Lorenzo Lawrence and Simon Anawangmane brought three captive women and eleven children to Fort Ridgely. By the time the war ended, Lawrence alone had saved seventeen people (including his own family). The missionaries also credited John Other Day with saving sixty-two settlers. Other Day "advised the whites to make their escape, and offered to pilot them out of danger." Although the group at first doubted "his faithfulness," in the end they agreed to follow him, which saved their lives. According to an article in the *Missionary Herald* titled "Noble Conduct of a Christian Indian," the actions of Other Day "[have] done more for missions than any event during the whole history of the Sioux mission."[23]

John Other Day, 1862.

ANPETU-TOKECA (Other Day.)
Who rescued Sixty-two persons from the Indian Massacre at Yellow Medicine, Minnesota, and piloted them safely to Shakopee. Aug. 19th, 1862.

Martha Riggs stressed that Christian Dakotas made these rescues *"at the peril of their lives."* Indeed, the actions of the Christians made them targets in their own right. Throughout the war, Dakota soldiers destroyed the homes and farms of Christian Dakotas. Stephen Riggs reported that the "hostile party . . . set fire to every house belonging to a Christian Indian on the upper Reservation." Nancy McClure recalled that more than $3,000 of her property was taken or destroyed during the war. John Other Day also reported that "all of his worldly possessions" were burned during the six weeks of fighting. In addition to destroying their homes and property, the warriors also threatened to kill Christian Dakotas if they failed to support the war. Riggs stated that when Paul Mazakutemani, the former president of the Hazelwood Republic, pleaded for the release of some white captives, Dakota warriors "said they would kill [him]."[24]

The divisions between pro- and anti-war Dakotas intensified as the war drew to a close. Riggs touted the fact that several members of the church took their opposition one step further by creating a *tiyotipi* (soldiers' lodge) to counter the war effort. This *tiyotipi* "formed a nucleus around which the Dakotas who desired to be loyal might rally." Paul Mazakutemani became spokesman for this "peace *tiyotipi*." As his first task, Mazakutemani demanded the return of property taken from Dakota farms by the Dakota warriors. Mazakutemani and other members of the peace *tiyotipi* also played a prominent role in the end of the war by helping to free captives and taking them to the hastily constructed Camp Release. When the war ended, Camp Release was filled with freed captives, peaceful Dakotas, and Dakotas who had participated in the conflicts but hoped to blend in with those who had rescued the captives. Without regard to their actions during the war, General Sibley imprisoned almost all Dakotas—men, women, and children.[25]

Conflicts over Post-war Treatment of the Dakotas

The missionaries did not support Sibley's actions; they believed that Christian Dakotas, especially members of the peaceful *tiyotipi*, should be released from prison and rewarded for their valor during the war. This did not happen. In the hysteria that followed the end of the war, the missionaries were dismayed to learn of calls for the annihilation of all Dakotas, regardless of whether they were Christian, had remained peaceful, or had rescued captives. During his work as chaplain for the army, Riggs was shocked to read a letter from Judge Charles E. Flandrau to General Sibley that counseled "killing all off, men, women and children . . . [as] they will only grow up like their fathers." Riggs wrote to his wife that he was "horrified at the way officers and soldiers in this camp talk about killing Indians." This evaluation must have included General John Pope, Lincoln's appointment to head the war effort against the Dakotas, who wrote that it was his "purpose to utterly exterminate the Sioux . . . They are to be treated as maniacs or wild beasts."[26]

Newspaper articles across Minnesota echoed the calls for extermination Riggs heard in the military. On August 22, the *Pioneer and Democrat* published remarks made by the sheriff of Brown County, an area that was especially affected by the war, as the village of New Ulm was located within its boundaries. The sheriff informed Governor Ramsey that the conflict with the Dakotas would end in one of two ways. One was to have a strong army "hold these Indians on their reservation." The other was to "kill them all at once, *and that would be the best.*" The press continued to publish these incendiary stories throughout the conflict. On September 12, before the Dakotas' surrender at Camp Release, the *Weekly Pioneer* printed an article entitled "Let the Sioux Race be Annihilated." The author praised soldiers for pledging to "persecute a war of utter extermination of the entire Sioux race." Indeed, this should "be the spirit which should actuate every white man. The race must be annihilated—every vestige of it blotted from the face of God's green earth. Otherwise our State will be ruined and white men slaughtered or driven from our noble young state. ANNIHILATION;—that is the word."[27]

Various methods were suggested for killing Dakotas. Some settlers proposed bringing together the Dakotas and massacring the assembled group. Others recommended infecting them with smallpox or poisoning the entire population. Three private citizens actually took steps to encourage vengeance. I. C. George, E. B. Ames, and William Caine, agents for the railroad and steamship lines, offered to pay $25 for every five Dakota scalps they received. The bounties for scalps eventually rose to over $200. Other settlers who did not want to kill Dakotas personally prayed for divine intervention. Riggs reported that he heard one woman wish "that the Mississippi River would suddenly rise and drown a whole camp of fifteen hundred Dakota women and children."[28]

As calls for the extermination of all Dakotas reverberated across Minnesota, others demanded that all Dakotas—and other Indians as well—be completely removed from the state. Agent Galbraith articulated this viewpoint: "[T]he recent atrocities of the Sioux have so exasperated the people of the State, as a body politic, that these people and the Sioux Indians can never again exist together with safety or benefit to either in the same State limits." Thus, the "Indians must be sent out and kept out of the State." The press strongly supported Galbraith's recommendation, crying that "*Exile*—EXILE—EXILE, can be our only compromise of this matter."[29]

Advocates of removal suggested that Isle Royale, in Lake Superior, be established as an "Indian penal colony," where all Dakotas (and other Minnesota Indians as well) would be forced to relocate. The colony would be organized under "severe military surveillance," with guards stationed at all entrances and exits. The prisoners would have no contact with whites, except for missionaries or government officials. Moreover, the Indians living on the island would be disarmed, except for a fishhook. The idea of sending the Dakotas to Isle Royale gained immense popularity among the general population and many of the government officials in charge of making policy. In a letter to President Lincoln, Governor Ramsey recommended "their removal to some distant locality 'far beyond our borders.'"[30]

Certainly, all Minnesotans did not advocate the extermination or removal of the Dakotas. Some former captives defended their captors. The most frequently cited example is that of Sarah Wakefield, who defended Chaska, or We-Chank-Wash-ta-don-pee, at his trial. She reported that he had protected her and her children throughout the war. Because of his actions, she did not think that he should be executed. Despite her testimony, the tribunal found Chaska guilty and sentenced him to hang. Although he received a pardon from Lincoln, a mix-up of names led to his execution with thirty-seven other Dakotas at Mankato. Rather than attempting to make amends for hanging an innocent man, many accused Wakefield of having adulterous relations with Chaska. Later, when she wrote her captivity narrative, Wakefield defended her actions. "I do not wish any one to think I uphold the Indians in their murderous work," she explained. "I should think I was insane, as many persons have said I was. I wish every murderer hanged, but those poor men who were dragged into this through fear I pity, and think ought to be spared."[31]

Like Wakefield, all of the missionaries spoke out against extermination. Thomas Williamson worried that innocent Dakotas "may be murdered by equally wicked white men." Likewise, John Williamson "detested the avowed determination of perhaps a majority of the citizens of this State that they will never rest till the race is exterminated by war or sent to a hangman['s] . . . grave." Stephen Riggs called the "great clamor all over the State for their execution . . . unreasonable and unreasoning." Riggs also worried about how all of the demands for "annihilation and extermination" in the Minnesota papers looked to people back east. He believed that easterners would "think us crazy and unfit" to deal with the Dakotas.[32]

Privately, most of the missionaries also opposed the removal of the Dakotas from Minnesota. For example, Jane Williamson was "hopeful that the Indians . . . might yet be located somewhere" in or near Minnesota. Thomas Williamson wanted the Dakotas "to occupy most of their late reservation." Even Secretary Treat, who usually opted to stay out of the political fray, called the demand for complete exile (in a masterpiece of understatement) "a little problematical."[33]

While the missionaries opposed removal in their private correspondence, most chose not to openly publicize their comments. John Williamson did not "consider it always safe or wise to give my opinion in regard to the treatment of many of these Indians." Likewise, while Stephen Riggs also called the removal of the Dakotas from Minnesota an "altogether unnecessary and bad policy," he chose not to publicly express his opinions. He defended his silence by stating that his "opinion will not avail much, especially expressed now." Perhaps later, when "the tide of public sentiment may turn . . . it may be worth while to express an opinion." Mary Riggs, however, urged him to take a public stance against removal to "repay the debt of gratitude we owe those who assisted all the whites they could to escape, and by their influence saved the captives from a general massacre and aided in their rescue."[34]

Riggs seems to have ignored his wife's plea. Indeed, the *Mankato Record* published an article stating that it was the "firm belief" of Riggs that the Dakota "must be removed beyond the State limits." Thus, Stephen Riggs and his colleagues perpetuated the missionaries' long-standing practice of saying one thing privately and another publicly about controversial policies. It certainly did not help the Dakotas to have their strongest potential allies against removal keep largely silent on the topic.[35]

The Missionaries in the Post-war Period

Amid calls for vengeance, extermination, and removal from Minnesota, the government began to try Dakota men for their roles in the war. On September 28, 1862, General John Pope created a five-man military commission and began to send men before the panel. By the time the trials ended, on November 5, 1862, the commission had tried 392 prisoners and convicted 323. Of those convicted, 303 were sentenced to be hanged, 20 received prison sentences, and 69 were acquitted. However, of those acquitted, only eight were released; the others remained imprisoned at Camp Release.[36]

Most of the missionaries, especially Thomas and John Williamson, believed that the trials were a severe miscarriage of justice. John Williamson bluntly stated that he was "not satisfied with . . . all the trials." His father called the court "incompetent to try Indians for their lives." Despite their fear of retribution for defending the Dakotas, the Williamsons felt they could not ignore what they saw as a mockery of the justice system. They began a campaign to publicize the injustices of the trials, which they hoped would lead to new trials for the hundreds of convicted Dakota men. At the same time they fought for new trials, however, they clearly stated that "those who [were] fairly convicted of murder should be sentenced to death."[37]

Operating under the assumption that "even a murderer deserves a fair trial," John Williamson and his fellow missionaries detailed numerous abuses. They criticized the tribunal for assuming that a man was considered guilty until proven innocent. Moreover, during the trials, the judges tried almost four hundred cases in the same time it generally took to try one white murder case. At times, the court resolved more than forty cases in one day. Many of the Dakota defendants did not understand the criminal justice system and, more fundamentally, the English language. Adequate translators were not provided. Dakota defendants also were forbidden from hiring counsel, the prosecution often browbeat the witnesses, and the defendants were not allowed to speak for themselves. Finally, different standards were applied to mixed- and full-blood Dakotas. While it was ruled that a mixed-blood Dakota could have been forced to participate in a battle against his will, full-blood Dakotas were barred from using this defense. In sum, Thomas Williamson declared the trials so unfair and prejudicial that they were insufficient to convict someone of "killing a dog worth five dollars."[38]

While Thomas and John Williamson criticized the trials in general, they were especially incensed about the guilty verdicts against three church members, including a ruling elder of the Pajutazee (Yellow Medicine) church known as Robert Hopkins Chaske. Because of his status as a ruling elder and the role he played in helping the missionaries escape, Thomas Williamson and several other missionaries began an intensive campaign for his retrial and release. Immediately after learning of the guilty verdict, Williamson requested all papers related to Chaske's trial. Looking over the transcripts convinced him that the "strong excitement" caused by the war had led the judges "to think the testimony stronger than it really was." To help prevent "perpetrating a wrong against these Indians," Williamson wrote a letter to the commissioner of Indian affairs asking for "a stay of proceedings till they can be tried by unprejudiced men, who must be obtained from some other state than Minnesota."[39]

In addition to writing to the commissioner, Williamson fired off letters to Board members in Boston, urging them to write the Massachusetts congressmen about the miscarriage of justice in Minnesota. He also begged

Robert Hopkins Chaske, standing to right of tipi poles, with his family at his home at Pajutazee mission, August 1862. (Adrian John Ebell)

them to pressure the president to "appoint two or three men of high standing as honest unprejudiced jurists more influenced by the fear of God than popular clamor to come to Minnesota and give these Indians a fair trial, that the guilty many be punished and the innocent liberated." Jane Williamson, who worked as a teacher at her brother's mission, also wrote letters to Lincoln and General Sibley in Chaske's defense. She claimed that he was a victim of circumstance and had played no role in the war except to save whites. Sophia Huggins, despite the fact that her husband had been killed, "wrote . . . in behalf of Sacred Nest," another church member. John Williamson informed evangelical readers of the *Missionary Herald* that a "grievous wrong" was about to be committed "in the execution of some, perhaps many, innocent" Dakotas.[40]

The missionaries' letter-writing campaign influenced several officials back east to take action. At Williamson's insistence, Secretary Treat wrote to commissioner William Dole asking him to review the trials. Dole forwarded the letter to the secretary of the interior, noting that it was likely that "unprejudiced men [would] be appointed by the President to give them a fair trial." While it is unclear how much the missionaries ultimately influenced his decision, Lincoln appointed two men to review the trial materials. Although they would not offer new trials, they could confirm or negate rulings based on the trial transcripts. After reading the men's recommendations, Lincoln reduced the number of Dakotas to be hanged from 303 to 39.[41]

In the context of calls for complete annihilation, an outcry arose across Minnesota over Lincoln's decision. Subsequent historians have questioned Lincoln's handling of the situation. Most of the missionaries, however, applauded the president's verdict. Thomas Williamson expressed his support for the president's leniency in the *Missionary Herald*. "We thank God that he gave wisdom and firmness to President Lincoln to resist the repeated demands of the people of Minnesota for a general execution," he wrote, "and only ordered those convicted of participating in the murders to be put to death." Samuel Pond likewise praised Lincoln for "mercifully and wisely [intervening] to prevent this second wholesale massacre."[42]

Stephen Riggs and the Post-war Period

Stephen Riggs disagreed with his fellow missionaries over the trials and Lincoln's decision, primarily because he, unlike his brethren, worked closely with the military. After reaching safety with the help of Christian Dakotas in August 1862, Riggs left his family and volunteered to serve as chaplain for General Sibley's expedition. He justified this decision by saying that his church members "might need help." He also hoped to "deliver if possible our people [Christian Dakotas]." His colleagues initially supported his military work; John Williamson noted, "The services of Mr. Riggs in connection with the expedition have been invaluable to the cause of justice and mercy."[43]

Riggs's involvement with the trials, however, strained his relationship with the Williamsons. From September 27 until mid-November, Riggs worked behind the scenes to gather evidence for use in the trials. At first he interviewed women in private about "any acts of cruelty or wrong which they had suffered at the hands of Dakota men during their captivity." Soon, however, his role "expanded to include interviewing all potential witnesses and helping to record the Dakota names of witnesses and defendants in court papers." Through these interviews, he "gather[ed] the information for the Adjutent [sic] to prepare the charges." Because of Riggs's actions, Isaac

Heard, who published a history of the Dakota War in 1865, claimed that Riggs "furnished the grounds for the charges." As such, he called Riggs "the Grand Jury of the court."[44]

As a result of "having passed through those weeks of trials," Riggs noted that his "point of observation is different from ... [the Williamsons]." During the trials, he came "to see a beauty and a fitness in justice which I never saw before." Although Riggs did not relish the idea of hanging more than three hundred men, he believed that justice required "that the great majority of those who are condemned, should be executed ... not only to satisfy the white people, but as a lesson to the Indians and protection for the women and children and innocent men who remain ... duty must always take precedence o[ver] feeling." He called the executions a "terrible necessity." Because the Dakotas had "accomplished their own destruction," Riggs felt that Lincoln's decision to reduce the number to be hung was misplaced.[45]

While he generally supported the trials, Riggs admitted that they were not perfect. His main criticism involved the issue of race. Riggs firmly believed that one's actions and character were more important than one's race. In a letter to the *St. Paul Pioneer,* Riggs complained that mixed-blood and full-blood Dakotas were treated differently during their trials. He referenced two trials, where a "half breed" and a "full blood" Dakota were charged with the same crimes, but "one is to be turned loose and the other put in irons ... They should be treated alike in my judgment."[46]

Riggs later downplayed his support of the trials in his memoirs *Mary and I* and *Tah-Koo Wah-Kan.* In *Mary and I* he repeated some of the Williamsons' criticisms of the trials, writing that "the greater part of these were condemned on general principles, without any specific charges proved." As such, many of the convictions had "no good foundation." He also claimed that he had merely recorded the names of Dakotas for trial, instead of interviewing and finding potential witnesses. Finally, he later praised Lincoln's reduction in the number who were hung at Mankato. These statements clearly contradict his writings at the time, in which he supported the trials and their outcome.[47]

Although he attempted to rewrite his role in the trials, Riggs could not hide the fact that he continued his close alliance with government officials after the hearings. He served as the government interpreter at the prison camp in Mankato and, along with Sibley, identified which Dakotas were to hang and read the charges against them. He also delivered the last words to the condemned prisoners. On the day of the hangings, he informed the prisoners that they had "sinned against their fellow-men . . . except in the mercy of God through the merits of the Blessed Redeemer." He then "earnestly exhorted" the men to "apply to him as their only source of consolation."[48]

Many Dakotas evidently mistrusted Riggs, as seen by their failure to turn to Riggs as their source of consolation before the hangings. Thomas Williamson, Father Augustin Ravoux, and Stephen Riggs were given the opportunity to baptize the condemned prisoners. By the time of the hanging, twenty-five men had accepted baptism from Father Ravoux, fifteen from Williamson, and none from Riggs. Riggs even questioned Williamson's baptism of one prisoner named Tataymena, saying he was not "satisfied that he was a Christian." It is not surprising that the Dakotas did not choose to entrust their salvation to Riggs. His close association with the government and the trials clearly lost him what little trust he had gained over the years.[49]

Defenders of "Savages"

Despite Riggs's close connection to the government, all of the missionaries (including Riggs) were condemned as defenders of the Dakotas. The missionaries reported that they were "subjected to insults and wrongs all winter." Riggs noted, "It was hard . . . to stand consistently and wisely on the side of the Indians, among this community, at the present time . . . the majority of the people will damn any man who speaks for them." In general, the public perceived all of the missionaries as apologists for war atrocities, defenders of savages, and traitors to their race. Before the war ended, the *Pioneer and Democrat* predicted that all those who did not forcefully condemn the Dakotas would "be overwhelmed with popular indignation." This accurately described the missionaries' treatment by the public and popular press in the tense post-war era.[50]

The local media and Minnesotans ridiculed the missionaries for their defense of the Dakotas, no matter how limited. In fact, the *St. Paul Pioneer* dubbed the missionaries "hare-brained, mistaken, and sometimes crazy, philanthropic humanitarians." Mary Riggs reported that the missionaries were called "'fools for Christ's sake,' on account of our interest in the Dakotas." Thomas Williamson complained that the press and public accused him of seeing "only one side—that he was always the apologist of the Indians." Stephen Riggs noted that all the Dakota missionaries were called "old Indian men" for defending the Dakotas. John Williamson, the youngest missionary, took "the obloquy and scorn of" Minnesotans for his work with the Dakota. As a final insult, the *St. Paul Pioneer* suggested that if the missionaries trusted the Dakotas so much, they should leave Minnesota and "follow their proteges [sic] to the plains of the west" (which some actually did). The missionaries were ridiculed by their community much as Dakotas had faced ridicule for attending the mission church or school, an irony lost on the missionaries.[51]

The condemnation only increased when the missionaries suggested that some of the actions of "civilized" white soldiers and settlers were actually as savage as the lurid outrages attributed to Dakota warriors by the Minnesota press. According to Stephen Riggs, "the late war has shown the white race to be capable of systematic cruelties which throw the barbarities of Indian massacres into the shade." While settlers protested against the destruction of their property, John Williamson noted that American soldiers had destroyed the homes of civilized Indians living on the lower reservation. They also had burned down his meeting house at Redwood. In the punitive campaign after 1863, General Alfred Sully's soldiers attacked a hunting camp of Yanktonai, Lakota, and Dakota people at Whitestone Hill, Dakota Territory, killing several hundred people, including women and children; soldiers seized "immense supplies of buffalo meat which they had [dried] for the winter, [destroyed] five hundred of their lodges, captur[ed] a large lot of ponies, and an immense stock of robes, furs, etc."[52]

Even worse, some settlers and soldiers adopted the "savage" practice of scalping Indian men, and, as Samuel Pond bluntly commented, "[c]ivilized soldiers do not take scalps." While serving as an army chaplain, Stephen Riggs personally witnessed numerous scalpings and other mutilations of Indians' bodies. After one of the battles, Riggs reported that he saw "sixteen dead and *scalped* Indians being buried." Another time, Riggs reported that soldiers "scalped most of the Indians and manifested very much savagism in reference to them." Riggs was so upset that he "took the occasion to speak of it at the grave of the last man we buried." Around Wood Lake, Riggs wrote to his wife that he was "ashamed" to see that the bodies of the Indians were "mutilated—scalped, the head of one cut off, hearts cut out ... [It was] unchristian and uncivilized." Because of their "savage" actions, Gideon Pond, in a letter to the *New York Evangelist,* called some settlers and soldiers "unjust, passionate, vindictive, barbarous, and cruel." Thomas Williamson described white treatment of the Dakotas as "madness," which had taken away people's Christian charity and restraint and made them into the savages they hoped to eradicate. Of course, white settlers and soldiers did not share the missionaries' view of their actions.[53]

The passage of time did not diminish the anger of many whites toward the missionaries. Two years after the hangings, Thomas Williamson was scheduled to speak at a church in Mankato about "dealing justly with the African and the Indian." As he arrived in town, "a war party from Canada" raided a nearby village. The townspeople immediately "connected this outrage with the presence of Dr. Williamson in their city." In response to the raid, the city council met and "characterized the missionaries as inciters and abettors of the murderous Indian, and Dr. Williamson they termed a dangerous character." After their meeting, members from the city council came to Williamson's talk, stopped him mid-sentence, and ordered him to leave town.[54]

Likewise, in 1863 Stephen Riggs applied to be chaplain of the Minnesota state senate. Most likely he sought this position because his family needed money. Mary Riggs told her son that his father was denied the job "because our senators regarded your father as feeling a stronger sympathy for Indians than for white people!!" After losing this position, Riggs worried that he would not be able "to find a place to preach within the limits of Minnesota." Because of their close association with the Dakotas over the years and their calls for leniency, the missionaries lost much of the support and good will they had enjoyed in the early years of their missions.[55]

While the missionaries faced criticism and some mild retribution for their defense of Dakotas, in actuality their support was ambiguous and filled with qualifications. The missionaries admitted that the Dakotas had legitimate reasons for going to war but condemned all bloodshed and violence as a way to redress their claims. They defended Dakotas, but mainly those who had adopted Christianity and saved whites. Indeed, the missionaries exhibited a paternalistic attitude toward Christian Dakotas, consistently calling them "our" Indians throughout their correspondence and reports. (Interestingly, some Christian Dakotas called the missionaries "our missionaries.") Riggs condemned the actions of soldiers who wanted to exterminate all Dakotas but continued to serve as chaplain for the duration of the war. While he downplayed his involvement in later years, Riggs actually played an extremely important role in the trials and subsequent hangings. In sum, even though the missionaries were derided by white society for their defense of the Dakotas, most Dakotas (except for a few Christians) did not benefit from their support. In fairness, given the hysterical climate following the war, it is unlikely that the missionaries could have prevented the executions (although they did play a role in getting a number of death sentences commuted) or eventual removal of the Dakotas from Minnesota even if they had offered an unambiguous defense of all Dakotas.[56]

Conclusion: "Darkness and Light"

When faced with extreme anger against both the Dakotas and the ABCFM missionaries after the war, Riggs's first thought was "What will become of our quarter-century's work among the Dakotas? It seemed to be lost." Upon reflection, both Williamson and Riggs decided that all was not lost. Indeed, according to Riggs, the war brought both *"darkness* and *light."* Of course, darkness referred to bloodshed, the destruction of property, the post-war hysteria that gripped Minnesotans, and the calls for the extermination or removal of all Dakotas. It also referred to the fact that both mission stations were destroyed during the war. Although their problems in no way compared to the suffering endured by the Dakotas, the Protestant missionaries faced condemnation for their (however limited) support of the Dakotas. After looking at the burned buildings of his mission station and desolated fields, Riggs found it was "hardly possible not to regard the efforts . . . as having been a failure. The labor seemed to be lost."[57]

Within this darkness, however, came light. The missionaries saw signs that Christianity was gaining ground among the Dakotas both during and immediately after the war. The missionaries believed that a growing acceptance of Christianity had helped to cause the war in the first place. During the war, loyal Christian Dakotas risked everything to rescue the missionaries and other captives. The missionaries also continued to believe that the Dakotas belonged "to the same race . . . [and were] capable of being civilized and Christianized," although most Minnesotans rejected this outright. For these reasons, the missionaries hoped that their war against heathenism finally would tip in favor of Christianity. While the missionaries realized that "It is not yet light," they had every hope that "day is beginning to dawn."[58]

"But oh, how changed the times"

The Immediate Aftermath of the Dakota War of 1862

In November 1862, approximately 2,100 Dakota men, women, and children were transferred to prison camps at Fort Snelling and Mankato. Dakotas who had not been tried—mainly women, children, and the elderly—were sent to Fort Snelling, whereas the condemned men were imprisoned in a hastily constructed Mankato jail. Angry settlers attacked the captives, causing injuries and deaths, during the relocation to both prisons. In spring 1863, the men held at Mankato were transported to a prison at Davenport, Iowa, where they remained for three years. Those held at Fort Snelling were relocated to an isolated and undeveloped reservation called Crow Creek in Dakota Territory.[1]

As the Dakotas struggled to adapt to imprisonment, the appalling conditions at the camps, and eventual removal from Minnesota, something happened that the missionaries considered miraculous. At the camps, "opposition to education and the gospel of Christ had vanished . . . the prison became a school of letters and religion, and the camp at Fort Snelling was not much behind." Missionary letters and reports tell of hundreds of conversions at both prisons, as well as the overwhelming desire of Dakotas to learn to read and write. The missionaries rejoiced that the seeds they had struggled to cultivate over twenty-five years with the Dakotas finally had flowered. As Mary Riggs later wrote, "but oh, how changed the times."[2]

While the times certainly had changed, long-standing conflicts remained. The missionaries had hoped that this new chapter of their work would finally end the struggles that had defined their labors with the Dakotas since 1835. The post-war period, however, simply translated these conflicts into the new situation. First, the missionaries divided with government officials and other Minnesotans over the treatment of the prisoners and their removal outside the borders of Minnesota. Second, the missionaries argued among themselves about the validity of the conversions in the two prison camps. Third, the missionaries experienced conflict with the Dakotas over the purpose of education, and with the government over the use of Dakota instead of English in the prison schools. Finally, as in earlier times, the mission press hid these conflicts from the evangelical public, instead publishing stories about the triumphant success of the Dakota mission after years of failure.

As usual, the Dakotas had a different frame of reference than the Protestant missionaries. Unlike the missionaries, they did not keep a tally of the number of baptisms and conversions in the prisons; rather, they focused on survival in a hostile post-war Minnesota. After the war, Gabriel Renville (the stepson of Joseph Renville) summarized the Dakotas' situation: "We had no land, no homes, no means of support, and the outlook was most dreary and discouraging," he mourned. "How can we get lands and have homes again, were the questions which troubled many thinking minds, and were hard questions to answer."[3]

Conflict over the Post-war Treatment of the Dakotas

Most Minnesotans would not have responded sympathetically to Renville's difficult questions. Indeed, the hysteria that swept across Minnesota during the Dakota War remained into the post-war period. Many settlers and government officials continued to call for harsh reprisals against all Dakotas.

Historian Jennifer Graber argues that the U.S. victory in the war prompted ABCFM missionaries "to embrace evangelistic methods that featured state violence and confinement as acceptable, if not providentially prompted means for effecting American Indian conversion." While Graber is correct that the ABCFM missionaries reveled in the prison camp conversions that followed the war, Stephen Riggs, Thomas and John Williamson, and the Ponds never advocated the use of violence as a legitimate method to achieve this end. In fact, throughout their twenty-five years with the Dakota mission in Minnesota and into the post-war period, the missionaries remained consistent in denouncing violence and government policies and actions they viewed as contrary to their evangelical beliefs.[4]

Amid the cries for further executions and removal, the missionaries attempted to walk an ineffective middle path between the two sides. The Williamsons, Riggs, and Gideon Pond acknowledged that many Minnesotans had suffered due to the war. However, they spoke out in both their public and private correspondence against settler attacks on the Dakotas as they moved to prison camps and questioned the prisoners' detention and treatment at Mankato and Fort Snelling. They also opposed the removal of the prisoners to Davenport, as well as the location of the new Crow Creek reservation. Even their guarded defense of the Dakotas, however, led to continued conflict with many Minnesotans and government officials. As John Williamson commented, to "befriend an Indian was not a popular thing to do in those days."[5]

Conflict over Attacks by Settlers on Dakotas

During the war, the missionaries strongly criticized the vigilantism and calls for extermination that rang throughout Minnesota. They continued their pleas against violence into the post-war period, when angry mobs attacked—and in some cases killed—prisoners as they were transferred between jails. Gabriel Renville reported that as the three hundred Dakota prisoners were moved to Mankato, a mob attacked them "with stones, bricks, and pitchforks, and everything they could lay their hand on." Once the group reached Mankato, another mob attempted to kill them. The prisoners on their way to the Fort Snelling camp also suffered, especially as they moved through New Ulm, a German community that saw extensive fighting during the war. According to John Williamson, as the group of mostly women, children, and the elderly traveled to Fort Snelling, a mob threw stones and sticks, "to say nothing of the curses which were heaped upon them from the doorways and hillsides." By the time the group reached the camp, a woman and a child had been killed.[6]

Published accounts of Dakota oral traditions also tell of mobs attacking families on their way to prison. Dakota historian Waziyatawin Angela Wilson recorded the stories recounted by her grandmother, Elsie Cavender. Cavender reported that as the women and children traveled through towns on the way to Fort Snelling "people were real hostile to them . . . They would throw rocks, cans, sticks, and everything they could think of: potatoes, even rotten tomatoes and eggs . . . It was on this trip that my maternal grandmother's grandmother was killed by white soldiers." Vine Deloria Sr. reported hearing a similar story from his uncle. Although his relatives did not participate in the war, they "one day woke to find themselves completely surrounded by soldiers." They were ordered to line up, and they "had to leave everything, including their tipis and horses, as they marched south." During the journey, Deloria's uncle recalled in vivid detail the brutal murder of a Dakota baby by one of the soldiers.[7]

As they did during the war, the missionaries attempted to walk an impossible line between acknowledging that settlers had legitimate grievances against the Dakotas while at the same time refusing to sanction the use of violence to settle those grievances. Riggs, Williamson, and Pond empathized with settlers who had suffered during the war and continued to face difficulties in its aftermath. Stephen Riggs wrote, "All along the line of the frontier, where the Sioux raids had been made, were many families who had returned to desolate homes." Because of the loss of lives and property, Riggs understood why there was a "highly exasperated state of feeling which existed in the minds of all whites on the border against all Indians." Likewise, John Williamson noted that "it was not strange" that white settlers were bitter, as "some of them had lost friends, and many more property."[8]

While the missionaries sympathized with the settlers, they did not condone violence against the Dakota prisoners. Gideon Pond called the attacks against the prisoners "unjust, passionate, vindictive, and cruel." Using similar terminology, Riggs described the violence directed at the prisoners as they passed through New Ulm as "insane." Thomas Williamson also condemned the guards for the death of prisoners because they refused to "keep the mob off" as they traveled through New Ulm in chains. Hugh Cunningham, a teacher at the Dakota mission, summarized the missionaries' view of the violence against prisoners, condemning Minnesotans and the United States in general as "verily guilty concerning this people."[9]

Conflict over the Prisons

Thomas and John Williamson and Gideon Pond (but not Riggs) earned further enmity from the public for questioning the imprisonment of Dakotas at Mankato and Fort Snelling. They argued that most of the guilty Dakota warriors had fled to the western plains immediately after the Battle of Wood Lake; thus, the vast majority who remained in Minnesota were innocent and should not be imprisoned for crimes they did not commit. According to John Williamson, "the real desperadoes succeeded in making their escape towards the British possessions." Because the trials had failed to convict the real culprits, justice demanded that the majority of prisoners be set free. Thomas Williamson believed that most prisoners had "done nothing worthy of death or bonds." Gideon Pond also was "fully persuaded that a large majority are suffering unjustly—suffering for the crimes of others."[10]

Innocent prisoners suffered doubly because of the conditions in the prisons. All of the missionaries—including Stephen Riggs—believed that the prisoners (even if guilty) should be treated humanely. The missionaries visited both prisons and uniformly condemned the conditions. Their letters and reports describe the Fort Snelling prison as a depressing, unhealthy place. According to the missionaries, one of the main problems was that families were separated from each other, with the men at Mankato and their families at Fort Snelling. John Williamson wrote, "It is a sad sight to see so many women and children . . . not knowing whether they will ever see their husbands and fathers again."[11]

The missionaries also complained about the location and small size of the Fort Snelling prison. Stephen Riggs noted that the prison's location was a "low, flat place, in part of which water stands." In addition to the unhealthy location, the government only allocated three acres for approximately 1,600 prisoners, which led to severe overcrowding. Even though most of the prisoners had not committed any crimes, or even had a trial, they were not allowed to leave the camp to hunt or gather, as they were surrounded by a "board fence, twelve or fourteen feet high, having one gate where a guard is kept."[12]

Finally, the missionaries criticized the prisoners' insufficient and unhealthy diets. Thomas Williamson complained that the prison diet "constipates their bowels and almost universally they are suffering from hard coughs." Historians have found evidence that confirms Williamson's complaints about the prisoners' diets. After searching through military records, historian Walt Bachman concluded that the Dakotas were fed much less than white prisoners. Indeed, in a telegram to Washington, General Sibley advised that "complete rations are not necessary" for the Dakota prisoners.[13]

Missionaries who visited the prison commented upon the high death rate caused by the crowded, unhealthy conditions and poor diet. After visiting the Fort Snelling prison, Thomas Williamson wrote that the "wailing hardly ever ceases" and from "five to ten die daily." Stephen Riggs described the mortality rate at Fort Snelling as "fearful . . . The shock, the anxiety of confinement, and the pitiful diet were naturally followed by sickness." John

Williamson reported that "Within 6 months, more than 200 have died, many of them in consequence of their confinement."[14]

The Mankato prisoners suffered many of the same hardships as their Fort Snelling counterparts, including illness, hunger, and cramped and unsanitary conditions. These prisoners, however, faced additional problems. While the Fort Snelling inmates were restricted by a board fence and an armed guard, they could move freely within the small camp. Thomas Williamson noted that the Mankato men did not have this liberty, as "some 400 Indian men and boys [were] chained by the ankle two and two . . . with a bar or chain about a foot long between." They were seated on the frozen ground covered with only a thin layer of straw. In addition to their shackles, the men lived in constant fear of the future. Immediately after the hangings, a rumor circulated among the prisoners that the thirty-eight men were only the first group to be hung and that the others would be executed at a later date. As the months passed and no other men were hung, another rumor circulated that they would be enslaved or removed to a distant island. The guards did nothing to dispel the prisoners' anxieties.[15]

Conflict over Removal from Minnesota

The unhealthy prisons were intended to be temporary. Most Minnesotans demanded the complete removal of all Dakota people (and other tribes including the Ho-Chunk) from Minnesota. In spring 1863, the prisoners at Fort Snelling were placed on steamboats and transferred to the newly established Crow Creek reservation in present-day central South Dakota. In the same year the men at the Mankato prison were transported by steamboat to another military prison in Davenport, Iowa. John Williamson accompanied the families to Crow Creek, while his father traveled with the Mankato prisoners to Iowa. Stephen Riggs again signed on to work with Sibley in 1863, only visiting the prisoners in Davenport months after their removal from Minnesota.

While only John Williamson traveled to Crow Creek to witness the conditions firsthand, all of the missionaries condemned the location of the new reservation even before the transfer began. They universally called Crow Creek a terrible choice for a reservation. Riggs described Crow Creek as "a miserable country" where it would be "impossible to make a living by agriculture." John Williamson characterized the land as "inhospitable." The missionaries also correctly pointed out that because many of the men were imprisoned in Davenport, women, children, and the elderly were the ones who would have to make a living on this difficult terrain. John Williamson admonished that it would not do "for the Government to take this company of women and children off to the deserts and turn them loose to shift for themselves, while they have all their men shut up in the Penitentiary at Davenport. They have to protect them from the neighboring tribes and do something towards giving them a start at farming to say the least."[16]

Unfortunately, the missionaries' predictions of distress and problems farming on the reservation proved to be correct. After nearly a year, John Williamson described failed crops, missing government rations, and overall terrible conditions. Williamson summarized the dire situation at Crow Creek: "The year had been one of much trial to the people—great scarcity of provisions, threatening starvation, much sickness, and great mortality."[17]

When faced with widespread starvation, Williamson made the same choice that his father had made years earlier—he told Dakota hunters to leave the reservation and attempt to find meat. He advised "as many of them as could do so, to scatter off, wherever there was any prospect of their picking up a living." While he realized that hunting was "contrary to our usual course" and that Indians were supposed to remain on their reservation, Williamson believed that averting starvation was more important than blindly adhering to farming under impossible conditions.[18]

Williamson did not, however, give up his single-minded devotion to converting the Crow Creek families to Christianity. He accompanied the Dakota hunters and attempted to show them "that they could travel over these wide prairies and keep the Sabbath; that they could kill buffalo without making charms; that they could live by the chase and worship God." Thus, Williamson continued to display some of the flexibility that had defined his father's missionary work over the years. Like his father, John Williamson made choices that contradicted the dictates of the ABCFM or the Indian agent based on issues that arose in the field. Williamson also continued the missionaries' long-standing focus on Christianization over civilization; it was more important for Williamson to impart instruction in Christianity than it was to stress "civilized" farming or living on a reservation.[19]

While John Williamson accompanied the Dakota refugees to Crow Creek, his father and Stephen Riggs focused their attention on the transfer of the prisoners from Mankato to Davenport. Both Riggs and Williamson believed that some (Riggs) or all (Williamson) of the prisoners should be released and sent to Crow Creek with their families rather than remain incarcerated in another prison. Secretary Treat, following Williamson's lead, asked the commissioner of Indian affairs for clemency for most of the Mankato prisoners. "Though we condemn the massacres in the strongest terms," he wrote, "we believe that the guilty parties, so far as arrested, have been sufficiently punished; that many, indeed, have been treated with undue severity; while not a few of the innocent have suffered grievous injustice. Nor can we forget the provocations which the Dacotas [sic] have received through many years."[20]

Unlike Williamson and Treat, Riggs did not ask for clemency for all the prisoners. He did, however, fight for the release of forty-eight men who had been acquitted in their trials but were still held in Minnesota. After learning of the transfer of all Mankato prisoners to Iowa, Riggs lay awake "thinking of the injustice." He believed that the small number who had been exonerated in their trials should be freed. The next morning, Riggs wrote to General Sibley asking that the forty-eight acquitted prisoners be sent to Crow Creek. Riggs's intervention was successful, and these prisoners were not transferred to Iowa. The pleas of Treat and Williamson to release all prisoners, however, were ignored.[21]

When the rest of the prisoners arrived in Iowa, the commander of the prison, General Benjamin S. Roberts, was so upset with the ABCFM's meddling and criticism that he barred Thomas Williamson from entering the prison, even though the elderly missionary had accompanied the prisoners to continue his ministry. When Stephen Riggs learned that Williamson could not minister to the prisoners, he appealed to General Sibley to help the ABCFM gain entrance to the prison. Sibley "kindly offered me his influence with General Roberts," and by the time Riggs joined Williamson in Iowa, "Roberts had re[s]cinded his order ... He at once gave me a very full and free permission to visit them at such times as I desired." Again, as happened repeatedly throughout the Dakota mission, the experiences of Williamson and Riggs diverged. Williamson's long-standing challenges to government policies resulted in punitive action against him at the prison. Riggs's close relationship with the government, however, resolved the issue of prison visitation in the ABCFM's favor. While the two missionaries interacted differently with the government, they still were united in their unwavering belief that every Dakota needed to accept Christianity and that their mission should continue in the prison.[22]

Conflict over Conversions

Although the missionaries criticized the government prisons and removals, they reveled in the post-war conversions that swept through both prisons prior to the Dakotas' removal from Minnesota. After years of conflict, it appeared that the Dakota mission would finally be successful. All missionary letters and reports jubilantly recounted that widespread conversions followed in the wake of war. Thomas Williamson proclaimed that he witnessed "the most remarkable displays of God's grace of which we have any record." After the war, "The barriers which had been impregnable and impenetrable in the past were suddenly broken down. Their ancestral religion had departed." John Williamson never would have predicted that the aftermath of the war would have "such a rich blessing in store for us."[23]

The missionaries' letters and reports triumphantly included the number of conversions. In January 1863 at the Mankato prison the missionaries reported that 230 men agreed to "renounc[e] heathenism and desir[ed] to embrace Christianity." A few weeks later, all 346 men in the camp added their names to the list. Gideon Pond described the scene at the Mankato prison. The men "huddle themselves together in the prison, every morning and evening," he wrote, "and read portions of the Scriptures, sing hymns, confess their sins one to another, and pray together." After witnessing the men's pious conduct, Thomas Williamson and Gideon Pond "baptized 274 people [and later] received 305 or 306 into the church that winter." In March, Pond reported that "Three hundred embittered defeated Indian warriors, manacled, fettered, with balls and chains,—but clothed in their right minds,— were sitting in groups upon the wintry grounds reverently observing the Lord's supper," he enthused. "It was like a 'nation born in a day.'"[24]

The missionaries described a similar religious awakening at Fort Snelling before the move to Crow Creek. The Williamsons erected a tent to accommodate hundreds of worshippers; when the group outgrew the tent, they met in the "garret of a large warehouse which had been prepared for a hospital." When the missionaries could not preach at the camp, native Christians took over the growing congregations. As a result of the combined efforts of the missionaries and native church members, more than 100 men and women converted during the first four or five months of their imprisonment at Fort Snelling. By spring 1863, approximately 140 had been received into the church. Thomas Williamson summarized the amazing success of the ABCFM's programs after years of failure. "I suppose as many readers and writers have been made among the prisoners in less than two years, as were made by our mission in the 27 previous years, and more converts."[25]

While all of the missionaries publicly touted the large numbers of new Christians, they privately divided over the sincerity of these conversions. Among themselves, the missionaries asked the difficult questions that had plagued their mission since 1835. Did all of the converts truly understand and accept Christianity? Did they meet the strict criteria for conversion? Especially in the context of imprisonment, did some Dakota men and women convert because the church offered tangible benefits and not because they embraced Christianity? In sum, were most of the conversions real or just a means to an end? The long-standing debate over what it meant to become and remain a Christian continued—as it had throughout their long years of work among the Dakota.

By this point in the missionaries' story, it should not come as a surprise that John and Thomas Williamson and Gideon Pond tended to accept the sincerity of these conversions. They also were more willing to compromise the all-or-nothing standards of what it meant to become, and remain, a Christian. Although the Williamsons and Pond understood that some people might question the Dakotas' motives, they believed that many of the conversions were legitimate because the Dakotas' "old superstitions [had been] dashed to pieces, like a potter's vessel." Moreover, the Williamsons and Pond promised that they had given all new converts a rigorous examination "as thoroughly as [we] have been accustomed to see in any of our churches." During the examinations, John Williamson wrote of "their pointed confessions of their sin and folly and expressions of detirmination [sic] to serve their Savior."[26]

As usual, and contrary to his brethren, Stephen Riggs, along with Secretary Treat of the ABCFM, questioned the sincerity of some of the conversions. Riggs believed that "the genuineness of their professions might be doubted and disbelieved." Although he saw the large number of new church members as "a very wonderful reformation, and as *a most amazing work of God's Spirit*," he had no doubt that many of the converts had "been influenced by *mixed* motives, and that *deliverance from the chain on the ankles has been one of the motives.*" In the end, Riggs worried that "there is not a great deal of reality there. Doubtless, there is much that is specious or that will not be enduring." Likewise, Secretary Treat wondered if many of the conversions were made "to escape hanging?" Thomas Williamson summarized the divide between Riggs and himself over the conversions. "The professions of a considerable number appeared to me well but . . . brother Riggs had doubts about the propriety of baptizing any of them."[27]

In addition to questioning whether the converts truly accepted Christianity, Riggs brought up the long-standing issue of whether men involved in polygamous marriages should be allowed to join the church. Riggs visited the Mankato prison and was appalled to see that Pond and Williamson had agreed to baptize several men who were involved in polygamous marriages. Riggs immediately called a meeting and informed the potential converts that any man who wanted to be baptized could have only one wife. After a lengthy discussion, "nineteen men were called upon to select which of two [wives] they would retain." In his correspondence, Riggs noted that Williamson and Pond were not at the prison at this time, so he was able to overturn their more lenient standards and make sure that polygamous marriages were not sanctioned by the church. As usual, the *Missionary Herald* failed to mention this internal struggle among its missionaries. In May 1863, the *Missionary Herald* informed its readers that the issue of polygamy had been "amicably settled."[28]

Conflicts over Education

The missionaries bickered among themselves about the validity of conversions and who could become, and remain, a Christian. However, they universally applauded the desire of the Dakota prisoners to learn to read and write. Indeed, the missionaries reported that a "perfect mania" for reading had swept through the prisons. They called the camps "one great school." The demand for the ABCFM's elementary readers (mainly translated biblical texts) became so great that the missionaries had to place an emergency order to print hundreds more in Minneapolis. The missionaries proudly informed the evangelical public that almost everyone, except the oldest Dakotas, attempted to learn to read and write. Stephen Riggs was thrilled with the strikingly different attitude toward education that followed in the wake of war. "As much progress has been made during the present winter in reading and writing," he proclaimed, "as was made during the twenty six or seven years preceding, by all the Dakotas."[29]

Dakota students, however, undoubtedly wanted to learn to read and write for reasons of their own. From the beginning of their mission, the ABCFM missionaries used literacy to promote Christianity. They continued this focus in the prison by distributing biblical translations as teaching materials. Indeed, they linked the numerous conversions directly to the growing literacy in the prisons. Most of the Dakota men, women, and children, however, probably had more secular goals in mind as they learned to read and write in Dakota. Following the war, families and kin groups were separated in distant prison camps. The ability to read and write letters allowed them to communicate while confined in the prisons. The amount of mail passing between the Mankato and Fort Snelling camps supports this assertion. In early March, Stephen Riggs carried three hundred letters from Fort Snelling to the prisoners at Mankato. He returned from the prison with about the same number. In late March, he delivered more than four hundred letters to prison. Later, the missionaries also carried daguerreotypes of friends and relatives between the prisons, supplied reams of paper, and made purchases for the men in Mankato with money sent by their Fort Snelling relatives. Literacy allowed the Dakotas to have some contact with their relatives despite their physical separation. The missionaries helped to maintain these ties by serving as mail carriers.[30]

Dakota parents imprisoned at Fort Snelling also asked the missionaries to establish a boarding school for their children. Hugh Cunningham, who had been in charge of the small Hazelwood boarding school before the war, visited the Fort Snelling camp with his wife, where he was surprised to learn that Dakota parents offered "as many [of their children] as we could accommodate." Prior to the war, the boarding school had suffered from poor attendance and boycotts. The parents' desire to enroll their children in school at this time can be explained at least in part by the camp conditions. They likely concluded that a mission education was preferable to continuous exposure to disease and hunger in the camp. Stephen Riggs conceded this point. "Their changed circumstances are such as to make their parents and friends desire more than ever that they should be in a Boarding School," he wrote. "During this winter ... [the children] will be subjected to evils of various kinds from the presence of white people, soldiers and others that makes it desirable that they should be taken from the camp."[31]

Perhaps the prison schools and the potential boarding school were received positively because the missionaries continued to teach in Dakota, rather than English. Indeed, even as Minnesotans and government officials derided the "savagery" and "barbarism" of Dakota cultural and religious practices, the missionaries continued to define Dakota as a civilized language. In defending the fact that the letters sent between prisons were written in Dakota, Thomas Williamson noted, "It is generally supposed that the language of a savage people, recently reduced to writing, must be imperfect and defective." However, he found that it was "easier to get the sense of those written in Dakota than those written in English." Thus, Williamson's view of Dakota continued to evolve. After twenty-five years of learning, speaking, and translating Dakota, Williamson had come to see the Dakota language as equal to English, and obviously for the Dakota, superior.[32]

The Conclusion of the Dakota Mission in Minnesota

Conflict had been a defining feature of the ABCFM Dakota mission since its inception. Beginning in 1835, the missionaries had divided with each other, government officials, the ABCFM, settlers, and, of course, the Dakotas. Many of these conflicts revolved around the issue of change. The missionaries were not supposed to be changed by their work with the Dakota. They were not supposed to question (or quietly alter) conversion standards. They were not supposed to challenge government officials, speak out against federal Indian policy, or question the settlers' actions. They were not supposed to change their evaluation of "inferior" Dakota practices, such as warfare, hunting, feasting, or polygamy. They were not supposed to focus on promoting civilization or on reading for the sake of literacy; every action must contribute to Christianizing the Dakotas. They were not supposed to reevaluate the Dakota language, first characterizing it as potentially equal to English, then as equal to English, and finally as superior to English in some cases. Female missionaries were supposed to contribute to the conversion of the Dakotas in the home and not question the lack of time they could spend proselytizing.

The missionaries were not supposed to change. Life in the field, however, led each of the missionaries to individually question, and occasionally re-evaluate, the directives of the Board and some of their own religious and cultural assumptions. This was not an easy process; changes caused tension within the overall mission community, as well as within each individual missionary. Throughout their time in Minnesota, the missionaries consciously attempted to hide, or at least obscure, the reality of their work among the Dakota. They deliberately omitted information from their letters and reports. At times, they included information they specified was not to be published. They told their relatives one story and the ABCFM another. Wives attempted to hide their disillusionment from their husbands. Most important, the missionaries never openly acknowledged that the Dakota influenced them as much as they hoped to influence the Dakota. Their collective letters and writings, however, provide many examples of these changes and challenges over time.

In the period following the war, the mission press continued to gloss over these conflicts. Instead, all of the ABCFM publications informed readers about the growing number of conversions and touted the success of the Dakota mission, which followed the Minnesota Dakota to reservations at Santee, Nebraska, and at Flandrau and Sisseton, South Dakota. One specific story was told numerous times, both in the immediate post-war period and in several of the missionaries' memoirs. The missionaries assuredly saw this tale as an important reflection of their efforts to convert the Dakotas. It begins with the transfer of the Dakota prisoners from Mankato. According to the missionaries, in the dark of night, 270 male prisoners were transferred to a steamship. They were not allowed to say farewell to their relatives at Fort Snelling. As the prisoners passed St. Paul on their way to their new prison in Iowa, they sang a hymn in Dakota—the words of David set to the tune of "Old Hundred," a popular hymn. Stephen Riggs included the first stanzas of the translated hymn in his memoir *Tah-Koo Wah-Kan*. It stressed sin, repentance, and acceptance by Christ.[33]

Likewise, John Williamson reported that prisoners from Fort Snelling sang hymns in Dakota as they were transferred to Crow Creek. Approximately 770 Dakota women, children, and elders boarded a steamboat at dusk under the guard of soldiers. As darkness set in and the steamer sailed from Fort Snelling, "these Indians looked out upon their native hills . . . for the last time." As Minnesota slipped away, the Dakota prisoners began to sing hymns, "like the murmur of many waters." They continued to sing and pray every morning and evening "without any suggestion from any one else." This is the image that the missionaries and the ABCFM wanted to leave with government officials, Minnesotans, evangelical readers, and Board members in Boston as they sailed into the next chapter of their story of Christianizing Dakotas—beautiful Christian hymns sung in the Dakota language. The singing on the steamboats proved that the "years of consecrated, self-sacrificing labours of Dr. Williamson and Dr. Riggs among the Indians bore rich fruit . . . in saving souls."[34]

The story of pious Dakota Christians singing hymns brought the ABCFM's Dakota mission full circle for antebellum evangelical readers. In the beginning, Thomas Williamson, Stephen Riggs, Gideon and Samuel Pond, and numerous other men and women of the Dakota mission had been inspired to devote their lives to the work of Christ by the stories of an earlier generation of missionaries. Now, their own purported success was used to inspire the next generation. This storybook ending, however, glossed over the quarter century of conflicted relations that had defined the Dakota mission.

Indeed, the story of the Dakota mission had not come full circle. The Dakota mission remained mired in contradictions, conflict, and challenges beyond Minnesota's borders. No amount of singing could prevent the Dakotas' removal from Minnesota or end the vitriolic rhetoric used against Dakotas in the press and by many settlers. While the public saw the missionaries as "friends of the Indians," the Protestants were ambiguous allies at best. They continued see the Dakotas in paternalistic terms and mainly supported Christian Dakotas. Likewise, they only challenged federal Indian policy when it contradicted their own goals and view of the world. They also failed to present a united front in their criticism, which may have diluted their overall ability to produce an effective critique of events in Minnesota. Thus, Dakotas and ABCFM missionaries were moving on to a new chapter in their lives, but it was neither the unambiguously glorious future that the missionaries had envisioned when they first arrived in Minnesota in 1835, nor the image of hope and salvation that they promoted to the evangelical public in 1863.

Acknowledgments

Over the years, I have written and rewritten this book. Because of the long process, I have accumulated an extensive list of people and institutions that I need to thank. Several institutions provided financial assistance for this project over the years. The University of Illinois at Urbana, Illinois State University, the Newberry Library Spencer Fellowship, and the American Philosophical Society, Philips Fund for Native American Research all provided support for this project. The Newberry Library's Scholar in Residence program also gave me space to work on this project, access to their collections, and amazing colleagues to critique my chapters.

Many archives across the country provided access to their extensive collections of primary and secondary sources related to ABCFM missionaries and the Dakotas. I would specifically like to thank the librarians and staff at the Minnesota Historical Society Library, the Center for Western Studies at Augustana College in Sioux Falls, South Dakota, and the Houghton Rare Book Library at Harvard University. Vanette Schwartz, the history librarian at Illinois State University, found obscure citations for me almost as soon as I sent my requests.

This project began in graduate school and benefitted from the critique of my dissertation committee—Sonya Michel, Martin Bruegel, and my advisor Robert Johannsen, who recently passed away. Dr. Johannsen always will serve as my model for the highest standards of scholarship and teaching. Donald Fixico also served as a de facto advisor and has continued to be an inspiration to me with his own scholarship. Julie Davis, Elisa Miller, Ed Tenace, Robert Galler, and Jessie Betts stand out among graduate school colleagues who helped me talk through this project and continue to make me laugh even though I mainly interact with them electronically.

My colleagues at Illinois State University also have helped me work through this project, both at our faculty seminars and in the hallways. Although my entire department was supportive, I would specifically like to thank Kyle Ciani, John Freed, Ron Gifford, Monica Noraian, Patrice Olsen,

Katrin Paehler, Lou Perez, Touré Reed, Georgia Tsouvala, Christine Varga-Harris, Ray Clemens, who has since moved on to Yale University, and Silvana Siddali, at St. Louis University. Kyle especially has helped me out, even teaching classes for me when I was on maternity leave. Roger Biles walked me though the unfamiliar world of publishing. Anthony Crubaugh, the chair of the history department, has also been highly supportive of my work. Linda Spencer, Faith Ten Haken, and Sharon Foiles in the ISU history office provided assistance throughout this project.

This book would not have happened without the support of the Minnesota Historical Society Press, especially editor in chief Ann Regan and managing editor Shannon Pennefeather. They both believed in this project and saw it through to its completion. I also would like to thank the anonymous reader for her helpful comments for my revision, as well as Tamara St. John, Sisseton-Wahpeton Oyate, for her encouraging comments and additions to the Dakota language sections of my work. David Deis drew the map that is included in the book.

I would like to thank my husband, Bill Jackson, and my three children for all of their support and inspiration throughout this very long process. This project began long before the birth of my oldest son, Charlie, who is now almost twelve, and continued through the births of Sam and Ellie, who are now nine and seven. Bill took care of them while I sat in libraries and my office writing and rewriting. I thank all of them for their love, patience, and support. Charlie, Sam, and Ellie: you wanted to make sure that your names appeared in my book, so here you are!

Finally, I would like to thank my parents, Rod and Margaret Clemmons, for their support and encouragement. I have chosen to dedicate this book to my mother, Margaret Clemmons. She has always supported and encouraged me in everything I have done. She has read this project in all of its many iterations and offered incisive comments and observations. She also has spent many hours babysitting my children as I worked on this project, and has taught them with the same patience and love that she taught me.

Notes

Notes to Introduction

1. Morris, *Old Rail Fence Corners*, 261.

2. Case, *An Unpredictable Gospel*, 7. Pointer, in *Encounters of the Spirit*, also commented that "receptive or not, though, European contact with native others changed both groups" (13). For additional scholarship discussing the transformative aspects of missionary life, see Bourne, *Gods of War, Gods of Peace*; Burkhart, *The Slippery Earth*; Merritt, *At the Crossroad*; Pruitt, *"A Looking-Glass for Ladies"*; Reeves-Ellington, "Women, Protestant Missions, and American Cultural Expansion, 1800 to 1938," 199; and Seat, *"Providence Has Freed our Hands."* Jennifer Graber, *The Furnace of Affliction*, described a similar process among antebellum prison reformers: working within the prison system forced evangelicals to adopt more secular ideas and goals.

3. See Case, *An Unpredictable Gospel*, 260; Merritt, *At the Crossroad*, 105–6; David Murray, "Spreading the Word: Missionaries, Conversion and Circulation in the Northeast," in Griffiths and Cervantes, *Spiritual Encounters*, 43–44; and Pointer, *Encounters of the Spirit*, 118, 120, 121, 204.

4. Hall and Newell, *The Conversion of the World*, 5.

5. Canku and Simon, *The Dakota Prisoner of War Letters*, 215.

6. Pointer, *Encounters of the Spirit*, 71; Case, *An Unpredictable Gospel*, 8, 9, 28.

7. For general information on the ABCFM, see Anderson, *Memorial Volume*; Andrew, *Rebuilding the Christian Commonwealth*; Berkhofer, *Salvation and the Savage*; and Phillips, *Protestant America and the Pagan World*.

8. Case, *An Unpredictable Gospel*, 11, 12.

9. Harris, *Nothing but Christ*, 3, 35.

10. Salisbury, "Red Puritans," 28. See also Hyman, *Dakota Women's Work*, 68; and Satz, *American Indian Policy in the Jacksonian Era*, 246. Many other historians have discussed the close links between imperialism and missionaries; indeed, this was the primary interpretation offered by historians in the 1960s–70s and beyond. See, for instance, Comaroff and Comaroff, *Of Revelation and Revolution*; Robert, "From Foreign Missions to Missions to beyond Missions;" Tinker, *Missionary Conquest*; and Craig, "Christianity and Empire."

11. For further information on the Cherokees and missionaries, see McLoughlin, *Champions of the Cherokees*; and McLoughlin, *Cherokees and Missionaries*. Satz, *American Indian Policy in the Jacksonian Era*, 252. Kidwell also discusses the relationship between missionaries, Choctaws, and the government: see Kidwell, *Choctaws and Missionaries*.

12. Perdue, *"Mixed Blood" Indians*, 71. For additional information on race in antebellum America, see Berkhofer, *The White Man's Indian;* Graves, *The Emperor's New Clothes;* Horsman, *Race and Manifest Destiny;* Sheehan, *Seeds of Extinction;* Stanton, *The Leopard's Spots;* Takaki, *Iron Cages;* and Vaughan, *Roots of American Racism.*

Vaughan, *Roots of American Racism,* 3. Higham, *Noble, Wretched and Redeemable,* 33. Quoted in Michael Hicks, "Noble Savages," in Eliason, *Mormons and Mormonism,* 181.

13. Peyer, *The Tutor'd Mind,* 123. Higham, *Noble, Wretched and Redeemable,* 37. Perdue, *"Mixed Blood" Indians,* 81.

14. Gray, *New World Babel,* 26, 65. See also Murray, "Joining Signs with Words."

15. Spack, *America's Second Tongue,* 3. Gray, *New World Babel,* 97. For references to the supposed inferiority of Indian languages, see Harvey, "'Must Not Their Languages Be Savage and Barbarous Like Them,'" 507; and Murray, "Joining Signs with Words," 62.

16. Several historians have argued that missionary attitudes toward race continued to reflect the Enlightenment notion of racial equality. See Coleman, *Presbyterian Missionary Attitudes,* 140. See also Coleman, "Not Race, But Grace," and Horsman, *Race and Manifest Destiny,* 205. Other historians, however, have argued that missionaries' views of race changed after extensive interaction with Indians. See Perdue, *"Mixed Blood" Indians,* 89; and Whaley, "'Trophies' for God," 25.

17. According to historian Michael Coleman, missionaries viewed tribal languages as "permeated by heathenism"; as such, these "impoverished and contaminated languages were hardly appropriate means of communication to or between converts of Christian civilization": Coleman, *Presbyterian Missionary Attitudes,* 117. Likewise, author C. L. Higham noted that antebellum missionaries believed that Indian "languages did not equal English and other 'civilized' European languages": Higham, *Noble, Wretched and Redeemable,* 78. See also Spack, *America's Second Tongue.*

The Dakota missionaries themselves initially offered a negative assessment of Dakota; before arriving in Minnesota the Dakota missionaries assumed that "in terms to express abstract ideas the Dakota language is undoubtedly defective." Quoted in Siems, "How do you say 'God' in Dakota," 170.

18. For example, see Kugel, "Of Missionaries and Their Cattle."

19. Dakota historian Waziyatawin (Angela Wilson) has written about Dakota history, the Dakota War of 1862, and the importance of Dakota oral tradition. See Wilson, "Grandmother to Granddaughter"; Wilson, *Remember This;* and Waziyatawin, *What Does Justice Look Like.* For information on Dakota interaction with Euro-Americans and Americans, see Anderson, *Kinsmen of Another Kind;* and Meyer, *History of the Santee Sioux.* Editors Zeman and Derounian-Stodola, in *A Thrilling Narrative of Indian Captivity,* offer a unique blend of historical background about the Dakota as well as a fully annotated reproduction of Renville's book. Several authors have written biographies of prominent Dakotas. For example, see Anderson, *Little Crow;* and Beck, *Inkpaduta.* Several books have successfully used ethnohistory to examine Dakota society and history. See Hyman, *Dakota Women's Work;* and Spector,

What this Awl Means. For a detailed look at Dakotas in Minnesota, see Westerman and White, *Mni Sota Makoce.* Charles Eastman, a Dakota doctor working in the mid- to late nineteenth century, wrote many books on Dakota culture, religion, and history. For example, see Eastman, *From Deep Woods to Civilization.*

20. See Higham, "Saviors and Scientists."

21. Nicholas Griffiths, "Introduction," in Griffiths and Cervantes, *Spiritual Encounters,* 2, 7.

Notes to Chapter 1

1. Riggs, *Mary and I,* v, vii, x, 27.

2. Riggs, *Mary and I,* ix, 26.

3. Higham, *Noble, Wretched and Redeemable,* 27. David Green to Thomas Williamson, 11 August 1836, ABCFM Indians Letter Book, 1:161, ABCFM Papers.

4. Nord, *Evangelical Origins of Mass Media in America,* 4. Kelley, "Pen and Ink Communion," 558, 561. Morgan, *Protestants and Pictures,* 6.

5. Higham, *Noble, Wretched and Redeemable,* 10. Pruitt, *"A Looking-Glass for Ladies,"* 28–29. Conforti, "David Brainerd," 310, 314, 322. See also Conforti, "Jonathan Edwards." See also Grigg, *The Lives of David Brainerd.*

6. Case, *An Unpredictable Gospel,* 46. Porterfield, *Mary Lyon,* 56. See also Brumberg, *Mission for Life,* 107.

7. Conforti, "Mary Lyon." The Library Company of Philadelphia, "Harriet Newell," Portraits of American Women in Religion, available: http://www.librarycompany.org/women/portraits_religion/newell.htm. Porterfield, *Mary Lyon,* 5. Kelley, "Pen and Ink Communion," 566. Jeffrey, *Converting the West,* 45.

8. Higham, *Noble, Wretched and Redeemable,* 19. Coleman, *Presbyterian Missionary Attitudes,* 12. Quoted in Brumberg, *Mission for Life,* 68.

9. Porterfield, *Mary Lyon,* 66. Higham, *Noble, Wretched and Redeemable,* 19. Gideon Pond to Samuel Pond, 30 October 1843, Pond Papers.

10. Pruitt, *"A Looking-Glass for Ladies,"* 69. Quoted in Joseph Conforti, "Mary Lyon," 80. *Annual Report of the ABCFM* (1841), 68.

11. For information on the years of the Second Great Awakening, see Andrew, *Rebuilding the Christian Commonwealth;* Butler, *Awash in a Sea of Faith;* and Marsden, *The Evangelical Mind.* For information on camp revivals and Cane Ridge in particular, see Conklin, *Cane Ridge,* and Eslinger, *Citizens of Zion.*

Handy, *A History of the Churches,* 163. Carwardine, *Evangelicals and Politics,* xv. See also Brumberg, *Mission for Life,* xi. McLoughlin, *The American Evangelicals,* 1. See also McLoughlin, *Revivals, Awakenings, and Reform,* xiii.

12. For information on the incorporation of other churches and missions into the ABCFM, see Willard, *Lac qui Parle and the Dakota Mission,* 1; and Phillips, *Protestant America and the Pagan World,* 235. Abzug, *Passionate Liberator,* 44. Noll, *Protestants in America,* 60. Marsden, *The Evangelical Mind,* 46–47.

13. Clark, "The Sacred Rights of the Weak," 465. Wacker, *Religion in Nineteenth*

Century America, 35. For information on the theological changes in the Second Great Awakening, see Ahlstrom, *A Religious History of the American People*, 405–9; Andrew, *Rebuilding the Christian Commonwealth*, 60; Banker, *Presbyterian Missions and Interaction in the Far Southwest*, 11–12; Bedell, Sandon, and Wellborn, *Religion in America*, 155; Carwardine, *Evangelicals and Politics*, 2–5; Conkin, *The Uneasy Center*; Hutchinson, *Errand to the World*, 49–51; Johnson, *Redeeming America*, 57–60; McLoughlin, *Revivals, Awakenings, and Reform*, 98–122; Noll, *A History of Christianity*, 158–60; and Olmstead, *History of Religion*, 257–300.

14. For information on the 1837 split within the Presbyterian Church, see Coleman, *Presbyterian Missionary Attitudes*, 11–13. Kling, "The New Divinity," 794.

15. Nevin, *Encyclopaedia of the Presbyterian Church*, 344. *Annual Report of the ABCFM* (1813), 67.

16. Braude, *Women and American Religion*, 18, 37. See also Johnson, *Redeeming America*, 55, 56–57. Kling, "The New Divinity," 801. See also Bratt, "The Reorientation of American Protestantism," 58. Kelley, "Pen and Ink Communion," 563.

17. Quoted in McCoy, "The Women of the ABCFM," 74.

18. For information on the different tactics used by the ABCFM missionaries and the Baptists and Methodists among the Cherokees, see McLoughlin, "Cherokees and Methodists;" and McLoughlin, *Cherokees and Missionaries*, 150–79. Anderson, *Memorial Volume*, 274.

19. Mary Riggs to Alfred Longley, 24 November 1834, in Riggs, *Family Correspondence*. This curriculum matched that of Mount Holyoke; see Porterfield, *Mary Lyon*, 42.

20. Anderson, *Memorial Volume*, 277, 333.

21. For the exact totals from each state, see ABCFM, *Report on Anti-Slavery Memorials*, 18. Porterfield, *Mary Lyon*, 5. ABCFM, *Report on Anti-Slavery Memorials*, 6. For a critique of the ABCFM's slave policy, see [Whipple,] *Slavery and the American Board of Commissioners for Foreign Missions*. For links between antebellum missionaries and abolitionists, see Bolt and Drescher, *Anti-Slavery, Religion, and Reform*, 209.

22. For examples of references to the missionaries' anti-slavery rhetoric, see Stephen R. Riggs to David Greene, 10 April 1848, mss. 244, no. 222, ABCFM Papers; Dakota Missionaries (Williamson, Riggs, and Hopkins) to the American Board, "Memorial to the American Board on the Subject of Slavery," September 1850, mss. 244, no. 21, ABCFM Papers; and Ruth Pond to Samuel Pond, November and 7 December 1839, Pond Papers. For a reference to missionary efforts to encourage temperance among the Indians, see Thomas Williamson to Samuel Pond, 3 August 1842, Pond Papers.

23. Harris, *Nothing but Christ*, 6. Thomas Williamson to Samuel Pond, 21 February 1839, Pond Papers.

24. Stephen Riggs to Selah Treat, 28 July 1860, mss. 310, no. 6, ABCFM Papers. Quoted in Pruitt, "A Looking-Glass for Ladies," 50.

25. Quoted in Pruitt, "A Looking-Glass for Ladies," 53. Mary Riggs to Mrs. Longley, 8 October 1837, Riggs Family Papers, Minnesota Historical Society (hereafter, MHS).

26. Anderson, *Memorial Volume*, 186. At least one example exists of a married woman who chose to pursue missionary work without her husband in the antebellum era. Clorinda Strong Minor became a missionary in Palestine while her husband remained in the United States. She did not have the backing of a missionary organization, however. See Kreiger, *Divine Expectations*. For information on the ABCFM's policy toward single women, see Welter, "She Hath Done What She Could"; and White, "Countering the Cost of Faith."

27. Grimshaw, *Paths of Duty*, 5. For additional information about missionary women in Hawaii, see Putney, *Missionaries in Hawai'i*. Jeffrey, *Converting the West*, 53. Sweet, *The Minister's Wife*, 92.

28. Mary Riggs to Mrs. Longley, 8 October 1837, Riggs Family Papers. Riggs, *A Small Bit of Bread and Butter*, 12, 13.

29. Riggs, *A Small Bit of Bread and Butter*, 13, 14.

30. See Bendroth, "Women and Missions," 52–53. Other historians have also studied women missionaries and argued that missionary work extended their sphere of action. See Alexander, "Gentle Evangelists"; Baker, "A Doorkeeper in the House of God"; Hill, *The World Their Household*; and Hunter, *The Gospel of Gentility*. Brumberg, *Mission for Life*, 82, 105. Also see, for example, Jeffrey, *Converting the West*.

31. See Lovejoy, "Satanizing the American Indian"; and Mandell, "The Indian's Pedigree." Riggs, *Tah-Koo Wah-Kan*, 92. Pond, *Two Volunteer Missionaries*, 18, 176. Pond, *Paganism, a Demon Worship*. Stephen R. Riggs to Greene, October 1838, mss. 141, no. 48, ABCFM Papers. Pond, *The Dakotas or Sioux in Minnesota*, 181.

32. Miller, *The Earth Filled with the Glory of the Lord*, 21. Magie, *A Sermon Preached at Buffalo, New York*, 6. Riggs, *Tah-Koo Wah-Kan*, 89. McMurray, *The Spiritual Contest of the Church*, 29. Jedediah Stevens to David Greene, 20 November 1838, mss. 141, no. 37, ABCFM Papers.

33. Pond, *The Dakotas or Sioux in Minnesota*, 3. David Greene to Stephen Riggs, 11 March 1837, ABCFM Indians Letter Book, 2:95, ABCFM Papers. Riggs, *A Small Bit of Bread and Butter*, 31. Stephen Riggs, "Sermon, 1860," mss. 310, no. 8, ABCFM Papers.

34. Perdue, "Race and Culture," 719. See also Vaughan, "From White Man to Redskin." Horsman, "Scientific Racism."

35. Coleman, "Not Race, but Grace," 60. Kling, "The New Divinity," 802.

36. Pond, *The Dakota or Sioux in Minnesota*, 71, 183–84. Commissioner of Indian Affairs, *Annual Report* (1850), 82.

37. Whaley, "'Trophies' for God," 48. Porterfield, *Mary Lyon*, 112.

38. Neill, "A Memorial of the Brothers Pond," 161, 162.

39. For information on Eatonville, see Anderson, "The Removal of the Mdewakanton Dakota in 1837," 316, 318; Folwell, *History of Minnesota*, 1:184–86; Forbes, "Evangelization and Acculturation," 24–25; and Meyer, *History of the Santee Sioux*, 49–50, 52. For information on Lawrence Taliaferro, see Neill, "Autobiography of Major Lawrence Taliaferro."

40. *Annual Report of the ABCFM* (1834), 121, 122.

41. The members of the three families included Thomas and Margaret

Williamson; Jedediah and Julia Stevens, who had taught the Stockbridge Indians near Green Bay for a number of years; Alexander and Lydia Huggins, friends of Williamson from his home state of Ohio; and two single women, Sarah Poage (the sister of Margaret Williamson) and Lucy Stevens (the niece of Jedediah Stevens). The Board appointed Thomas Williamson and Jedediah Stevens as full missionaries. The rest of the men and women served as assistant missionaries.

42. The ABCFM was the largest missionary organization of the era. By 1850, the Board sponsored 40 percent of all the missionary personnel in the United States. See Kling, "The New Divinity," 9. McLoughlin, *Cherokees and Missionaries*, 34.

43. Report of the Commissioner of Indian Affairs, Senate Documents, 26th Congress, 1st session, 1839–40, no. 354, 494–97.

44. The Teton (also called the Lakota, or Western Sioux by the missionaries) consisted of the Hunkpapa, Sicangu/Brulé, Itazipo/Sans Arc, Sihasapa/Blackfeet, Oglala, Oohenumpa/Two Kettles, and Mniconjou.

45. Gideon Pond to Miss Ruth Pond, 17 September 1839, Pond Papers. Case, *An Unpredictable Gospel*, 24.

Notes to Chapter 2

1. Riggs, *Mary and I*, 28, 32, 37.
2. Holmquist, *They Chose Minnesota*, 1, 8.
3. Riggs, *A Small Bit of Bread and Butter*, 22, 25, 91.
4. Riggs, *Mary and I*, 41, 47, 53.
5. Anderson, *Memorial Volume*, 350. Samuel Pond to Mrs. Phebe Mitchell, 23 November 1841, Pond Papers. Mary Riggs to her mother, 8 November 1838, in Riggs, *Family Correspondence*. Mary Riggs to her brothers, 23 October 1838, in Riggs, *Family Correspondence*.
6. Jedediah Stevens to David Greene, 8 June 1838, mss. 74, no. 11, ABCFM Papers; and Samuel Pond to Rebecca Hine, 10 December 1840, Pond Papers. Jedediah Stevens to Rev. David Greene, 2 January 1837, mss. 74, no. 13, ABCFM Papers; see also Thomas Williamson to David Greene, 30 December 1839, mss. 141, no. 13, ABCFM Papers.
7. Gideon Pond to Herman Hine, 15 May 1837, Pond Papers.
8. David Greene to Jedediah Stevens, 30 March 1837, ABCFM Indians Letter Book, 2:139, ABCFM Papers. David Greene to Stephen Riggs, 20 July 1837, ABCFM Indians Letter Book, 2:284, ABCFM Papers.
9. See David Greene to Thomas Williamson, 20 September 1837, ABCFM Indians Letter Book, 2:264, ABCFM Papers. See also David Greene to Stephen Riggs, 7 July 1838, ABCFM Indians Letter Book, 3:328, ABCFM Papers. For information on ABCFM policy with regard to new missionaries, see David Greene to Jedediah Stevens, 30 March 1837, ABCFM Indians Letter Book, 2:139, ABCFM Papers. *Annual Report of the ACBFM*, vol. 27 (1836–40), 145. Thomas Williamson to Samuel Pond, 23 July 1840, Pond Papers.
10. David Greene to Stephen Riggs, 11 March 1837, ABCFM Indians Letter Book,

2:95, ABCFM Papers. Stephen Riggs and Thomas Williamson to Rufus Anderson, 20 June 1857, mss. 244, no. 40, ABCFM Papers.

11. Thomas Williamson to David Greene, 30 September 1837, mss. 141, no. 3, ABCFM Papers. Thomas Williamson to Samuel Pond, 28 May 1840, Pond Papers.

12. David Greene to Jedediah Stevens, 17 July 1835, ABCFM Indians Letter Book, July 3–August 1837, 312.

13. Thomas Williamson to David Greene, 14 August 1837, mss. 141, no. 2, ABCFM Papers. Commissioner of Indian Affairs, *Annual Report* (1838), 523. Anderson, "The Removal of the Mdewakanton Dakota," 317.

14. Stephen Riggs to David Greene, 17 June 1837, mss. 74, no. 34, ABCFM Papers.

15. For information on slaveholding among the military at Fort Snelling, see Bachman, *Northern Slave, Black Dakota,* 10–11. Bachman notes that from 1828 to 1837, 85 percent of officers stationed at Fort Snelling held slaves at some point. Jedediah Stevens to David Greene, 8 June 1836, mss. 74, no. 11, ABCFM Papers. Thomas Williamson to David Greene, 13 July 1837, mss. 141, no. 1, ABCFM Papers. Riggs, *Mary and I,* 46. Riggs, *A Small Bit of Bread and Butter,* 44.

16. Thomas Williamson to David Greene, 15 October 1835, mss. 74, no. 26, ABCFM Papers.

17. Prucha, *The Great Father,* 151. Commissioner of Indian Affairs, *Annual Report* (1834), 255. Commissioner of Indian Affairs, *Annual Report* (1839), 516.

18. Samuel Pond to Gideon Pond, 10 January 1839, Pond Papers. Samuel Pond to David Greene, 10 May 1842, mss. 141, no. 97, ABCFM Papers.

19. David Greene to Stephen Riggs, 11 March 1837, ABCFM Indians Letter Book, 2:95, ABCFM Papers. David Greene to Jedediah Stevens, 13 October 1835, ABCFM Indians Letter Book, 1:375, ABCFM Papers. David Greene to Jedediah Stevens, 17 July 1835, ABCFM Indians Letter Book, July 3–August 1837, 312.

20. Pond, *Two Volunteer Missionaries,* 215.

21. Folwell, *History of Minnesota,* 1:188.

22. Samuel Pond to Preston Hollister, 28 March 1835, Pond Papers. See also Hedin, "The Minnesota Constitution in the Language of the Dakota," 2.

23. Siems, "How do you say 'God' in Dakota," 164. Powers, *Sacred Language,* 104–5. Stephen Riggs to David Greene, 27 September 1839, mss. 141, no. 57, ABCFM Papers.

24. Bray and Bray, *Joseph N. Nicollet on the Plains and Prairies,* 264. *Missionary Herald* 36.8 (August 1840): 325. See also Stephen Riggs to David Greene, 27 September 1839, mss. 141, no. 57, ABCFM Papers. Riggs, *Mary and I,* 41. Mary Riggs to Thomas and Joseph [Longley], 9 November 1837, Riggs Family Papers.

25. For an extensive bibliography of the missionaries' religious translations, see *Collections of the Minnesota Historical Society* 3 (1870–80): 37–42.

26. Thomas Williamson to David Greene, 4 May 1836, mss. 74, no. 27, ABCFM Papers. Samuel Pond to his sister, 28 October 1838, Pond Papers. For example, see Stephen Riggs to Samuel W. Pond, 17 April 1841, Pond Papers.

27. Samuel Pond to Sarah Pond, 24 August 1834, Pond Papers. Riggs, *A Small Bit*

of Bread and Butter, 66–67. Mary Riggs to her mother, 31 July 1837, in Riggs, *Family Correspondence.*

28. Bartlett, *Historical Sketch,* 28. Pond, *Two Volunteer Missionaries,* 50. See Stephen Riggs to Samuel Pond, 21 June 1839, Pond Papers; Riggs, *Tah-Koo Wah-Kan,* 12–13; Thomas Williamson to David Greene, 14 August 1837, mss. 141, no. 2, ABCFM Papers; and Mary Riggs to her father, 14 August 1837, in Riggs, *Family Correspondence.*

29. Thomas Williamson to David Greene, 14 August 1837, mss. 141, no. 2, ABCFM Papers. Riggs, *Tah-Koo Wah-Kan,* 10. Riggs, "The Dakota Language," 97.

30. Riggs, "The Dakota Language," 106. Thomas Williamson to David Greene, 14 August 1837, mss. 141, no. 2, ABCFM Papers. Thomas Williamson to David Greene, 1 October 1836, mss. 74, no. 29, ABCFM Papers.

31. Riggs, *Mary and I,* 59. Pond, *The Dakotas or Sioux in Minnesota,* 77. Riggs, *Tah-Koo Wah-Kan,* 13–14.

32. Riggs, *Mary and I,* 60.

33. Mary Riggs to Henrietta Longley, 27 June 1837, in Riggs, *Family Correspondence.*

34. Hyman, *Dakota Women's Work,* 4. Riggs, *A Small Bit of Bread and Butter,* 40. Mary Riggs to her parents, 9 November 1839, Riggs Family Papers. Mary Riggs to her mother, 9 September 1837, in Riggs, *Family Correspondence.*

35. Mary Riggs to her parents, 9 November 1839, Riggs Family Papers. Mary Riggs to her mother, 8 November 1838, in Riggs, *Family Correspondence.*

36. Fanny Huggins to Cordelia Pond, 1 October 1844, Pond Papers. Mary Riggs to her grandfather, 22 June 1837, in Riggs, *Family Correspondence.* Mary Riggs to [unknown], 3 April 1839, Riggs Family Papers.

37. Mary Huggins Kerlinger, *Reminiscences of Missionaries among the Dakotas,* 125–26, Huggins Papers. For further information on Dakota boarders, see Clemmons, "We find it a difficult work."

38. Stephen Riggs, "Biography of Men Connected with the Dakota Mission, 1835–1860," Riggs Family Papers. Mary Riggs to Alfred Longley, 30 January 1851, Longley Papers. Huggan, "The Story of Nancy McClure," 443.

39. Riggs, *A Small Bit of Bread and Butter,* 51, 71. Jedediah Stevens to David Greene, 26 September 1837, mss. 141, no. 31, ABCFM Papers.

40. Mary Riggs to Alfred Longley, 28 September 1837, Riggs Family Papers. Morris, *Old Rail Fence Corners,* 23. Mary Riggs to her parents, 5 April 1836, in Riggs, *Family Correspondence.*

41. Stephen Riggs to Cooley, 31 October 1843, Riggs Family Papers. See also Pettijohn *Autobiography, Family History,* 40. Mary Riggs to her mother, 9 September 1837, in Riggs, *Family Correspondence.* For examples of Dakota trade with the missionaries, see Kerlinger, *Reminisces of Missionaries Among the Dakotas,* 156, Huggins Papers; Diary of Janet Pond, 25 April 1850, Pond Papers; Mary Riggs to Mr. and Mrs. Longley, 27 June 1839, Riggs Family Papers; and Riggs, *Mary and I,* 45.

42. Mary Riggs to Mr. and Mrs. Longley, 6 December 1837, Riggs Family Papers.

43. Throughout the missionaries' letters and publications, Catharine's name is

spelled in various ways; I chose the one most commonly used by the missionaries. See Riggs, *Tah-Koo Wah-Kan*, 179. Jonas Pettijohn to Samuel Pond and Fanny Pettijohn to Cordelia Pond, 1 September 1848, Pond Papers.

44. Jonas Pettijohn to Samuel Pond and Fanny Pettijohn to Cordelia Pond, 1 September 1848, Pond Papers.

45. Miller, *The Earth Filled with the Glory of the Lord*, 24. Riggs, *A Small Bit of Bread and Butter*, 40; Mary Riggs to her parents, 4 June 1839, Riggs Family Papers. Mary Riggs to Alfred Longley, 14 May [1838], in Riggs, *Family Correspondence*.

46. Jedediah D. Stevens to David Greene, 20 June 1838, mss. 141, no. 35, ABCFM Papers. David Greene to Jedediah Stevens, 27 September 1838, ABCFM Indians Letter Book, 4:73, ABCFM Papers.

47. David Greene to Thomas Williamson, 27 September 1838, Pond Papers.

48. Stephen Riggs to David Greene, 24 October 1838, mss. 141, no. 47, ABCFM Papers.

49. Thomas Williamson to David Greene, 8 November 1838, mss. 141, no. 6, ABCFM Papers.

50. Jedediah Stevens to David Greene, 20 June 1838, mss. 141, no. 35, ABCFM Papers. Jedediah Stevens to David Greene, 19 November 1838, mss. 141, no. 36, ABCFM Papers. Jedediah Stevens to David Greene, 20 November 1838, mss. 141, no. 37, ABCFM Papers.

51. David Greene to Jedediah Stevens, 18 March 1839, ABCFM Indians Letter Book, 4:250, ABCFM Papers.

52. Stephen Riggs to David Greene, 1 August 1839, mss. 141, no. 54, ABCFM Papers. See also Mary Riggs to her parents, 9 November 1839, in Riggs, *Family Correspondence*. Thomas Williamson to David Greene, 15 August 1839, mss. 141, no. 12, ABCFM Papers.

53. Jedediah Stevens to David Greene, 6 September 1839, mss. 141, no. 43, ABCFM Papers. David Greene to Jedediah Stevens, October 1, 1839, ABCFM Indians Letter Book, 4:521, ABCFM Papers. *Annual Report of the ABCFM*, vol. 27 (1836–40), 145. Samuel Pond to Rebecca Hine, 23 October 1838, Pond Papers.

54. Jedediah Stevens to David Greene, 6 September 1839, mss. 141, no. 43, ABCFM Papers.

55. Thomas Williamson to David Greene, 10 May 1837, mss. 74, no. 32, ABCFM Papers. Samuel Pond to David Greene, 21 May 1838, mss. 141, no. 87, ABCFM Papers.

56. Riggs, *Mary and I*, 42.

57. Thomas Williamson to Samuel Pond, 21 February 1839, Pond Papers.

Notes to Chapter 3

1. For information on Rufus Anderson and his policies, see Harris, *Nothing but Christ*. Quoted in Congregational Library, "Rethinking Strategy," Of Faith and Courage: The History of the ABCFM, available: http://exhibits.congregationallibrary.org/exhibits/show/abcfm200/strategy. Magie, *A Sermon Preached at Buffalo, NY*, 11.

2. The missionaries offered various spellings of Eagle Help, including Wanmdi-Okiye, Wamde-Okeya, and Wande-Okeya. See *Two Volunteer Missionaries* and *Mary and I*, 339. I chose the spelling used most frequently by modern historians; see Zeman and Derounian-Stodola, *A Thrilling Narrative*, 8.

Stephen Riggs to David Greene, 26 March 1839, mss. 141, no. 49, ABCFM Papers; Samuel Pond to David Greene, 14 June 1839, mss. 141, no. 89, ABCFM Papers; and Thomas Williamson to David Greene, 12 July 1839, mss. 141, no. 12, ABCFM Papers.

3. Pond, *Two Volunteer Missionaries*, 91, 103.

4. Commissioner of Indian Affairs, *Annual Report* (1840), 1. David Greene to Stephen Riggs, 12 October 1839, ABCFM Indians Letter Book, 4:527, ABCFM Papers.

5. Wamdiokiye to Thomas Williamson, 18 April 18 —. In Ella Cara Deloria "Letters and Miscellaneous Materials in Dakota from the Minnesota Manuscript," American Philosophical Society Library, Philadelphia (hereafter, Deloria Papers). Riggs, *Mary and I*, 53. Mary Riggs to Mrs. Longley, 1 August 1839, in Riggs, *Family Correspondence*.

6. Stephen Riggs to David Greene, 13 July 1839, mss. 141, no. 53, ABCFM Papers. Stephen Riggs to David Greene, 10 September 1839, mss. 141, no. 56, ABCFM Papers. Jedediah Stevens to David Greene, 8 July 1839, mss. 141, no. 42, ABCFM Papers.

7. Stephen Riggs to Thomas Longley, 9 April 1839, in Riggs, *Family Correspondence*.

8. Stephen Riggs to David Greene, 13 July 1839, mss. 141, no. 53, ABCFM Papers; and Mary Riggs to Mr. and Mrs. Longley, 27 June 1839, Riggs Family Papers. See also Thomas Williamson to David Greene, 12 July 1839, mss. 141, no. 12, ABCFM Papers.

9. Riggs, *A Small Bit of Bread and Butter*, 101–2. Bray and Bray, *Joseph N. Nicollet on the Plains and Prairies*, 21. Stephen Riggs to David Greene, 10 September 1839, mss. 141, no. 56, ABCFM Papers. For information on Joseph N. Nicollet, see DeMallie, "Joseph N. Nicollet's Account."

10. Wamdiokiye to unknown, 9 February 1839, Deloria Papers.

11. Stephen Riggs to David Greene, 16 March 1839, mss. 141, no 51, ABCFM Papers.

12. Mary Riggs to Mr. and Mrs. Longley, 16 February 1839, Riggs Family Papers.

13. Mary Riggs to Mr. and Mrs. Longley, 4 June 1839, Riggs Family Papers.

14. Stephen Riggs to David Greene, 13 July 1839, mss. 141, no. 53, ABCFM Papers. Riggs, "Dakota Portraits," 564.

15. Thomas Williamson to David Greene, 13 July 1839, mss. 141, no. 12, ABCFM Papers. Pond, *The Dakotas or Sioux in Minnesota*, 60–61.

16. Lucas, "Civilization or Extinction," 242–43.

17. For a discussion of Dakota gift-giving practices, see Pond, *The Dakota or Sioux in Minnesota*, 169–73. See also White, "Give Us a Little Milk"; and White, "A Skilled Game of Exchange," 229–240.

18. Robert Hopkins to Selah Treat, 26 December 1848, mss. 244, no. 141, ABCFM Papers.

19. Pond, *The Dakota or Sioux in Minnesota*, 93–96, 98.

20. Deloria, *Speaking of Indians*, 24. For information on Dakota kinship practices, see Albers, "Regional System of the Devil's Lake Sioux," 33–35, 148–49; Landes, *The*

Mystic Lake Sioux, 95–160; Lesser, "Siouan Kinship"; Pond, *The Dakotas or Sioux in Minnesota,* 147; and Wozniak, *Contact, Negotiation, and Conflict,* 6, 24.

21. Stephen Riggs to Moses Longley, 10 October 1849, Riggs Family Papers, the Center for Western Studies, Augustana College. Because both the Minnesota Historical Society Library and the Center for Western Studies use the same name for their collections, I will note when I am using the Augustana collection. Citations without notation come from the Minnesota collection. Riggs, "Dakota Portraits," 500. Riggs, *A Small Bit of Bread and Butter,* 41.

22. Pond, *Two Volunteer Missionaries,* 94. Riggs, *A Small Bit of Bread and Butter,* 77–78. Robert Hopkins to Selah Treat, 26 December 1848, mss. 244, no. 141, ABCFM Papers.

23. Riggs, *Tah-Koo Wah-Kan,* 221.

24. Mary Riggs to Henrietta Longley, 28 July 1838, in Riggs, *Family Correspondence.*

25. Stephen Riggs to David Greene, 1842, mss. 141, no. 109, ABCFM Papers.

26. Jedediah Stevens to David Greene, 27 January 1836, mss. 74, no. 9, 27, ABCFM Papers; and Riggs, *Mary and I,* 60. Mary Riggs to Mrs. Longley, 25 March 1840, Riggs Family Papers. Mary Riggs to her mother, 2 October 1839; and Mary Riggs to her father, 14 August 1837, in Riggs, *Family Correspondence.*

27. Stephen Riggs to David Greene, 25 September 1837, mss. 141, no. 44, ABCFM Papers.

28. White, "Indian Visits," 100. Kugel, *To Be the Main Leaders of Our People,* 19.

29. *Missionary Herald* 45.6 (June 1849): 212.

30. Neill, "A Sketch of Joseph Renville," 198. Riggs, *Tah-Koo Wah-Kan,* 171.

31. Riggs, *Tah-Koo Wah-Kan,* 164–65.

32. Riggs, *Mary and I,* 73. Riggs, *Tah-Koo Wah-Kan,* 165. See Thomas Williamson to David Greene, 12 June 1846, mss. 244, no. 372, ABCFM Papers.

33. See Williamson, "Napeshneedoota"; and Riggs, *Mary and I,* 89, 124. See Zeman and Derounian-Stodola, *A Thrilling Narrative,* 6. Thomas Williamson to David Greene, 2 January 1846, mss. 244, no. 367, ABCFM Papers. Craig, "Christianity and Empire," 10.

34. Stephen Riggs to Selah Treat, 16 February 1853, mss. 244, no. 290, ABCFM Papers. Thomas Williamson to David Greene, 13 July 1837, mss. 141, no. 1, ABCFM Papers. Riggs, "The Indian Question," 255.

35. Gideon Pond to Selah Treat, 25 September 1849, mss. 244, no. 174, ABCFM Papers. See also Samuel Pond to Selah Treat, 12 September 1849, mss. 244, no. 12, ABCFM Papers.

36. Pond, *Two Volunteer Missionaries,* iii.

37. Neill, *The History of Minnesota,* 478. Blegan, "Two Missionaries in Sioux Country," 275. Thomas Williamson to David Greene, 13 July 1837, mss. 141, no. 1, ABCFM Papers; and Thomas Williamson to David Greene, 10 May 1837, mss. 74, no. 32, ABCFM Papers.

38. Thomas S. Williamson to Samuel Pond, 4 April 1845, Pond Papers. Stephen Riggs to David Greene, 27 September 1839, mss. 141, no. 57, ABCFM Papers.

39. For other references of infractions that resulted in suspensions, see Mary Riggs to Mrs. Longley, 8 October 1837, Riggs Family Papers; Thomas Williamson to David Greene, 3 January 1845, mss. 244, no. 362, ABCFM Papers; Thomas Williamson to David Greene, 2 January 1846, mss. 244, no. 376, ABCFM Papers; Stephen Riggs, "Lac qui Parle Church Report," September 1848, Riggs Family Papers; Riggs, *Tah-Koo Wah-Kan,* 231; *Missionary Herald* 38.10 (October 1842): 393; *Missionary Herald* 42.2 (February 1846): 50; *Missionary Herald* 42.5 (May 1846): 174, and Riggs, *Mary and I,* 88. Heard, *History of the Sioux War,* 219.

40. Mary Riggs to Mr. and Mrs. Longley, 9 February 1839, Riggs Family Papers.

41. Pond, *The Dakota or Sioux in Minnesota,* 139. For other references to polygamy in Dakota society, see Lesser, "Siouan Kinship," 253; and Wozniak, *Contact, Negotiation and Conflict,* 17–18. Thomas Williamson to David Greene, 14 August 1837, mss. 141, no. 2, ABCFM Papers. Riggs, "The Dakota Mission," 120. "The Polygamy Question," *The Boston Recorder,* found in ABCFM Papers, no. 389, n.d.

42. David Greene to Jedediah Stevens, 30 March 1837, ABCFM Indians Letter Book, 7: 139, ABCFM Papers. Stephen Riggs to David Greene, 27 September 1839, mss. 141, no. 57, ABCFM Papers.

43. Thomas Williamson to David Greene, 10 May 1837, mss. 74, no. 32, ABCFM Papers.

44. Stephen Riggs to David Greene, 20 June 1838, mss. 141, no. 34, ABCFM Papers. For other references to Renville breaking the church rules but not receiving a suspension, see Stephen Riggs to David Greene, 26 March 1839, mss. 141, no. 59, ABCFM Papers; and Thomas Williamson to David Greene, 19 December 1843, mss. 141, no. 29, ABCFM Papers. Pond, *The Dakotas or Sioux in Minnesota,* 19. See also Riggs, *Tah-Koo Wah-Kan,* 166–67, and Thomas Williamson to David Greene, 19 December 1843, mss. 141, no. 20, ABCFM Papers. Thomas Williamson to David Greene, 13 July 1837, mss. 141, no. 1, ABCFM Papers. Pond, *Two Missionaries in Sioux Country,* 275.

45. Mary Riggs to Mr. and Mrs. Longley, 9 February 1839, Riggs Family Papers. Riggs, "Dakota Portraits," 556. Porterfield, *Mary Lyon,* 72.

46. For information on Dakota burial practices, see Pond, *The Dakota or Sioux in Minnesota,* 162–69. Mary Riggs to Mr. and Mrs. Longley, 9 February 1839, Riggs Family Papers.

47. Riggs, *Mary and I,* 95. Riggs, "The Dakota Mission," 120.

48. "The Polygamy Question," *The Boston Recorder,* found in ABCFM Papers, no. 389, n.d. Thomas Williamson to David Greene, 15 June 1847, mss. 244, no. 378, ABCFM Papers.

49. Riggs, *Mary and I,* 95. Stephen Riggs to Selah Treat, n.d., mss. 244, no. 252, ABCFM Papers.

50. Pointer, *Encounters of the Spirit,* 72.

51. Anderson, *Memorial Volume,* 310. Riggs, *Tah-Koo Wah-Kan,* 402.

52. *Annual Report of the ABCFM* 28 (1837), 117, and Commissioner of Indian Affairs, *Annual Report* (1851), 437. See also *Missionary Herald* 33.7 (July 1837): 318; *Report*

of the ABCFM (1843), 173; Thomas Williamson to Samuel Pond, 25 April 1839, Pond Papers; and Commissioner of Indian Affairs, *Annual Report* (1851), 439–40. Stephen Riggs to David Greene, 26 March 1839, mss. 141, no. 49, ABCFM Papers. Pond, *Two Volunteer Missionaries*, 157.

53. Newcomb, *Cyclopedia of Missions*, 584.

54. Joseph Hancock to Selah Treat, 2 May 1854, mss. 244, no. 119, ABCFM Papers. Abel Stewawinika to David Greene (translated by Stephen Riggs), 23 September 1844, mss. 244, no. 1, ABCFM Papers.

55. Stephen Riggs to Selah Treat, 24 March 1849, mss. 244, no. 245, ABCFM Papers. Thomas Williamson to David Greene, 13 July, 1838, mss. 141, no. 1, ABCFM Papers.

56. Alexander Huggins to his brother, 18 January 1838, Huggins Papers. Rockman (?) to Mr. Renville, n.d., Deloria Letters.

57. *Missionary Herald* 38.10 (October 1842): 394. Stephen Riggs to ABCFM, 2 January 1862, mss. 309, no. 173, ABCFM Papers.

58. See Pond, *The Dakota or Sioux in Minnesota*, 142–44. Stephen Riggs to Selah Treat, 11 July 1856, mss. 244, no. 336, ABCFM Papers.

59. For information on Dakota child-rearing practices, see Pond, *The Dakota or Sioux in Minnesota*, 144–45.

60. Mary Riggs to Mrs. Longley, 28 August 1838, Riggs Family Papers. Samuel Pond to David Greene, 18 September 1844, mss. 244, no. 186, ABCFM Papers.

61. *Annual Report of the ABCFM* (1836), 99–100.

62. Stephen Riggs to David Greene, 27 September 1839, mss. 141, no. 57, ABCFM Papers. Thomas Williamson to David Greene, 6 April 1839, mss. 141, no. 9, ABCFM Papers.

63. Pond, *Two Volunteer Missionaries*, 229.

64. Thomas Williamson to David Greene, 6 April 1839, mss. 141, no. 9, ABCFM Papers.

65. Thomas Williamson to Gideon Pond, 24 and 26 February 1840, Pond Papers. Thomas Williamson to Samuel Pond, 28 May 1840, Pond Papers.

66. Gideon Pond to Rebecca Hine, 18 March 1840, Pond Papers. Thomas Williamson to Samuel Pond, 23 July 1840, Pond Papers.

67. Riggs, *Tah-Koo Wah-Kan*, 222. Pond, *Two Volunteer Missionaries*, 161–63.

68. Stephen Riggs to David Greene, 16 May 1839, mss. 141, no. 51, ABCFM Papers.

69. Thomas Williamson to David Greene, 15 August 1839, mss. 141, no. 12, ABCFM Papers.

Notes to Chapter 4

1. Holmquist, *They Chose Minnesota,* 8. Harris, *Nothing but Christ,* 23.

2. The Report of the Commissioner of Indian Affairs, issued in December 1837, clearly defines Jacksonian Indian policy. See Commissioner of Indian Affairs, *Annual Report* (1837), 525. Anderson, "The Removal of the Mdewakanton Dakota," 310.

3. Dakota-Lakota-Nakota Human Rights Advocacy Coalition, "DLN Nation: Treaties, Laws, Executive Orders Concerning the DLN Nation," available: http://www.dlncoalition.org/dln_nation/1837_treaty.htm. For a more complete explanation of the Treaty of 1837 and its ramifications for the Dakotas, see Clemmons, "We will talk of nothing else."

4. Riggs, *Mary and I*, 79. Stephen Riggs to David Greene, 22 June 1838, mss. 141, no. 46, ABCFM Papers.

5. Samuel Pond to David Greene, 14 June 1839, mss. 141, no. 89, ABCFM Papers. Thomas Williamson to David Greene, 10 May 1838, mss. 141, no. 5, ABCFM Papers. Riggs, *A Small Bit of Bread and Butter*, 60.

6. Thomas Williamson to David Greene, 12 July 1839, mss. 141, no. 12, ABCFM Papers. Thomas Williamson to David Greene, 10 May 1838, mss. 141, no. 5, ABCFM Papers.

7. Riggs, *A Small Bit of Bread and Butter*, 62. Mary Riggs to Mrs. Longley, 4 April 1839, in Riggs, *Family Correspondence*. Mary Riggs to Mr. Longley, 14 August 1837, in Riggs, *Family Correspondence*.

8. Mary Riggs to Mrs. Longley, 31 July 1837, in Riggs, *Family Correspondence*.

9. Stephen Riggs to David Greene, 23 January 1847, mss. 244, no. 231, ABCFM Papers. *Annual Report of the ABCFM* (1850), 191.

10. Anderson, "The Removal of the Mdewakanton Dakota," 310–33.

11. Stephen Riggs to David Greene, 1 May 1844, mss. 141, no. 83, ABCFM Papers. Thomas Williamson to David Greene, 25 August 1840, mss. 141, no. 15, ABCFM Papers. Thomas Williamson to David Greene, 2 January 1846, mss. 244, no. 367, ABCFM Papers.

12. Thomas Williamson to the Commissioner of Indian Affairs, 26 February 1850, Letters Received from the Office of Indian Affairs, 1824–70, St. Peter's Agency, 1845–50, reel 76, Record Group 75, Records of the Bureau of Indian Affairs, Washington, DC, National Archives. Thomas Williamson to David Greene, 20 June 1846, mss. 244, no. 371, ABCFM Papers. Riggs, *Mary and I*, 79. For information on education and the Treaty of 1837, see Westerman and White, *Mni Sota Makoce*, 162–63.

13. Thomas Williamson to Samuel Pond, 16 November 1843, Pond Papers. Riggs, *Mary and I*, 79.

14. Stephen Riggs to David Greene, 1 May 1844, mss. 141, no. 83, ABCFM Papers. Thomas Williamson to David Greene, "State and Prospects of the Mission Station at Lac qui Parle in September 1846," mss. 244, no. 374, ABCFM Papers. Thomas Williamson to Amos Bruce, 30 June 1846, Letters Received by the Office of Indian Affairs, 1824–70, St. Peter's Agency, 1845–50, reel 760. Robert Hopkins to Selah Treat, 20 July 1849, mss. 244, no. 145, ABCFM Papers. Riggs, *Tah-Koo Wah-Kan*, 245.

15. Stephen Riggs to Selah Treat, 24 March 1849, mss. 244, no. 245, ABCFM Papers. Riggs, *Mary and I*, 79. Jedediah Stevens to David Greene, 23 March 1839, mss. 141, no. 39, ABCFM Papers. Riggs, "The Indian Question," 263. Cordelia Pond to her sister, 25 September 1843, Pond Papers.

16. Samuel Pond to Selah Treat, 12 September 1849, mss. 244, no. 12, ABCFM Papers. Commissioner of Indian Affairs, *Annual Report* (1843), 385.

17. For references to killing cattle, see Thomas Williamson to Samuel Pond, 23 July 1840, Pond Papers; Stephen Riggs to Pond, 15 August 1843, Pond Papers; and Pond, *Two Volunteer Missionaries*, 170.

Annual Report of the ABCFM (1844), 221, 222; Cordelia Pettijohn to Gideon Pond, 26 February 1844, Pond Papers; and Thomas Williamson to David Greene, "Ninth Annual Report of the Lac qui Parle Mission School for the Year Ending June 30 1844," mss. 244, no. 360, ABCFM Papers. Commissioner of Indian Affairs, *Annual Report* (1844), 360. Moses Adams to Selah Treat, 17 August 1849, mss. 244, no. 55, ABCFM Papers. Commissioner of Indian Affairs, *Annual Report* (1849), 1059. Riggs, *Mary and I*, 128.

18. Eastman, *Old Indian Days*, 64. Pond, *The Dakotas or Sioux in Minnesota*, 69.

19. Robert Hopkins and Alexander Huggins to David Greene, 22 June 1848, mss. 244, no. 34, ABCFM Papers. Robert Hopkins to Selah Treat, 26 December 1848, mss. 244, no. 141, ABCFM Papers. Sioux Missionaries to the ABCFM, 31 August 1848, mss. 244, no. 10, ABCFM Papers.

20. *Missionary Herald* 38.10 (October 1842): 395. Gideon Pond to Selah Treat, 9 July 1849, mss. 244, no. 173, ABCFM Papers. *Annual Report of the ABCFM* (1844), 221.

21. Pond, *Paganism, a Demon Worship*, 22. Robert Hopkins to Selah Treat, 20 July 1849, mss. 244, no. 145, ABCFM Papers. Williamson, "Napeshneedoota," 189.

22. Catherine Price defined *akicita* as "enforcer of decisions." Price, "Lakotas and Euroamericans," 449. According to anthropologist William Powers, *akicita* means a soldier or marshal in Lakota; it also means "a messenger of a supernatural being or power." Powers, *Sacred Language*, 201. Although both authors referred to the Lakota language, the same general translation is also applicable to Dakota. Riggs defined *akicita* as a "warrior or soldier." Riggs, *A Dakota-English Dictionary*, 26. See also Williamson, *An English-Dakota Dictionary*, 215.

Eastman, *Indian Boyhood*, 259. See also Riggs, *Dakota Grammar, Texts, and Ethnography*, 195, 200, 220. Hassrick, *The Sioux*, 30.

23. Huggan, "The Story of Nancy McClure," 444.

24. Mary Riggs to Julia Longley, 5 February 1840, Longley Papers. Riggs, *Tah-Koo Wah-Kan*, 199. Robert Hopkins to Selah Treat, 18 June 1851, mss. 244, no. 154, ABCFM Papers.

25. Thomas Williamson and Stephen Riggs to Selah Treat, "Annual Report of the Dakota Mission," September 1850, mss. 244, no. 14, ABCFM Papers. Thomas Williamson to David Greene, 3 January 1845, mss. 244, no. 362, ABCFM Papers. Thomas Williamson to David Greene, "State and Prospects of the Mission Station at Lac qui Parle in September 1846," mss. 244, no. 374, ABCFM Papers.

26. David Greene to Samuel Pond, 20 April 1840, ABCFM Indians Letter Book, 5:137, ABCFM Papers. Thomas Williamson to Samuel Pond, 23 September 1840, Pond Papers.

27. Thomas Williamson to Samuel Pond, 23 September 1840, Pond Papers. Thomas Williamson to David Greene, 15 December 1840, ABCFM Indians Letter Book, 5:405, ABCFM Papers. Thomas Williamson to David Greene, 21 March 1843, ABCFM Indians Letter Book, 7:45, ABCFM Papers.

28. Samuel Pond to Rebecca Hine, 10 December 1840, Pond Papers.

29. Stephen Riggs and Gideon Pond to David Greene, 10 September 1846, "Report of the Committee on the Subject of Occupying Little Crow's Village as a Mission Station," ABCFM mss. 244, no. 5, ABCFM Papers. Thomas Williamson to David Greene, 30 November 1846, mss. 244, no. 375, ABCFM Papers.

30. John Aiton to Selah Treat, 21 June 1849, mss. 244, no. 87, ABCFM Papers; and the Sioux Missionaries to Selah Treat, "Annual Report of the Sioux Mission to the Year Ending September 1849," mss. 244, no. 11, ABCFM Papers. Gideon Pond to Selah Treat, 9 July 1849, mss. 244, no. 173, ABCFM Papers.

31. Pond, *Two Volunteer Missionaries*, 133–34.

32. Thomas Williamson to David Greene, 20 July 1841, mss. 141, no. 19, ABCFM Papers. Stephen Riggs to David Greene, 1 September 1842, mss. 141, no. 73, ABCFM Papers. See also Riggs, *Mary and I*, 49.

33. Riggs, "Dakota Portraits," 497. Stephen Riggs to Gideon Pond, 15 August 1843, Pond Papers. Williamson, Riggs, and Samuel Pond to David Greene, 1 October 1845, mss. 244, no. 4, ABCFM Papers.

34. Riggs, *Mary and I*, 111.

35. Pond, *Two Volunteer Missionaries*, 65.

36. Mary Riggs to Mrs. Cleland, 27 November 1842, Riggs Family Papers.

37. Mary Riggs to Mrs. Longley, 13 July 1844, in Riggs, *Family Correspondence*.

38. Mary Riggs to her brother and sister, 25 February 1847, in Riggs, *Family Correspondence*.

39. Sabrina Stevens to Mrs. Samuel Pond, 4 November 1843, Pond Papers. Mary Riggs to her parents, 18 January 1840, in Riggs, *Family Correspondence*.

40. Mary Riggs to Alfred Longley, 10 November 1849, Longley Papers. Riggs, *Mary and I*, 65. Diary of Marjorie Cunningham, 1861–63, MHS. Mary Riggs to Alfred Longley, 23 September 1840, in Riggs, *Family Correspondence*. Pond, *Two Volunteer Missionaries*, 200.

41. Mary Riggs to Julia Kephart, 2 February 1840, in Riggs, *Family Correspondence*. Mary Riggs to her parents, 10 December 1841, in Riggs, *Family Correspondence*.

42. For a timeline of Mary Riggs's life and birthdates of her eight children, see Riggs, *A Small Bit of Bread and Butter*, viii–ix. See Pond, *Two Volunteer Missionaries*, 200–208. Pond, *Two Volunteer Missionaries*, 255.

43. Mary Riggs to Miss Hallock, 24 April 1840, in Riggs, *Family Correspondence*. Mary Riggs to Mrs. Longley, 10 January 1848, in Riggs, *Family Correspondence*. Stephen Riggs to Selah Treat, 12 November 1849, mss. 244, no. 299, ABCFM Papers.

44. Mary Riggs to Mrs. Longley, 25 March 1840, in Riggs, *Family Correspondence*. Mary Riggs to Mr. and Mrs. Longley, 10 December 1841, Riggs Family Papers.

45. Riggs, *Sunset to Sunset*, 191. Mary Riggs to Mr. and Mrs. Longley, 10 December 1841, Riggs Family Papers.

46. Riggs, *Mary and I*, 74. Riggs, *Sunset to Sunset*, 110.

47. Gideon Pond to Samuel Pond, 30 November 1849, Pond Papers. Mary Riggs to her brother and sister, 24 March 1849, in Riggs, *Family Correspondence*.

48. Mary Riggs to Mrs. Longley, 31 May 1849, in Riggs, *Family Correspondence.* Mary Riggs to her parents, 9 May 1843, in Riggs, *Family Correspondence.* Mary Riggs to her parents, 24 March 1846, in Riggs, *Family Correspondence.* Stephen Riggs to Selah Treat, 12 November 1849, mss. 244, no. 299, ABCFM Papers.

49. Thomas Williamson to David Greene, 15 June 1847, mss. 244, no. 378, ABCFM Papers.

50. Thomas Williamson to David Greene, 8 November 1838, mss. 141, no. 6, ABCFM Papers. Gideon Pond to Sarah Pond, 2 February 1844, Pond Papers; and Gideon Pond to Samuel Pond, 15 January 1844, Pond Papers. Alexander Huggins to Selah Treat, 31 May 1849, mss. 244, no. 162, ABCFM Papers.

51. Mary Riggs to Alfred Longley, 28 April 1841, in Riggs, *Family Correspondence.*

52. Mary Riggs to Alfred Longley, 28 April 1841, in Riggs, *Family Correspondence.* Cordelia Pond to her sister Ruth, 25 September 1843, Pond Papers. Cordelia Pond to Agnes Hopkins, 29 May 1844, Pond Papers.

53. Samuel Pond to Selah Treat, 12 July 1849, mss. 244, no. 197, ABCFM Papers. Stephen Riggs to David Greene, 24 July 1843, mss. 141, no. 78, ABCFM Papers. Samuel Pond to David Greene, 4 October 1845, mss. 244, no. 188, ABCFM Papers.

54. Pond, *Two Volunteer Missionaries,* 203. Thomas Williamson to Selah Treat, 7 May 1849, mss. 244, no. 390, ABCFM Papers; Joshua Potter to Selah Treat, 3 June 1849, mss. 247, no. 26, ABCFM Papers. Robert Hopkins to Selah Treat, 9 April 1849, mss. 244, no. 142, ABCFM Papers.

Notes to Chapter 5

1. Samuel Pond to Selah Treat, 19 October 1854, mss. 244, no. 210, ABCFM Papers.

2. Anderson, *Kinsmen of Another Kind,* 210; Folwell, *History of Minnesota,* 1:211; Forbes, "Evangelization and Acculturation," 66.

3. Pointer, *Encounters of the Spirit,* 113.

4. Thomas Williamson to Selah Treat [June 1850], mss. 244, no. 13, ABCFM Papers.

5. Thomas Williamson to Selah Treat [June 1859], mss. 244, no. 13, ABCFM Papers. Robert Hopkins to Selah Treat, 7 June 1850, mss. 244, no. 147, ABCFM Papers. Thomas Williamson to Selah Treat, "Annual Report of the Dakota Mission Adopted at Lac qui Parle, September 1850," mss. 244, no. 14, ABCFM Papers. Samuel Pond to Selah Treat, 23 June 1851, mss. 244, no. 201, ABCFM Papers. "Report of the Commissioner of Indian Affairs," Senate Documents, 31st Congress, 2nd session, 1850–51, no. 587, 115.

6. Samuel Pond to Selah Treat, 13 February 1851, mss. 244, no. 200, ABCFM Papers

7. Gideon Pond to Selah Treat, 10 June 1851, mss. 244, no. 177, ABCFM Papers. Robert Hopkins to Selah Treat, 7 June 1850, mss. 244, no. 147, ABCFM Papers.

8. Robert Hopkins to Selah Treat, 7 June 1850, mss. 244, no. 147, ABCFM Papers.

9. Stephen Riggs, 28 June 1850, mss. 244, no. 255, ABCFM Papers. For the copy of the "Outline," see Alexander Ramsey to Luke Lea, 6 February 1851, Letters Received by the Office of Indian Affairs, 1824–81, St. Peter's Agency, 1851–54, reel 761.

10. Gideon Pond to Selah Treat, 10 June 1851, mss. 244, no. 177, ABCFM Papers. Samuel Treat to Samuel Pond, 21 October 1852, Pond Papers. Pond, *Two Volunteer Missionaries*, 211; and Samuel Pond to Selah Treat, 23 June 1851, mss. 244, no. 201, ABCFM Papers.

11. Robert Hopkins to Selah Treat, 1 October 1850, mss. 244, no. 149, ABCFM Papers.

12. LeDuc, *Minnesota Year Book for 1852*, 59. Meyer, *History of the Santee Sioux*, 80. Thomas Williamson to Selah Treat, 7 August 1851, mss. 244, no. 402, ABCFM Papers.

13. Fay, *A Grand Compendium*, 119. See also Folwell, *History of Minnesota*, 1:599–60.

14. Fay, *A Grand Compendium*, 126–28.

15. Riggs, *Mary and I*, 79. Meyer, *History of the Santee Sioux*, 84. LeDuc, *Minnesota Year Book for 1852*, 77, 84, and Anderson, *Kinsmen of Another Kind*, 188–89. Thomas Williamson to Selah Treat, 8 June 1852, mss. 244, no. 407, ABCFM Papers.

16. Commissioner of Indian Affairs, *Annual Report* (1851), 280–81, 416. Hubbard, et al., *Minnesota in Three Centuries*, 294. Minnesota Legislature, *Legislative Manual of the State of Minnesota* (1893), 198.

17. LeDuc, *A Brief Sketch*. Thomas Williamson to Selah Treat, 16 July 1851, mss. 244, no. 401, ABCFM Papers.

18. LeDuc, *Minnesota Year Book for 1852*, 60–61. Commissioner of Indian Affairs, *Annual Report* (1852–53), 332.

19. *Annual Report of the ABCFM* (1852), 151. See also Gilman, "How Minnesota Became the 32nd State," 162. Stephen Riggs to Selah Treat, 28 August 1852, mss. 244, no. 283, ABCFM Papers.

20. Commissioner of Indian Affairs, *Annual Report* (1853), 315. Beck, *Inkpaduta*, 39.

21. Commissioner of Indian Affairs, *Annual Report* (1852), 350. Commissioner of Indian Affairs, *Annual Report* (1853), 296.

22. Stephen Riggs to Selah Treat, 31 July 1852, mss. 244, no. 279, ABCFM Papers.

23. Stephen Riggs to Selah Treat, 31 July 1852, mss. 244, no. 279, ABCFM Papers. See also Thomas Williamson to Selah Treat, 28 September 1852, mss. 244, no. 411, ABCFM Papers; and Thomas Williamson to Selah Treat, 30 June 1852, mss. 244, no. 110, ABCFM Papers.

24. See Anderson, *Kinsmen of Another Kind*, 187, 199; Diedrich, *Dakota Oratory*, 44; Folwell, *History of Minnesota* 1:282–83; and Meyer, *History of the Santee Sioux*, 80, 81.

25. "The United States and the Indians," 32nd Congress, vol. 36 (1852–53), 25. Diedrich, *Dakota Oratory*, 49–52. Pond, *The Dakota or Sioux in Minnesota*, 173.

26. "Report of the Secretary of the Interior," 32nd Congress, 2nd Session, (1852–53), ex. doc 29, 14.

27. 33rd Congress, 1st session (1853–54), sen. doc. 16, 319.

28. Stephen Riggs to Selah Treat, 9 March 1854, mss. 244, no. 304, ABCFM Papers.

29. Holmquist, *They Chose Minnesota*, 8. Diedrich, *Dakota Oratory*, 46. Riggs, *Tah-Koo Wah-Kan*, 256. Frankyln Curtiss-Wedge, *History of Goodhue County Minnesota* (Chicago: H. C. Cooper, Jr. and Co., 1909), 533; Madeline Angell, *Red Wing, Minnesota: Saga of a River Town* (N.p.: Dillon Press, 1977), 64. Quoted on Goodhue County Historical Society website, available: http://www.goodhuehistory.mus .mn.us/GrandExcursionPartIII.html.

30. Joseph Hancock to Selah Treat, March 1853, mss. 244, no. 113, ABCFM Papers. Thomas Williamson to Selah Treat, 22 January 1850, mss. 244, no. 383, ABCFM Papers.

31. Stephen Riggs to Selah Treat, 5 December 1853, mss. 244, no. 300, ABCFM Papers. Stephen Riggs to Selah Treat, 30 January 1854, mss. 244, no. 302, ABCFM Papers. Thomas Williamson to Selah Treat, 17 February 1854, mss. 244, no. 434, ABCFM Papers

32. Joseph Hancock to Selah Treat, 14 June 1853, mss. 244, no. 114, ABCFM Papers. Thomas Williamson to Selah Treat, 13 October 1854, mss. 244, no. 426, ABCFM Papers.

33. For information about the response of the ABCFM missionaries to the aftermath of the Treaty of 1851, see Riggs, *Tah-Koo Wah-Kan*, 255; *Annual Report of the ABCFM* (1854), 173; and Gideon Pond to Selah Treat, 1 October 1852, mss. 244, no. 183, ABCFM Papers.

34. Riggs, *Mary and I*, 154. "Sketches of the Dakota Mission," *Iapi Oaye: The Word Carrier* 2.3 (March 1873): 12.

35. Riggs, *Mary and I*, 389.

36. Thomas Williamson to Selah Treat, 30 June 1852, mss. 244, no. 409, ABCFM Papers. Thomas Williamson to Selah Treat, 13 April 1852, mss. 244, no. 405, ABCFM Papers. Riggs, *Mary and I*, 154.

37. Thomas Williamson to Selah Treat, 7 August 1851, mss. 244, no. 402, ABCFM Papers.

38. Thomas Williamson to Selah Treat, 30 July 1852, mss. 244, no. 409, ABCFM Papers; Stephen Riggs to Selah Treat, 31 July 1852, mss. 244, no. 279, ABCFM Papers. Selah Treat to G. W. Manypenny, 16 February 1854, ABCFM Indians Letter Book, 18:120, ABCFM Papers. Selah Treat, February 1854, "Notes," mss. 244, no. 42, ABCFM Papers. Stephen Riggs to Selah Treat, 16 February 1853, mss. 244, no. 290, ABCFM Papers.

39. Thomas Williamson to Selah Treat, 3 December 1853, mss. 244, no. 422, ABCFM Papers. Thomas Williamson to Selah Treat, 2 December 1853, mss. 244, no. 421, ABCFM Papers, and Stephen Riggs to Selah Treat, 5 December 1853, mss. 244, no. 300, ABCFM Papers. Thomas Williamson to Selah Treat, 7 August 1851, mss. 244, no. 402, ABCFM Papers.

40. Thomas Williamson to Selah Treat, 2 December 1853, mss. 244, no. 421, ABCFM Papers. Stephen Riggs to Selah Treat, 5 December 1853, mss. 244, no.

300, ABCFM Papers. Stephen Riggs to Selah Treat, 22 June 1853, mss. 244, no. 294, ABCFM Papers. Stephen Riggs to Selah Treat, 18 September 1853, mss. 244, no. 297, ABCFM Papers.

41. Selah Treat to Gideon Pond, 7 May 1852, ABCFM Indians Letter Book, 15:378, ABCFM Papers. Selah Treat to Stephen Riggs, 22 May 1852, ABCFM Indians Letter Book, 15:403, ABCFM Papers.

42. Riggs, Williamson, and Sibley, "Memorial Notices," 362, 365, 369, 371.

43. Thomas Williamson to Selah Treat, June 1850, mss. 244, no. 13, ABCFM Papers. Thomas Williamson to S. L. Pomroy, 30 September 1850, mss. 244, no. 22, ABCFM Papers; and Thomas Williamson to ABCFM, 25 June 1850, mss. 244, no. 395, ABCFM Papers. John Aiton to Selah Treat, 14 February 1850, mss. 244, no. 89, ABCFM Papers.

44. Selah Treat to John Aiton, 24 January 1850, ABCFM Indians Letter Book, 12:440, ABCFM Papers. Thomas Williamson to the ABCFM, 25 June 1850, mss. 244, no. 395, ABCFM Papers. Robert Hopkins to Selah Treat, 7 June 1850, mss. 244, no. 147, ABCFM Papers. John Aiton to "Rev. Gentlemen, and Lay Members of the Sioux Mission," 5 October 1849, in Aiton and Family Papers, MHS. Thomas Williamson to Selah Treat, 10 February 1851, mss. 244, no. 397, ABCFM Papers. J. Fletcher Williams, "History of West St. Paul, Minnesota," available: http://history.rays-place.com/mn/dak-w-st-paul.htm.

45. Stephen Riggs to Selah Treat, 14 July 1851, mss. 244, no. 260, ABCFM Papers. Robert Hopkins to Selah Treat, 19 May 1851, mss. 244, no. 152, ABCFM Papers. Robert Hopkins to Selah Treat, 7 June 1850, mss. 244, no. 147, ABCFM Papers. Robert Hopkins to Selah Treat, 14 January 1850, mss. 244, no. 146, ABCFM Papers.

46. Jonas Pettijohn to Selah Treat, 6 December 1851, mss. 244, no. 167, ABCFM Papers. For references to the issue of the ABCFM and slavery, see Oshatz, *Slavery and Sin*, 83–91; and, Oshatz, "No Ordinary Sin." See Willand, *Lac qui Parle and the Dakota Mission*, 220.

47. Riggs, *Mary and I*, 147.

48. Alexander Huggins, 6 January 1852, mss. 244, no. 164, ABCFM Papers.

49. Alexander Huggins, 6 January 1852, mss. 244, no. 164, ABCFM Papers. Thomas Williamson to Selah Treat, 9 August 1852, mss. 244, no. 410, ABCFM Papers.

50. Joseph Hancock to Selah Treat, 2 May 1854, mss. 244, no. 119, ABCFM Papers. Joseph Hancock to Selah Treat, 23 June 1852, mss. 244, no. 110, ABCFM Papers.

51. Joseph Hancock to Selah Treat, 2 May 1854, mss. 244, no. 119, ABCFM Papers. Goodhue County, Minnesota, "Biographies," available: http://genealogytrails.com/minn/goodhue/bios_h.htm.

52. Moses Adams to Selah Treat, 12 January 1850, mss. 244, no. 59, ABCFM Papers.

53. Moses Adams to Selah Treat, 1 August 1853, mss. 244, no, 81, ABCFM Papers. Selah Treat, 2 June 1854, mss. 244, no. 32, ABCFM Papers.

54. Selah Treat to Moses Adams, 6 June 1853, ABCFM Indians Letter Book, 17:156, ABCFM Papers. Moses Adams to Selah Treat, 30 June 1853, mss. 244, no. 80,

ABCFM Papers. Thomas Williamson to Selah Treat, 18 July 1853, mss. 244, no. 417, ABCFM Papers.

55. Thomas Williamson to Selah Treat, 6 May 1853, mss. 244, no. 415, ABCFM Papers. Stephen Riggs to Selah Treat, 12 April 1853, mss. 244, no. 291, ABCFM Papers.

56. Selah Treat to Stephen Riggs, 7 March 1853, ABCFM Indians Letter Book, 17:45, ABCFM Papers. Selah Treat to Thomas Williamson, 22 August 1853, ABCFM Indians Letter Book, 17:280, ABCFM Papers. Selah Treat to Moses Adams, 23 August 1853, ABCFM Indians Letter Book, 17:304, ABCFM Papers. Riggs, *Mary and I,* 147. See Sterling, "Moses N. Adams."

57. Gideon Pond to Selah Treat, 1 October 1852, mss. 244, no. 183, ABCFM Papers. Gideon Pond to Selah Treat, 20 February 1852, mss. 244, no. 178, ABCFM Papers.

58. Gideon Pond to Selah Treat, 3 August 1852, mss. 244, no. 181, ABCFM Papers. Gideon Pond to Selah Treat, 12 July 1852, mss. 244, no. 180, ABCFM Papers.

59. Gideon Pond to Selah Treat, 20 February 1852, mss. 244, no. 178, ABCFM Papers.

60. Gideon Pond to Selah Treat, 20 February 1852, mss. 244, no. 178, ABCFM Papers.

61. Gideon Pond to Selah Treat, 20 February 1852, mss. 244, no. 178, ABCFM Papers. Gideon Pond to Selah Treat, 10 June 1851, mss. 244, no. 177, ABCFM Papers.

62. Samuel Pond to Selah Treat, August 1852, mss. 244, no. 204, ABCFM Papers. Pond, *Two Volunteer Missionaries,* 219. Samuel Pond to Selah Treat, 19 October 1854, mss. 244, no. 210, ABCFM Papers. Samuel Pond to Selah Treat, 14 August 1854, mss. 244, no. 209, ABCFM Papers.

63. Pond, *Two Volunteer Missionaries,* 211. Gideon Pond to Selah Treat, 12 July 1852, mss. 244, no. 180, ABCFM Papers. Selah Treat to Samuel Pond, ABCFM Indians Letter Book, 16:257, ABCFM Papers; and Gideon Pond to Selah Treat, 8 January 1853, mss. 244, no. 184, ABCFM Papers.

64. Samuel Pond to his sister, 31 August 1855, Pond Papers. See also Samuel Pond to his sister, 25–26 September 1854, Pond Papers.

65. Selah Treat to Alexander Huggins, 26 March 1852, ABCFM Indians Letter Book, 15:298, ABCFM Papers. Selah Treat to Gideon Pond, 7 May 1852, ABCFM Indians Letter Book, 15:378, ABCFM Papers.

66. *Missionary Herald* 49.6 (1853): 180. Thomas Williamson to Selah Treat, 1 April 1853, mss. 244, no. 414, ABCFM Papers.

67. Selah Treat to Stephen Riggs, [May 1852,] ABCFM Indians Letter Book, 15:395, ABCFM Papers. Selah Treat to the Dakota Mission, 19 May 1853, ABCFM Indians Letter Book, 17:140, ABCFM Papers.

Notes to Chapter 6

1. Stephen Riggs to Selah Treat, 26 August 1854, mss. 244, no. 313, ABCFM Papers. Stephen Riggs to Selah Treat, 4 March 1858, mss. 244, no. 334, ABCFM Papers.

2. Stephen Riggs to Selah Treat, 11 January 1855, mss. 244, no. 320, ABCFM Papers.

3. Riggs, *Mary and I*, 156.

4. Stephen Riggs to Selah Treat, 19 February 1855, mss. 244, no. 324, ABCFM Papers. Stephen Riggs to Selah Treat, 11 January 1855, mss. 244, no. 320, ABCFM Papers. Stephen Riggs and Thomas Williamson to Rufus Anderson, 20 June 1857, mss. 244, no. 40, ABCFM Papers.

5. Stephen Riggs to Selah Treat, 30 January 1855, mss. 244, no. 322, ABCFM Papers. Treat wrote that "I am quite sure that I said nothing about furnishing boards gratuitously to the Indians." Selah Treat to Stephen Riggs, 12 March 1855, ABCFM Indians Letter Book, 19:265, ABCFM Papers.

6. Stephen Riggs to Selah Treat, 14 January 1856, mss. 244, no. 333, ABCFM Papers.

7. Stephen Riggs to Selah Treat, 30 January 1855, mss. 244, no. 322, ABCFM Papers. Stephen Riggs to Selah Treat, 11 January 1855, mss. 244, no. 320, ABCFM Papers; and Stephen Riggs to Selah Treat, 19 February 1855, mss. 244, no. 324, ABCFM Papers.

8. For a summary of boarding school policies and issues related to boarding schools, see Adams, *Education for Extinction*; Brenda J. Child, *Boarding School Seasons: American Indian Families, 1900–1940* (Lincoln: University of Nebraska Press, 1998); Michael Coleman, *American Indian Children at School, 1850–1930* (Jackson: University Press of Mississippi, 1993); Michael C. Coleman, "Motivations of Indian Children at Missionary and U.S. Government Schools," *Montana: The Magazine of History* 40.1 (Winter 1990): 30–45; Michael C. Coleman, "The Responses of American Indian Children to Presbyterian Schooling in the Nineteenth Century: An Analysis through Missionary Sources," *History of Education Quarterly* 27.4 (Winter 1987): 473–97; and Robert A. Trennert, "Educating Indian Girls at Nonreservation Boarding Schools, 1878–1920," *Western Historical Quarterly* 13.3 (July 1982): 271–90. For more specific studies on individual schools, see David Wallace Adams, "Schooling the Hopi: Federal Indian Policy Writ Small, 1887–1917," *Pacific Historical Review* 48.3 (August 1979): 335–56; Clyde Ellis, *To Change Them Forever: Indian Education at the Rainy Mountain Boarding School, 1893–1920* (Norman: University of Oklahoma Press, 1996); Sally Hyer, *One House, One Voice, One Heart: Native American Education at the Sante Fe Indian School* (Santa Fe: Museum of New Mexico Press, 1990); K. Tsianina Lomawaima, *They Called it Prairie Light: The Story of the Chilocco Indian School* (Lincoln: University of Nebraska Press, 1994); Sally McBeth, *Ethnic Identity and the Boarding School Experience of West-Central Oklahoma Indians* (Washington, DC: University Press of America, 1983); Scott Riney, *The Rapid City Indian School 1898–1933* (Norman: University of Oklahoma Press, 1999); and Widder, *Battle for the Soul,* chapter 5. For similar information on Progressive Era boarding schools, see Riney, *The Rapid City Indian School,* 138; and Ellis, *To Change Them Forever,* xii.

9. Thomas Williamson to Selah Treat, 23 June 1859, mss. 244, no. 451, ABCFM Papers. See also Commissioner of Indian Affairs, *Annual Report* (1858), 53.

10. Stephen Riggs to Selah Treat, 15 March 1861, mss. 310, no. 11, ABCFM Papers. See Clemmons, "We find it difficult work." Thomas Williamson to Selah Treat, 17 March 1857, mss. 244, no. 440, ABCFM Papers. Thomas Williamson to Selah Treat, 24 October 1855, mss. 244, no. 432, ABCFM Papers. Thomas Williamson to Selah Treat, 24 June 1856, mss. 244, no. 437, ABCM Papers.

11. Stephen Riggs, "Biography of Men Connected with the Dakota Mission, 1835–1860," Riggs Family Papers. Morris, *Old Rail Fence Corners*, 260.

12. *Friends' Intelligencer United with the Friends' Journal* 44 (1887): 645. Riggs, *Mary and I*, 157. *Friends' Intelligencer* 14 (1858): 79. Quoted in Green, *A Peculiar Imbalance*, 107.

13. Stephen Riggs to Selah Treat, 31 July 1856, mss. 244, no. 337, ABCFM Papers; and *Friends' Intelligencer United with the Friends' Journal* 44 (1887): 645.

14. Stephen Riggs to Selah Treat, 12 April 1855, mss. 244, no. 326, ABCFM Papers. Stephen Riggs to Selah Treat, 30 January 1855, mss. 244, no. 322, ABCFM Papers. Stephen Riggs to Selah Treat, 11 January 1855, mss. 244, no. 320, ABCFM Papers. Commissioner of Indian Affairs, *Annual Report* (1855), 383. *Annual Report of the ABCFM* (1855), 136.

15. Riggs, *A Small Bit of Bread and Butter*, 216. Riggs, "Biography of Men Connected with the Dakota Mission, 1835–1860," Riggs Family Papers; and Stephen Riggs to Selah Treat, 12 July 1860, mss. 310, no. 4, ABCFM Papers. Stephen Riggs to Selah Treat, 12 June 1858, mss. 244, no. 346, ABCFM Papers. *Annual Report of the ABCFM* (1855), 136. For attendance figures at the boarding school, see Commissioner of Indian Affairs, *Annual Report* (1856), 64.

16. Joseph Brown to William Cullen, 6 February 1860, Letters Received by the Office of Indian Affairs, 1824–81, St. Peter's Agency, 1859–61, reel 763; and Heard, *History of the Sioux War*, 42–43. Stephen Riggs to Selah Treat, 27 November 1858, mss. 244, no. 348, ABCFM Papers. Stephen Riggs, "Sermon," 1860, mss. 310, no. 8, ABCFM Papers. Thomas Williamson to Selah Treat, 6 July 1858, mss. 244, no. 446, ABCFM Papers.

17. Thomas Williamson and Stephen Riggs to George Manypenny, December 1855, Letters Received by the Office of Indian Affairs, 1824–81, St. Peter's Agency, 1855–58, reel 762. Stephen Riggs to Selah Treat, 10 December 1855, mss. 244, no. 332, ABCFM Papers. Stephen Riggs to Selah Treat, 27 August 1860, mss. 310, no. 9, ABCFM Papers.

18. Stephen Riggs to the ABCFM, "A Sketch of the Missionary Labors among the Dakotas," 2 January 1862, mss. 309, no. 173, ABCFM Papers. Joseph Brown to William Cullen, 6 February 1860, Letters Received by the Office of Indian Affairs, 1824–81, St. Peter's Agency, 1859–61, reel 763. Joseph Brown to William Cullen, 15 April 1860, Letters Received by the Office of Indian Affairs, 1824–81, St. Peter's Agency, 1859–61, reel 763. Also unknown writer, 3 January 1856, Letters Received by the Office of Indian Affairs, 1824–81, St. Peter's Agency, 1855–58, reel 762.

19. Thomas Williamson to Selah Treat, 18 November 1859, mss. 244, no. 452, ABCFM Papers.

20. Stephen Riggs to Selah Treat, 24 August 1859, mss. 244, no. 355, ABCFM Papers. Commissioner of Indian Affairs, *Annual Report* (1860), 269.

21. John P. Williamson to Selah Treat, 2 August 1861, mss. 310, no. 148, ABCFM Papers.

22. Thomas Williamson to Selah Treat, 13 January 1855, mss. 244, no. 437, ABCFM Papers. Thomas Williamson to Selah Treat, 24 October 1855, mss. 244, no. 432, ABCFM Papers.

23. Thomas Williamson to Selah Treat, 13 June 1855, mss. 244, no. 430, ABCFM Papers. Thomas Williamson to Selah Treat, 24 October 1855, mss. 244, no. 432, ABCFM Papers. Thomas Williamson to Selah Treat, 18 November 1858, mss. 244, no. 448, ABCFM Papers.

24. Thomas Williamson to Selah Treat, 8 May 1856, mss. 244, no. 436, ABCFM Papers; and Thomas Williamson to Selah Treat, 13 June 1855, mss. 244, no. 430, ABCFM Papers. Stephen Riggs to Selah Treat, 30 October 1855, mss. 244, no. 331, ABCFM Papers.

25. Williamson, "The Diseases of the Dakota Indians." Amos Bruce to James Clarke, 12 September 1846, Letters received by the Office of Indian Affairs, 1824–70, St. Peter's Agency, 1845–50, reel 760.

26. Riggs, *Tah-Koo Wah-Kan*, 263–64. Stephen Riggs and Thomas Williamson to Rufus Anderson, 20 June 1857, mss. 244, no. 40, ABCFM Papers. For a general discussion off Inkpaduta and the Spirit Lake Massacre, see Beck, *Inkpaduta*; and Larson, "A New Look at the Elusive Inkpaduta." *Annual Report of the ABCFM* (1857), 151.

27. Stephen Riggs and Thomas Williamson to Rufus Anderson, 20 June 1857, mss. 244, no. 40, ABCFM Papers. Sibley, "Sketch of John Other Day," 100. *Annual Report of the ABCFM* (1857), 152. "Sketches of the Dakota Mission," *Iapi Oaye: The Word Carrier* 2.4 (April 1873): 16.

28. Thomas Williamson to Selah Treat, November 1857, mss. 244, no. 441, ABCFM Papers; and *Annual Report of the ABCFM* (1857), 152. Riggs, "The Indian Question," 263.

29. Stephen Riggs to Selah Treat, 13 August 1857, mss. 244, no. 341, ABCFM Papers.

30. Commissioner of Indian Affairs, *Annual Report* (1857), 339, 347.

31. Thomas Williamson to Selah Treat, 18 March 1858, mss. 244, no. 444, ABCFM Papers. *Annual Report of the ABCFM* (1858), 130.

32. Thomas Williamson to Selah Treat, 18 January 1858, mss. 244, no. 442, ABCFM Papers. Diedrich, *Dakota Oratory*, 57. See Stephen Riggs to Selah Treat, 17 May 1859, mss. 244, no. 353, ABCFM Papers.

33. Commissioner of Indian Affairs, *Annual Report* (1859), 452, 454. Anderson, *Kinsmen of Another Kind*, 231.

34. Wamditanka, "A Sioux Story of the War," 384.

35. Thomas Williamson to Selah Treat, 24 August 1858, mss. 244, no. 447, ABCFM Papers. Selah Treat to the Commissioner of Indian Affairs, 27 November, ABCFM Indians Letter Book, 21:426, ABCFM Papers.

36. Riggs, "The Dakota Mission," 124. *Annual Report of the ABCFM* (1861), 123. Riggs, *Tah-Koo Wah-Kan,* 397.

37. Report of the Commissioner of Indian Affairs, "An Extract from Agent Brown's Report for 1858," received 21 March 1861, mss. 309, no. 175, ABCFM Papers. Stephen Riggs to the ABCFM, [2 January 1862,] mss. 309, no. 173, ABCFM Papers.

38. Riggs, "The Indian Question," 267. Stephen Riggs to Selah Treat, 14 August 1861, mss. 310, no. 12, ABCFM Papers. Stephen Riggs to Selah Treat, 12 July 1859, mss. 244, no. 354, ABCFM Papers. Thomas Williamson to Selah Treat, 18 November 1859, mss. 244, no. 452, ABCFM Papers.

39. Thomas Williamson to Selah Treat, 18 November 1859, mss. 244, no. 452, ABCFM Papers. Thomas Williamson to Selah Treat, 30 April 1860, mss. 310, no. 209, ABCFM Papers.

40. Commissioner of Indian Affairs, *Annual Report* (1854), 283.

41. Thomas Williamson to Selah Treat, 18 November 1859, mss. 244, no. 452, ABCFM Papers. Riggs, "The Indian Question," 259.

42. Thomas Williamson to Selah Treat, 24 October 1855, mss. 244, no. 432, ABCFM Papers.

43. Riggs, *Mary and I,* 130. Stephen Riggs to Selah Treat, 17 May 1850, mss. 244, no. 253, ABCFM Papers.

44. Thomas Williamson to Selah Treat, 18 November 1858, mss. 244, no. 448, ABCFM Papers. Thomas Williamson to Selah Treat, 20 July 1860, mss. 310, no. 211, ABCFM Papers. Thomas Williamson to Selah Treat, 23 June 1859, mss. 244, no. 451, ABCFM Papers. Thomas Williamson to Selah Treat, 11 February 1861, mss. 310, no. 215, ABCFM Papers.

45. Stephen Riggs to ABCFM, "A Sketch of the Missionary Labors among the Dakotas," mss. 309, no. 173, ABCFM Papers. Although this letter was sent to the ABCFM, it was forwarded to the Commissioner of Indian Affairs. See Thomas Williamson to Selah Treat, 2 January 1862, mss. 310, no. 216, ABCFM Papers. Selah Treat to Dakota Mission, 16 January 1862, ABCFM Indians Letter Book, 23:29, ABCFM Papers.

46. Riggs, "The Dakota Language," 89.

47. Stephen Riggs to Selah Treat, 13 April 1857, mss. 244, no. 341, ABCFM Papers. Mary Riggs to Alfred Riggs, 29 November 1860, Riggs Family Papers.

48. Stephen Riggs to Selah Treat, 13 April 1857, mss. 244, no. 341, ABCFM Papers. *St. Paul Advertiser,* 31 March 1857, quoted in Hedin, "The Minnesota Constitution in the Language of the Dakota," 13. Green, *A Peculiar Imbalance,* 109.

49. Quoted in Folwell, *History of Minnesota,* 4:332. See also Minnesota State Constitution, Article 7, Section 1, available: http://www.house.leg.state.mn.us/cco/rules/mncon/preamble.htm.

50. Stephen Riggs to Selah Treat, 9 December 1859, mss. 244, no. 357, ABCFM Papers. Plane and Button, "The Massachusetts Indian Enfranchisement Act," 590, 591. Selah Treat to Stephen Riggs, 17 January 1859, ABCFM Indians Letter Book, 22:251, ABCFM Papers. Stephen Riggs to Selah Treat, 13 August 1857, mss. 244, no. 341, ABCFM Papers.

51. Selah Treat to Alexander Ramsey, 17 January 1860, ABCFM Indians Letter Book, 22:249, ABCFM Papers. Alexander Ramsey to Selah Treat, 30 January 1860, mss. 274, no. 411, ABCFM Papers.

52. Stephen Riggs to Selah Treat, 3 February 1860, mss. 310, no. 2, ABCFM Papers. Stephen Riggs to Selah Treat, 22 February 1861, mss. 310, no. 10, ABCFM Papers.

53. "Application of Sioux Indians," 21 June 1861, mss. 309, no. 176, ABCFM Papers. Stephen Riggs to Selah Treat, 30 November 1857, mss. 244, no. 342, ABCFM Papers.

54. "Application of Sioux Indians," 21 June 1861, mss. 309, no. 176, ABCFM Papers. Green, *A Peculiar Imbalance*, 115.

55. White, "The Power of Whiteness," 43.

56. Stephen Riggs to Selah Treat, 20 May 1852, mss. 244, no. 276, ABCFM Papers. Riggs, "The Indian Question," 273. Williamson, "The Indian Question," 617. Selah Treat to Stephen Riggs, ABCFM Indians Letter Book, 22:25, ABCFM Papers.

57. Riggs, "The Dakota Language," 92–93.

58. For references to the Semi-Jubilee, see Stephen Riggs to Selah Treat, 12 July 1860, mss. 310, no. 4, ABCFM Papers; Stephen Riggs to Selah Treat, 14 July 1862, mss. 310, no. 5, ABCFM Papers; Stephen Riggs to Selah Treat, 28 July 1860, mss. 310, no. 6, ABCFM Papers; and *Missionary Herald* 56:5 (May 1860): 156.

59. Stephen Riggs to Selah Treat, 12 July 1860, mss. 310, no. 4, ABCFM Papers.

60. Stephen Riggs to Selah Treat, 12 July 1860, mss. 310, no. 4, ABCFM Papers.

61. Riggs, "The Indian Question," 266. *Missionary Herald* 56:5 (May 1860): 156. Stephen Riggs to Selah Treat, 12 July 1860, mss. 310, no. 4, ABCFM Papers.

62. For example, see Selah Treat to the Commissioner of Indian Affairs, 27 November 1858, ABCFM Indians Letter Book, 21:428, ABCFM Papers; Selah B. Treat to W. P. Dole, 13 February 1862, ABCFM Indians Letter Book, 23:40, ABCFM Papers; and Selah Treat to G. B. Smith (Secretary of the Interior), 7 March 1861, ABCFM Indians Letter Book, 22, ABCFM Papers.

Notes to Chapter 7

1. The events of the U.S.–Dakota War (August–September 1862) can be told from the point of view of the Dakotas, Minnesota settlers, and government agents and officials. Because this book focuses on the ABCFM missionaries, their story is highlighted. As such, this chapter does not provide a chronological history of the military events of the war, nor does it include complete interpretations of the war by all involved groups. For a brief historiography of the U.S.–Dakota War of 1862, see Bachman, *Northern Slave Black Dakota*, 345–48; and Peacock, "An Account of the Dakota–US War," 185–87. Riggs titled his chapter on the Dakota War in *Tah-Koo Wah-Kan*, "The Dark Hour," 279.

2. Riggs, *Tah-Koo Wah-Kan*, 280. For general information on the U.S.–Dakota War of 1862, see Anderson, *Kinsmen of Another Kind*, 261–80; Anderson, *Little Crow*, 135–79; Black Thunder, *Ehanna Woyakapi*, 38–47; Carley, *The Sioux Uprising of 1862*;

Folwell, *History of Minnesota*, 2:109–211; Forbes, "Evangelization and Acculturation," 234–341, and Meyer, *History of the Santee Sioux*, 109–32.

There was never an official report on the number of white settlers who died during the war. Thus, the numbers given vary depending on the source cited. Most historians mention 500 deaths, but 400–800 also are given in other sources. For example, Graber, in "Mighty Upheaval on the Minnesota Frontier," 76, cites 500 as the number. See also Lewis, "Wise Decisions," 49. Carol Chomsky gives the precise number of 464: 77 American soldiers, 29 citizen-soldiers, and 358 settlers. See Chomsky, "The United States–Dakota War Trials," 21.

Anderson and Woolworth, *Through Dakota Eyes*, 1; and Peacock, "An Account of the Dakota–US War," 193. Thomas Williamson to S. Griffith, 10 April 1863, mss. 310, no. 328, ABCFM Papers. For a discussion of the post-war campaigns, see Beck, *Columns of Vengeance*.

3. Commissioner of Indian Affairs, *Annual Report* (1863), 395. Commissioner of Indian Affairs, *Annual Report* (1862), 177, 213.

4. Tolzmann, *The Sioux Uprising in Minnesota*, 128. Riggs, *Tah-Koo Wah-Kan*, 337. *St. Paul Pioneer*, 27 November 1862. "Extracts from [the] *Pioneer Democrat*," 26 August 1862, mss. 309, no. 179, ABCFM Papers. An article in the *St. Paul Pioneer* summarized the cause of the war in stark racial terms. It was a "war of the white race against the brutal, inhuman savage." *St. Paul Pioneer*, 23 October 1862.

5. Pond, *Dakota Life in the Upper Midwest*, 62. Adams, "The Sioux Outbreak in the Year 1862," 432. John Williamson to Selah Treat, mss. 310, no. 155, ABCFM Papers. Stephen Riggs to Selah Treat, 11 October 1862, mss. 310, no. 22, ABCFM Papers.

6. Riggs, *Tah-Koo Wah-Kan*, 323. Riggs, *Mary and I*, 204. *Missionary Herald* 59:10 (July 1863): 43.

7. Riggs, "Protestant Missions in the Northwest," 174; and Riggs, *Tah-Koo Wah-Kan*, 329. Riggs, *Mary and I*, 172.

8. Sweet, "Mrs. J. E. DeCamp Sweet's Narrative of her Captivity," 356, 357; and Folwell, *History of Minnesota*, 2:228. For information on the conflict over annuities at the Upper Agency, see Anderson and Woolworth, *Through Dakota Eyes*, 20; McClure, "The Story of Nancy McClure," 448; Wakefield, *Six Weeks in the Sioux Tepees*, 62–64; Riggs, *Mary and I*, 175–76; and Riggs, *Tah-Koo Wah-Kan*, 324–26.

9. Anderson and Woolworth, *Through Dakota Eyes*, 38. Meyer, *History of the Santee Sioux*, 117. For more information on Myrick, see Anderson, "Myrick's Insult." Riggs, *Mary and I*, 173.

10. Martha Riggs, "Flight of the Missionaries," 26 September 1862, 309, no. 177, ABCFM Papers. Adams, "The Sioux Outbreak in the Year 1862," 432.

11. Mary Riggs to Stephen Riggs, 13 October 1862, in Riggs, *Family Correspondence*.

12. Riggs, *Mary and I*, 217. Riggs, *Tah-Koo Wah-Kan*, 332. Thomas Williamson to Selah Treat, 17 October 1862, mss. 310, no. 223, ABCFM Papers.

13. Thomas Williamson to Walter S. Griffith, 10 April 1863, mss. 310, no. 228, ABCFM Papers.

14. John Mattocks to [ABCFM], 23 August 1862, 309, no. 190, ABCFM Papers.

See also Bryant and Murch, *A History of the Great Massacre*, 29. Riggs, *Tah-Koo Wah-Kan*, 336.

15. Quoted in Chomsky, "The United States–Dakota War Trials," 92.

16. Thomas Williamson to Selah Treat, 8 September 1862, mss. 310, no. 222, ABCFM Papers. *Annual Report of the ABCFM* (1863), 142–43. Martha Riggs, "The Flight of the Missionaries," 26 September 1862, mss. 309, no. 177, ABCFM Papers. *Missionary Herald* 58.10 (October 1862): 297.

17. Waziyatawin, *What does Justice Look Like*, 122. Canku and Simon, *The Dakota Prisoner of War Letters*, 214. Peacock, "An Account of the Dakota–US War," 202.

18. Canku and Simon, *The Dakota Prisoner of War Letters*, 214. See also Peacock, "An Account of the Dakota–US War," 199.

19. Riggs, *Mary and I*, 178. Thomas Williamson to Selah Treat, 8 September 1862, mss. 310, no. 222, ABCFM Papers.

20. For a description of the missionaries' journey to safety and the help they received from Christian Dakotas, see Mary Butler Renville, *A Thrilling Narrative of Indian Captivity*, 5–9, 49–52; Martha Riggs, "The Flight of the Missionaries," 26 September 1862, mss. 309, no. 177, ABCFM Papers; Stephen Riggs to Selah Treat, 24 August 1862, mss. 310, no. 17, ABCFM Papers; Stephen Riggs to Selah Treat, 15 September 1862, mss. 310, no. 20, ABCFM Papers; Riggs, "Protestant Missions in the Northwest," 175; Riggs, *Mary and I*, 176–87; Riggs, *Tah-Koo Wah-Kan*, 280–301; and Thomas Williamson to Selah Treat, 8 September 1862, mss. 310, no. 222, ABCFM Papers.

Riggs, *Mary and I*, 180. J. Mattocks to ABCFM, 23 August 1862, mss. 309, no. 190, ABCFM Papers. See also *Missionary Herald* 58:10 (October 1862): 297.

21. Riggs, *Mary and I*, 194.

22. Riggs, *Tah-Koo Wah-Kan*, 309–10. Zeman and Derounian-Stodola, *A Thrilling Narrative*, 19, 46, 49.

23. Commissioner of Indian Affairs, *Annual Report* (1863), 404. Riggs, *Mary and I*, 204. Stephen Riggs to Selah Treat, 10 September 1862, mss. 310, no. 19, ABCFM Papers. John George Nicolay, "The Sioux War" [magazine articles on the Sioux, Utes, etc.], [n.p., 1863–92], 198. See also *Missionary Herald* 58.10 (October 1862): 300; and "Extracts from *Pioneer and Democrat*," mss. 308, no. 178, ABCFM Papers.

24. Riggs, *Mary and I*, 204. Riggs, *Tah-Koo Wah-Kan*, 310. McClure, "The Story of Nancy McClure," 459. Sibley, "Sketch of John Other Day," 101. Riggs, "Narrative of Paul Mazakootemane," 86.

25. Riggs, *Tah-Koo Wah-Kan*, 319. See also Anderson and Woolworth, *Through Dakota Eyes*, 171, 178, 187, 188, 189, 198, 199, 202, 223, 229, 230, 232, 238.

26. Stephen Riggs to Mary Riggs, 25 October 1862, in Riggs, *Family Correspondence*. Stephen Riggs to Selah Treat, 11 October 1862, mss. 310, no. 22, ABCFM Papers. Quoted in Chomsky, "The United States–Dakota War Trials," 23.

27. *Pioneer and Democrat*, 22 August 1862. Various newspaper clippings sent to the ABCFM, "Let the Sioux Race be Annihilated," *Weekly Pioneer*, 12 September 1862, mss. 310, no. 225, ABCFM Papers.

28. Various newspaper clippings sent to the ABCFM, "Let the Sioux Race be Annihilated," *Weekly Pioneer,* 12 September 1862, mss. 310, no. 225, ABCFM Papers. Wilson, *Remember This,* 8. Riggs, *Tah-Koo Wah-Kan,* 336.

29. Following the war the Ho-Chunk (Winnebagos) were removed from Minnesota even though they had not fought alongside the Dakotas. They shared a reservation with the Dakotas at Crow Creek. Commissioner of Indian Affairs, *Annual Report* (1863), 409. Taylor, *The Sioux War,* 13.

30. Taylor, *The Sioux War,* 11–13. See also Nicolay, "The Sioux War," 204. Mary Riggs to Stephen Riggs, 5 November 1862, in Riggs, *Family Correspondence.*

31. Wakefield, *Six Weeks in the Sioux Tepees,* 4, 64.

32. Thomas Williamson to Selah Treat, 8 September 1862, 310, no. 222, ABCFM Papers. John P. Williamson to Selah Treat, 5 November 1862, mss. 310, no. 156, ABCFM Papers. Stephen Riggs to Selah Treat, 24 November 1862, mss. 310, no. 23, ABCFM Papers.

33. Mary Riggs to Stephen Riggs, 13 October 1862, in Riggs, *Family Correspondence.* Mary Riggs to Stephen Riggs, 7 November 1864, in Riggs, *Family Correspondence.* Thomas Williamson to Selah Treat, 1 December 1862, mss. 310, no. 226, ABCFM Papers. Selah Treat to John Williamson, 19 December 1862, ABCFM Indians Letter Book, 23:168, ABCFM Papers.

34. John Williamson to Selah Treat, 5 November 1862, mss. 310, no. 156, ABCFM Papers. Stephen Riggs to Mary Riggs, 18 October 1862, in Riggs, *Family Correspondence.* Mary Riggs to Stephen Riggs, 5 November 1862, in Riggs, *Family Correspondence.*

35. Quoted in Lewis, "Wise Decisions," 68.

36. Peacock, "An Account of the Dakota–US War," 194. See also Chomsky, "The United States–Dakota War Trials," 28.

37. John P. Williamson to Selah Treat, 5 November 1862, mss. 310, no. 156, ABCFM Papers. Thomas Williamson to Selah Treat, 21 November 1862, mss. 310, no. 224, ABCFM Papers.

38. John P. Williamson to Selah Treat, 5 November 1862, mss. 310, no. 156, ABCFM Papers. *Missionary Herald* 59.1 (January 1863): 15–16. Riggs, *Tah-Koo Wah-Kan,* 334. Thomas Williamson to John Smith, 13 November 1862, Letters received by the Office of Indian Affairs, 1824–70, St. Peter's Agency, 1862–65, reel 764.

39. The missionaries used the name "Robert Hopkins" and not "Robert Hopkins Chaske." See Riggs, *Mary and I,* 194; and Riggs, *Tah-Koo Wah-Kan,* 426. Thomas Williamson to Selah Treat, 21 November 1862, mss. 310, no. 224, ABCFM Papers.

40. Thomas Williamson to Selah Treat, 21 November 1862, mss. 310, no. 224, ABCFM Papers. Stephen Riggs to Mary Riggs, 13 November 18162, in Riggs, *Family Correspondence.* Riggs, *Tah-Koo Wah-Kan,* 349. *Missionary Herald* 58.1 (January 1862): 16.

41. W. P. Dole to Selah Treat, 22 December 1862, mss. 323, no. 221, ABCFM Papers.

42. See Nichols, *Lincoln and the Indians. Missionary Herald* 59.7 (July 1863): 204. Pond, *Two Volunteer Missionaries,* 221.

43. Riggs, *Mary and I,* 188. Stephen Riggs to Selah Treat, 29 August 1862, mss. 310, no. 18, ABCFM Papers. John Williamson to Selah Treat, 5 November 1862, mss. 310, no. 156, ABCFM Papers.

44. Riggs, *Mary and I,* 206. Bachman, *Northern Slave, Black Dakota,* 129. Stephen Riggs to Mary Riggs, 17 October 1862, in Riggs, *Family Correspondence.* Heard, *History of the Sioux War,* 251, 268.

45. Stephen Riggs to Selah Treat, 26 March 1863, mss. 310, no. 29, ABCFM Papers. Riggs, *Tah-Koo Wah-Kan,* 339. Stephen Riggs to Selah Treat, 24 November 1862, mss. 310, no. 23, ABCFM Papers. Stephen Riggs to Mary Riggs, 22 September 1862, in Riggs, *Family Correspondence;* and *Annual Report of the ABCFM* (1863), 144.

46. Stephen Riggs to Mary Riggs, 28 October 1862, in Riggs, *Family Correspondence.*

47. Riggs, *Mary and I,* 208. See also Riggs, *Tah-Koo Wah-Kan,* 333–34. Bachman, *Northern Slave, Black Dakota,* 129.

48. Bryant and Murch, *A History of the Great Massacre,* 472.

49. Mary Riggs to her son, 1 January 1863, in Riggs, *Family Correspondence.* Stephen Riggs to Mary Riggs, 22 December 1862, in Riggs, *Family Correspondence.* Riggs, *Mary and I,* 212.

50. *Annual Report of the ABCFM* (1863), 148. Stephen Riggs to Selah Treat, 20 February 1863, mss. 310, no. 26, ABCFM Papers. *Pioneer and Democrat,* 8 October 1862.

51. *St. Paul Pioneer,* 16 December 1862. Mary Riggs to her son, 10 January 1863, in Riggs, *Family Correspondence.* Riggs, *Mary and I,* 394. Stephen Riggs to Mary Riggs, 17 October 1862, in Riggs, *Family Correspondence.* Stephen Riggs to Selah Treat, 24 November 1862, mss. 310, no. 23, ABCFM Papers. *St. Paul Pioneer,* 8 October 1862.

52. Riggs, *Tah-Koo Wah-Kan,* 339. John P. Williamson to Selah Treat, 5 November 1862, mss. 310, no. 156, ABCFM Papers. *Harper's Weekly* 10.31 (1863): 695.

53. Pond, *The Dakota or Sioux in Minnesota,* 61. Riggs, *Mary and I,* 192. Stephen Riggs to Mary Riggs, 22 September 1862, in Riggs, *Family Correspondence.* Stephen Riggs to Mary Riggs, 24 September 1862, in Riggs, *Family Correspondence.* Gideon Pond to *New York Evangelist,* "The Indian Prisoners in Minnesota," 9 February 1863, mss. 309, no. 196, ABCFM Papers.

54. Barton, *John P. Williamson,* 57–58.

55. Mary Riggs to her son, 10 January 1863, in Riggs, *Family Correspondence.* Stephen Riggs to Selah Treat, 15 September 1863, mss. 310, no. 34, ABCFM Papers.

56. Zeman and Derounian-Stodola, *A Thrilling Narrative,* 145.

57. Riggs, *Mary and I,* 186. Stephen Riggs to Selah Treat, 29 August 1862, mss. 310, no. 18, ABCFM Papers. Riggs, *Tah-Koo Wah-Kan,* 399.

58. Riggs, *Tah-Koo Wah-Kan,* 400. Thomas Williamson to Selah Treat, 17 October 1862, mss. 310, no. 223, ABCFM Papers.

Notes to Epilogue

1. Waziyatawin, "Decolonizing the 1862 Death Marches," 185.
2. Riggs, "Protestant Missions in the Northwest," 182. Riggs, *A Small Bit of Bread and Butter*, 253.
3. Anderson and Woolworth, *Through Dakota Eyes*, 234.
4. Graber, "Mighty Upheaval on the Minnesota Frontier," 79.
5. Barton, *John P. Williamson*, 57.
6. Renville, "A Sioux Narrative of the Outbreak in 1862," 609–10. Morris, *Old Rail Fence Corners*, 177. John Williamson to Selah Treat, 28 November 1862, mss. 310, no. 157, ABCFM Papers.
7. Wilson, "Grandmother to Granddaughter," 10. Vine V. Deloria, "The Establishment of Christianity among the Sioux," in DeMallie and Parks, *Sioux Indian Religion*, 106–7.
8. Riggs, *Mary and I*, 210. Riggs, *Tah-Koo Wah-Kan*, 334. Barton, *John P. Williamson*, 57.
9. Gideon Pond to *New York Evangelist*, 9 February 1863, mss. 309, no. 196, ABCFM Papers. Riggs, *Mary and I*, 209. Thomas Williamson to Selah Treat, 1 December 1862, mss. 310, no. 226, ABCFM Papers. Hugh Cunningham to Selah Treat, 2 December 1862, mss. 309, no. 235, ABCFM Papers.
10. Thomas Williamson to Walter S. Griffith, 10 April 1863, mss. 310, no. 328, ABCFM Papers. Barton, *John P. Williamson*, 58. Thomas Williamson to Selah Treat, 1 December 1862, mss. 310, no. 226, ABCFM Papers. Gideon Pond to *New York Evangelist*, 9 February 1863, mss. 309, no. 196, ABCFM Papers.
11. John Williamson to Selah Treat, 5 November 1862, mss. 310, no. 156, ABCFM Papers.
12. See Stephen Riggs to Selah Treat, 21 January 1863, mss. 310, no. 25, ABCFM Papers. Folwell, *History of Minnesota*, 2:252. The missionaries also estimated that 1,600 Dakotas were being held at Fort Snelling: *Annual Report of the ABCFM* (1863), 148. R. J. Creswell reported that 1,500 Dakotas were held at Fort Snelling: Creswell, *Among the Sioux*, 35.
13. Thomas Williamson to Selah Treat, 1 December 1862, mss. 310, no. 226, ABCFM Papers. Bachman, *Northern Slave, Black Dakota*, 286.
14. *Annual Report of the ABCFM* (1863), 148. See also Stephen Riggs to Selah Treat, 21 January 1863, mss. 310, no. 25, ABCFM Papers. "Sketches of the Dakota Mission," *Iapi Oaye: The Word Carrier* 2.5 (May 1873): 24. *Missionary Herald* 59.7 (July 1863): 204.
15. Thomas Williamson to Selah Treat, 21 November 1862, mss. 310, no. 224, ABCFM Papers. Folwell, *History of Minnesota*, 2:255.
16. Stephen Riggs to Selah Treat, 15 September 1863, mss. 310, no. 34, ABCFM Papers. Barton, *John P. Williamson*, 75. John Williamson to Selah Treat, 7 May 1863, mss. 310, no. 58, ABCFM Papers.
17. *Missionary Herald* 60.9 (September 1864): 261.

18. *Missionary Herald* 60.7 (July 1864): 203.

19. *Missionary Herald* 60.7 (July 1864): 204.

20. Selah Treat to W. P. Dole, 17 December 1863, ABCFM Indians Letter Book, 23:280, ABCFM Papers.

21. Stephen Riggs to Selah Treat, 21 April 1863, mss. 310, no. 30, ABCFM Papers.

22. Stephen Riggs to Selah Treat, 12 May 1863, mss. 310, no. 31, ABCFM Papers. Stephen Riggs to Selah Treat, 7 November 1863, mss. 310, no. 36, ABCFM Papers.

23. Thomas Williamson to Walter S. Griffith, 10 April 1863, mss, 310, no. 328, ABCFM Papers. Barton, *John P. Williamson,* 62. John Williamson to Selah Treat, 7 May 1863, mss. 310, no. 58, ABCFM Papers.

24. Thomas Williamson to Selah Treat, 20 January 1863, mss. 310, no. 227, ABCFM Papers. Gideon Pond to *New York Evangelist,* "The Indian Prisoners in Minnesota," 9 February 1863, mss. 309, no. 196, ABCFM Papers. *Missionary Herald* 59.7 (July 1863): 204. Creswell, *Among the Sioux,* 33–34.

25. Stephen Riggs to Selah Treat, 10 March 1863, mss. 310, no. 38, ABCFM Papers. Riggs, *Tah-Koo Wah-Kan,* 359. *Annual Report of the ABCFM* (1865), 145. *Missionary Herald* 61.3 (March 1865): 71.

26. *Annual Report of the ABCFM* (1863), 146. John Williamson to Selah Treat, 7 May 1863, mss. 310, no. 58, ABCFM Papers. Thomas Williamson to Selah Treat, 20 January 1863, mss. 310, no. 227, ABCFM Papers.

27. Riggs, *Tah-Koo Wah-Kan,* 345. *Missionary Herald* 59.5 (May 1863): 150. Stephen Riggs to Selah Treat, 26 March 1863, mss. 310, no. 29, ABCFM Papers. Selah Treat to Stephen Riggs, 12 March 1863, ABCFM Indians Letter Book, 23:197, ABCFM Papers. Thomas Williamson to Selah Treat, 20 January 1863, mss. 310, no. 227, ABCFM Papers.

28. Stephen Riggs to Selah Treat, 26 March 1863, mss. 310, no. 29, ABCFM Papers. *Missionary Herald* 59.5 (May 1863): 149.

29. Stephen Riggs to Selah Treat, 26 March 1863, mss. 310, no. 29, ABCFM Papers. See also *Missionary Herald* 59.5 (May 1863): 149. Riggs, *Tah-Koo Wah-Kan,* 344, 345.

30. Riggs, *Tah-Koo Wah-Kan,* 344. See also Stephen Riggs to Selah Treat, 3 March 1863, mss. 310, no. 27, ABCFM Papers. Stephen Riggs to Selah Treat, 26 March 1863, mss. 310, no. 29, ABCFM Papers. "Indian Prisoners," *Mankato Weekly Record,* 28 March 1863, mss. 309, no. 182, ABCFM Papers.

31. Hugh Cunningham to Selah Treat, 15 November 1862, mss. 309, no. 234, ABCFM Papers. Stephen Riggs to Selah Treat, 1 December 1862, mss. 310, no. 24, ABCFM Papers.

32. *Missionary Herald* 60.5 (May 1864): 138.

33. Riggs, *Tah-Koo Wah-Kan,* 362.

34. John Williamson to Selah Treat, 7 May 1863, mss. 310, no. 58, ABCFM Papers. Barton, *John P. Williamson,* 57.

Works Cited

Manuscript Sources and Collections

American Philosophical Society, Philadelphia, Pennsylvania
  Ella Cara Deloria, ed. "Letters and Miscellaneous Materials in Dakota from the Minnesota Manuscript"
Center for Western Studies, Augustana College, Sioux Falls, South Dakota
  Riggs Family Papers
Minnesota Historical Society, St. Paul
  ABCFM Papers (typescript copies; originals available at Houghton Rare Book Library, Harvard University)
  Moses N. Adams and Family Papers
  John Felix Aiton and Family Papers
  Diary of Marjorie Cunningham, 1861–63
  Nancy McClure Huggan Reminiscences
  Alexander G. Huggins and Family Papers
  Alfred Longley and Family Papers
  Pond Family Papers
  Stephen Return Riggs and Family Papers
  Thomas S. Williamson Papers

Government Documents

Commissioner of Indian Affairs, *Annual Report*, 1830–65
National Archives, Washington, DC
  Minnesota Superintendency. Letters Received and Sent. Record Group 75.
  Office of Indian Affairs. Letters Received and Sent. Record Group 75.
  St. Peter's Agency. Letters Received and Sent. Record Group 75.
U.S. Congress. Congressional Serial Set.

Newspaper and Periodical Sources

Annual Report of the ABCFM, 1830–65
The Boston Recorder
Friends' Intelligencer
Friends' Intelligencer United with the Friends' Journal

Harper's Weekly, 1862–65
Iapi Oaye: The Word Carrier
Missionary Herald, 1830–65
Pioneer and Democrat
St. Paul Advertiser
St. Paul Pioneer

Published Primary Sources

Adams, Moses N. "The Sioux Outbreak in the Year 1862, with Notes of Missionary Work Among the Sioux." *Collections of the Minnesota Historical Society* 9 (1901): 431–52.

American Board of Commissioners for Foreign Missions. *Report of the Committee on Anti-Slavery Memorials, September 1845. With a Historical Statement of Previous Proceedings.* Boston: Press of T. R. Marvin, 1845.

Anderson, Gary Clayton, and Alan R. Woolworth, eds. *Through Dakota Eyes: Narrative Accounts of the Minnesota Indian War of 1862.* St. Paul: Minnesota Historical Society Press, 1988.

Anderson, Rufus. *Memorial Volume of the First Fifty Years of the American Board of Commissioners for Foreign Missions.* Boston: The Board, 1861.

Bartlett, S. C. *Historical Sketch of the Missions of the American Board among the North American Indians.* Boston: The Board, 1876.

Barton, Winifred W. *John P. Williamson: A Brother to the Sioux.* Grand Rapids, MI: Fleming H. Revell Company, 1919; reprint, Clements, MN: Sunnycrest Publishing, 1980.

Bray, Edmund C., and Martha Coleman Bray, eds. *Joseph N. Nicollet on the Plains and Prairies: The Expeditions of 1838–39 with Journals, Letters, and Notes on the Dakota Indians.* St. Paul: Minnesota Historical Society Press, 1993.

Canku, Clifford, and Michael Simon. *The Dakota Prisoner of War Letters: Dakota Kaškapi Okicize Wowapi.* St. Paul: Minnesota Historical Society Press, 2013.

Diedrich, Mark, ed. *Dakota Oratory: Great Moments in the Recorded Speech of the Eastern Sioux, 1695–1874.* Rochester, MN: Coyote Books, 1989.

Eastman, Charles A. *From Deep Woods to Civilization.* Boston: Little, Brown, 1916; reprint, Lincoln: University of Nebraska Press, 1977.

———. *Indian Boyhood.* Boston: Little, Brown, 1902; reprint, Lincoln: University of Nebraska Press, 1991.

———. *Old Indian Days.* New York: McClure Co., 1907; reprint, Lincoln: University of Nebraska Press, 1991.

Fay, George E., ed. *A Grand Compendium of United States Congressional Documentation of Relationships between the Bands of the Sioux and the United States.* Greeley, CO: Museum of Anthropology, University of Northern Colorado, 1975.

Hall, Gordon, and Samuel Newell. *The Conversion of the World: or, the Claims of Six*

Hundred Millions of Heathen, and the Ability and Duty of the Churches Respecting Them. Andover, MA: Flagg and Gould, 1818.

Heard, Isaac V. D. *History of the Sioux War and Massacres of 1862 and 1863.* New York: Harper and Brothers Publishers, 1865.

Hedin, Douglas A., ed. "The Minnesota Constitution in the Language of the Dakota." Available at the Minnesota Legal History Project: http://www .minnesotalegalhistoryproject.org/assets/Minn.%20Const.%20in%20%20 Dakota%20Language.pdf.

Heilbron, Bertha L., ed. *With Pen and Pencil on the Frontier in 1851: The Diary and Sketches of Frank Blackwell Mayer.* St. Paul: Minnesota Historical Society Press, 1986.

Huggan, Nancy McClure. "The Story of Nancy McClure: Captivity Among the Sioux." *Minnesota Historical Society Collections* 6 (1894): 438–60.

LeDuc, William. *A Brief Sketch and History of the Signing of the Treaty of Traverse des Sioux.* St. Peter, MN: Daughters of the American Revolution, 1900.

———. *Minnesota Year Book for 1852.* St. Paul, MN: W. G. LeDuc, 1852.

Magie, David. *Our True Encouragement: A Sermon Preached at Buffalo, New York, September 8, 1847, before the American Board of Commissioners for Foreign Missions, at Their Thirty-Eighth Annual Meeting.* Boston: T. R. Marvin, 1847.

McMurray, William. *The Spiritual Contest of the Church. A Sermon Preached in Philadelphia, Sept. 18, 1833, Before the American Board of Commissioners for Foreign Missions, at Their Twenty-Fourth Annual Meeting.* Boston: Crocker and Brewster, 1833.

Miller, Samuel. *The Earth Filled with the Glory of the Lord. A Sermon Preached at Baltimore, September 9, 1835, Before the American Board of Commissioners for Foreign Missions, at Their Twenty-Sixth Annual Meeting.* Boston: Crocker and Brewster, 1835.

Morris, Lucy Leavenworth Wilder, ed. *Old Rail Fence Corners: Frontier Tales Told by Minnesota Pioneers.* St. Paul: Minnesota Historical Society Press, 1976.

Neill, Edward D., ed. "Autobiography of Major Lawrence Taliaferro Written in 1864." *Minnesota Historical Society Collections* 6 (1894): 189–255.

———. *The History of Minnesota: From the Earliest Explorations to the Present Time.* Minneapolis: Minnesota Historical Company, 1882.

———. "A Memorial of the Brothers Pond, the First Resident Missionaries Among the Dakotahs." *Macalester College Contributions* 2:8. St. Paul, MN: The Pioneer Press Company, 1890.

———. "A Sketch of Joseph Renville: 'Bois Brule,' an Early Trader of Minnesota." *Collections of the Minnesota Historical Society* 1 (1872): 196–206.

Nevin, Alfred, ed. *Encyclopaedia of the Presbyterian Church in the United States of America: Including the Northern and Southern Assemblies.* Philadelphia: Presbyterian Encyclopaedia Co., 1884.

Newcomb, Harvey. *Cyclopedia of Missions: Containing a Comprehensive View of Missionary Operations Throughout the World.* New York: Charles Scribner, 1855.

Pettijohn, Jonas. *Autobiography, Family History and Various Reminiscences of the Life of Jonas Pettijohn.* Clay Center, KS: Dispatch Printing House, 1890.

Pond, Gideon H. *Paganism, a Demon Worship: A Discourse Delivered before the Synod of Minnesota, September 1860.* Philadelphia: William S. Young, Book and Job Printer, 1861.

Pond, Samuel W. "Dakota Life in the Upper Midwest." *Collections of the Minnesota Historical Society* 12 (1908); reprint, St. Paul: Minnesota Historical Society Press, 1986.

———. *The Dakotas or Sioux in Minnesota as They Were in 1834.* St. Paul: Minnesota Historical Society Press, 1986.

———. *Two Volunteer Missionaries among the Dakotas, or, the Story of the Labors of Samuel W. and Gideon H. Pond.* Boston: Congregational Sunday School and Publishing Society, 1893.

Renville, Gabriel. "A Sioux Narrative of the Outbreak in 1862 and of Sibley's Expedition in 1863." *Collections of the Minnesota Historical Society* 10 (1905): 595–618.

Riggs, Maida Leonard, ed. *A Small Bit of Bread and Butter: Letters from the Dakota Territory, 1832–1869.* South Deerfield, MA: Ash Grove Press, 1996.

Riggs, Stephen R. *A Dakota-English Dictionary.* Department of the Interior, U.S. Geographical and Geological Survey of the Rocky Mountain Region, as Contributions to North American Ethnology 7 (1890); reprint, St. Paul: Minnesota Historical Society Press, 1992.

———. *Dakota Grammar, Texts, and Ethnography.* Washington, DC: Government Printing Office, 1893.

———. "The Dakota Language." *Minnesota Historical Society Collections* 1 (1872): 89–107.

———. "The Dakota Mission." *Minnesota Historical Collections* 2 (1880): 115–28.

———. "Dakota Portraits." *Minnesota History Bulletin* 8 (November 1918): 481–568.

———. "The Indian Question." *New Englander* 15:58 (May 1857): 250–74.

———. *Mary and I: Forty Years with the Sioux.* Minneapolis, MN: Ross and Haines, Inc., 1969.

———. "Narrative of Paul Mazakootemane." *Collections of the Minnesota Historical Society* 3 (1870–80): 82–90.

———. "Protestant Missions in the Northwest." *Collections of the Minnesota Historical Society* 6 (1894): 117–88.

———. *Stephen R. Riggs and Family Correspondence, Concerning Lac qui Parle Mission and other Matters, 1832–1869.* Typescript. Available in the Minnesota Historical Society Library.

———. *Tah-Koo Wah-Kan; Or, The Gospel Among the Dakotas.* Boston: Congregational Publishing Society, 1869.

Riggs, Stephen, Thomas Williamson, and Henry Sibley. "Memorial Notices and Rev. Gideon H. Pond." *Collections of the Minnesota Historical Society* 3 (1870–80): 356–71.

Riggs, Thomas Lawrence. *Sunset to Sunset: A Lifetime with My Brothers, the Dakotas.* Pierre: South Dakota Historical Society Press, 1997.

Sibley, Henry Hastings. "Sketch of John Other Day." *Collections of the Minnesota Historical Society* 3 (1880): 99–102.

Sweet, J. E. DeCamp. "Mrs. J. E. DeCamp Sweet's Narrative of her Captivity in the Sioux Outbreak of 1862." *Collections of the Minnesota Historical Society* 6 (1894): 354–80.

Taylor, John Wickes. *The Sioux War: What shall we do with it? The Sioux Indians: What shall we do with them?* St. Paul: Minnesota Press Printing Company, 1862.

Tolzmann, Don, ed. *The Sioux Uprising in Minnesota, 1862: Jacob Nix's Eyewitness History.* Max Kade German-American Center, Indiana University–Purdue University at Indianapolis and Indiana German Heritage Society, 1994.

Wakefield, Sarah F. *Six Weeks in the Sioux Tepees: A Narrative of Indian Captivity.* June Namias, ed. Norman: University of Oklahoma Press, 1997.

Wamditanka. "A Sioux Story of the War. Chief Big Eagle's Story of the Sioux Outbreak of 1862." *Collections of the Minnesota State Historical Society* 6 (1894): 382–400.

[Whipple, Charles King]. *Slavery and the American Board of Commissioners for Foreign Missions.* New York: American Anti-Slavery Society, 1859.

Williamson, John P. *An English-Dakota Dictionary.* New York: American Tract Society, 1902; reprint, St. Paul: Minnesota Historical Society Press, 1992.

Williamson, Thomas. "The Diseases of the Dakota Indians." *The Northwestern Medical and Surgical Journal* 4 (1873–74): 418–19.

———. "The Indian Question." *Presbyterian Quarterly and Princeton Review* (1876): 608–24.

———. "Napeshneedoota: The First Male Convert to Christianity." *Minnesota Historical Collections* 2 (1860–67): 188–91.

Zeman, Carrie Reber, and Kathryn Zabelle Derounian-Stodola, eds. *A Thrilling Narrative of Indian Captivity: Dispatches from the Dakota War.* Lincoln: University of Nebraska Press, 2012.

Secondary Sources

Abzug, Robert H. *Passionate Liberator: Theodore Dwight Weld and the Dilemma of Reform.* New York: Oxford, 1982.

Adams, David Wallace. *Education for Extinction: American Indians and the Boarding School Experience, 1875–1928.* Lawrence: University Press of Kansas, 1995.

Ahlstrom, Sydney E. *A Religious History of the American People.* New Haven: Yale University Press, 1972.

Albers, Patricia. "The Regional System of the Devil's Lake Sioux: Its Structure, Composition, Development, and Function." PhD diss., University of Wisconsin, 1974.

Alexander, Ruth Ann. "Gentle Evangelists: Women in Dakota Episcopal Missions, 1867–1900." *South Dakota History* 24.3–4 (Fall/Winter 1994): 174–93.

Anderson, Gary Clayton. *Kinsmen of Another Kind: Dakota-White Relations in the Upper Mississippi Valley 1650–1862.* St. Paul: Minnesota Historical Society Press, 1997.

———. *Little Crow: Spokesman for the Sioux.* St. Paul: Minnesota Historical Society Press, 1986.

———. "Myrick's Insult: A Fresh Look at Myth and Reality." *Minnesota History* 48.5 (Spring 1983): 198–206.

———. "The Removal of the Mdewakanton Dakota in 1837: A Case Study for Jacksonian Paternalism." *South Dakota History* 10.4 (Fall 1980): 310–33.

Andrew, John. *Rebuilding the Christian Commonwealth: New England Congregationalists and Foreign Missions, 1800–1830.* Lexington: University Press of Kentucky, 1975.

Bachman, Walt. *Northern Slave, Black Dakota: The Life and Times of Joseph Godfrey.* Bloomington, MN: Pond Dakota Press, 2013.

Baker, Anne Marie, ed. "A Doorkeeper in the House of God: The Letters of Beatrice A. R. Stocker, Missionary to the Sioux, 1892–1893." *South Dakota History* 22.1 (Spring 1992): 38–63.

Banker, Mark T. *Presbyterian Missions and Cultural Interaction in the Far Southwest, 1850–1950.* Urbana: University of Illinois Press, 1993.

Beck, Paul N. *Columns of Vengeance: Soldiers, Sioux, and the Punitive Expeditions, 1863–1864.* Norman: University of Oklahoma Press, 2013.

———. *Inkpaduta: Dakota Leader.* Norman: University of Oklahoma Press, 2008.

Bedell, George C., Leo Sandon, Jr., and Charles J. Wellborn. *Religion in America.* New York: Macmillan Publishing Company, 1975.

Bendroth, Margaret L. "Women and Missions: Conflict and Changing Roles in the Presbyterian Church in the United States of America, 1870–1935." *Journal of Presbyterian History* 65.1 (Spring 1987): 49–59.

Berkhofer, Robert F. *Salvation and the Savage: An Analysis of Protestant Missions and American Indian Response, 1787–1862.* New York: Antheum, 1972.

———. *The White Man's Indian: Images of the American Indian from Columbus to Present.* New York: Alfred A. Knopf, 1978.

Black Thunder, Elijah, et al. *Ehanna Woyakapi: History and Culture of the Sisseton Wahpeton Sioux Tribe of South Dakota.* Sisseton, SD: Sisseton Wahpeton Sioux Tribe, 1971.

Blegan, Thomas C., ed. "Two Missionaries in Sioux Country." *Minnesota History* 21 (March 940): 272–83.

Bolt, Christine, and Seymour Drescher, eds. *Anti-Slavery, Religion, and Reform: Essays in Memory of Roger Anstey.* Folkestone Kent, England: Dawson, Archon, 1980.

Bourne, Russell. *Gods of War, Gods of Peace: How the Meeting of Native and Colonial Religions Shaped Early America.* New York: Harcourt, Inc., 2002.

Bratt, James D. "The Reorientation of American Protestantism, 1835–1845." *Church History* 67.1 (March 1998): 52–83.

Braude, Ann. *Women and American Religion.* New York: Oxford University Press, 2000.

Brumberg, Joan Jacobs. *Mission for Life: The Story of the Family of Adoniram Judson, the Dramatic Events of the First American Foreign Mission, and the Course of Evangelical Religion in the Nineteenth Century.* New York: The Free Press, 1980.

Bryant, Charles S., and Abel B. Murch. *A History of the Great Massacre by the Sioux Indians in Minnesota.* St. Paul, MN: E. Wainwright and Son, Publishers, 1872.

Burkhart, Louise M. *The Slippery Earth: Nahua-Christian Moral Dialogue in Sixteenth-Century Mexico.* Tucson: University of Arizona Press, 1989.

Butler, Jon. *Awash in a Sea of Faith: Christianizing the American People.* Cambridge: Harvard University Press, 1990.

Carley, Kenneth. *The Sioux Uprising of 1862.* St. Paul: Minnesota Historical Society Press, 1976.

Carwardine, Richard J. *Evangelicals and Politics in Antebellum America.* New Haven: Yale University Press, 1993.

Case, Jay Riley. *An Unpredictable Gospel: American Evangelicals and World Christianity, 1812–1920.* New York: Oxford University Press, 2012.

Chomsky, Carol. "The United States–Dakota War Trials: A Study in Military Injustice." *Stanford Law Review* 43.13 (November 1990): 13–98.

Clark, Elizabeth B. "'The Sacred Rights of the Weak': Pain, Sympathy, and the Culture of Individual Rights in Antebellum America." *The Journal of American History* 82.2 (September 1995): 463–93.

Clemmons, Linda M. "'Leagued together': Adapting Traditional Forms of Resistance to Protest ABCFM Missionaries and the Treaty of 1837," *South Dakota History* 37 (Summer 2007): 95–124.

———. "'We find it a difficult work': Educating Dakota Children in Missionary Homes, 1835–1862." *American Indian Quarterly* 24.4 (Fall 2000): 570–600.

———. "'We will talk of nothing else': Dakota Interpretations of the Treaty of 1837." *Great Plains Quarterly* 25.3 (Summer 2005): 173–85.

Coleman, Michael C. "Not Race, But Grace: Presbyterian Missionaries and American Indians, 1837–1893." *The Journal of American History* 67.1 (June 1980): 41–60.

———. *Presbyterian Missionary Attitudes toward American Indians, 1837–1893.* Jackson: University Press of Mississippi, 1985.

Comaroff, Jean, and Joan Comaroff. *Of Revelation and Revolution: Christianity, Colonialism and Consciousness in South Africa.* 2 vols. Chicago: University of Chicago Press, 1991.

Conforti, Joseph C. "David Brainerd and the Nineteenth Century Missionary Movement." *Journal of the Early Republic* 5.3 (Autumn 1985): 309–29.

———. "Jonathan Edwards's Most Popular Work: 'The Life of David Brainerd' and Nineteenth-Century Evangelical Culture." *Church History* 54.2 (June 1985): 188–201.

————. "Mary Lyon, The Founding of Mount Holyoke College, and the Cultural Revival of Jonathan Edwards." *Religion and American Culture: A Journal of Interpretation* 3.1 (Winter 1993): 69–89.

Conkin, Paul K. *Cane Ridge: America's Pentecost*. Madison: University of Wisconsin Press, 1990.

————. *The Uneasy Center: Reformed Christianity in Antebellum America*. Chapel Hill: University of North Carolina Press, 1995.

Craig, Robert. "Christianity and Empire: A Case Study of American Protestant Colonialism and Native Americans." *American Indian Culture and Research Journal* 21.2 (1997): 1–41.

Creswell, R. J. *Among the Sioux: A Story of the Twin Cities and the Two Dakotas*. Minneapolis, MN: The University Press, 1906.

Deloria, Ella Cara. *Speaking of Indians*. New York: Friendship Press, 1944.

DeMallie, Raymond J. "Joseph N. Nicollet's Account of the Sioux and Assiniboin in 1839." *South Dakota History* 5.4 (Fall 1975): 343–59.

DeMallie, Raymond J., and Douglas R. Parks, eds. *Sioux Indian Religion: Tradition and Innovation*. Norman: University of Oklahoma Press, 1987.

Eliason, Eric A. *Mormons and Mormonism: An Introduction to an American World Religion*. Urbana: University of Illinois Press, 2001.

Eslinger, Ellen. *Citizens of Zion: The Social Origins of Camp Meeting Revivalism*. Knoxville: University of Tennessee Press, 1999.

Folwell, William Watts. *A History of Minnesota*. St. Paul: Minnesota Historical Society, 1921.

Forbes, Bruce David. "Evangelization and Acculturation among the Santee Dakota Indians, 1834–1864." PhD diss., Princeton, NJ, 1977.

Gilman, Rhoda. "How Minnesota Became the 32nd State." *Minnesota History* 56.4 (Winter 1998): 154–71.

Graber, Jennifer. *The Furnace of Affliction: Prisons and Religion in Antebellum America*. Chapel Hill: University of North Carolina Press, 2011.

————. "Mighty Upheaval on the Minnesota Frontier: Violence, War, and Death in Dakota and Missionary Christianity." *Church History* 80.1 (March 2011): 76–108.

Graves, Joseph L. Jr. *The Emperor's New Clothes: Biological Theories of Race at the Millennium*. New Brunswick, NJ: Rutgers University Press, 2001.

Gray, Edward. *New World Babel: Languages and Nations in Early America*. Princeton, NJ: Princeton University Press, 1999.

Green, William D. *A Peculiar Imbalance: The Fall and Rise of Racial Equality in Early Minnesota*. St. Paul: Minnesota Historical Society Press, 2007.

Griffiths, Nicholas, and Fernando Cervantes, eds. *Spiritual Encounters: Interactions between Christianity and Native Religions in Colonial America*. Lincoln: University of Nebraska Press, 1999.

Grigg, John A. *The Lives of David Brainerd: The Making of an American Evangelical Icon*. New York: Oxford University Press, 2009.

Grimshaw, Patricia. *Paths of Duty: American Missionary Wives in Nineteenth-Century Hawaii.* Honolulu: University of Hawaii Press, 1989.

Handy, Robert T. *A History of the Churches in the United States and Canada.* New York: Oxford University Press, 1977.

Harris, Paul William. *Nothing but Christ: Rufus Anderson and the Ideology of Protestant Foreign Missions.* New York: Oxford University Press, 1999.

Harvey, Sean P. "'Must Not Their Languages Be Savage and Barbarous Like Them?': Philology, Indian Removal, and Race Science." *Journal of the Early Republic* 30.4 (Winter 2010): 505–32.

Hassrick, Royal B. *The Sioux: Life and Customs of a Warrior Society.* Norman: University of Oklahoma Press, 1964.

Higham, C. L. *Noble, Wretched and Redeemable: Protestant Missionaries to the Indians in Canada and the United States, 1820–1900.* Albuquerque: University of New Mexico Press, 2000.

———. "Saviors and Scientists: North American Protestant Missionaries and the Development of Anthropology." *Pacific Historical Review* 72.4 (November 2003): 531–59.

Hill, Patricia R. *The World Their Household: The American Woman's Mission Movement and Cultural Transformation, 1870–1920.* Ann Arbor: University of Michigan Press, 1985.

Holmquist, June Dremming. *They Chose Minnesota: A Survey of the State's Ethnic Groups.* St. Paul: Minnesota Historical Society Press, 2004.

Horsman, Reginald. *Race and Manifest Destiny: The Origins of American Racial Anglo-Saxonism.* Cambridge, MA: Harvard University Press, 1981.

———. "Scientific Racism and the American Indian in the Mid-Nineteenth Century." *American Quarterly* 27.2 (May 1975): 152–68.

Hubbard, Lucius Frederick, William Pitt Murray, James Heaton Baker, Warren Upham, Return Ira Holcombe, and Frank R. Holmes. *Minnesota in Three Centuries.* [New York]: Publishing Society of Minnesota, 1908.

Hunter, Jane. *The Gospel of Gentility: American Women Missionaries in Turn-of-the-Century China.* New Haven, CT: Yale University Press, 1984.

Hutchinson, William R. *Errand to the World: American Protestant Thought and Foreign Missions.* Chicago: University of Chicago Press, 1987.

Hyman, Colette A. *Dakota Women's Work: Creativity, Culture, and Exile.* St. Paul: Minnesota Historical Society Press, 2012.

Jeffrey, Julie Roy. *Converting the West: A Biography of Narcissa Whitman.* Norman: University of Oklahoma Press, 1991.

Johnson, Curtis D. *Redeeming America: Evangelicals and the Road to the Civil War.* Chicago: Ivan R. Dee, 1993.

Kelley, Mary. "'Pen and Ink Communion': Evangelical Reading and Writing in Antebellum America." *The New England Quarterly* 84.4 (December 2011): 555–87.

Kidwell, Clara Sue. *Choctaws and Missionaries in Mississippi, 1818–1918.* Norman: University of Oklahoma Press, 1995.

Kling, David W. "The New Divinity and the Origins of the American Board of Commissioners for Foreign Missions." *Church History* 72.4 (December 2003): 791–819.

Kreiger, Barbara. *Divine Expectations: An American Woman in 19th-Century Palestine.* Athens: Ohio University Press, 1999.

Kugel, Rebecca. "Of Missionaries and Their Cattle: Ojibwa Perceptions of a Missionary as Evil Shaman." *Ethnohistory* 41.2 (Spring 1994): 227–44.

———. *To Be the Main Leaders of Our People: A History of Minnesota Ojibwe Politics, 1825–1898.* East Lansing: Michigan State University, 1998.

Landes, Ruth. *The Mystic Lake Sioux: Sociology of the Mdewakantonwan Santee.* Madison: University of Wisconsin Press, 1968.

Larson, Peggy Rodina. "A New Look at the Elusive Inkpaduta." *Minnesota History* 48.1 (Spring 1982): 24–35.

Lesser, Alexander. "Siouan Kinship." PhD diss., Columbia University, 1958.

Lewis, Charles. "Wise Decisions: A Frontier Newspaper's Coverage of the Dakota Conflict." *American Journalism* 28.2 (2011): 48–80.

Lovejoy, David S. "Satanizing the American Indian." *The New England Quarterly* 67.4 (December 1994): 603–21.

Lucas, Joseph S. "Civilization or Extinction: Citizens and Indians in the Early United States." *The Journal of the Historical Society* 6.2 (June 2006): 235–50.

Mandell, Daniel R. "The Indian's Pedigree (1794): Indians, Folklore, and Race in Southern New England." *William and Mary Quarterly* 61.3 (July 2004): 1–13.

Marsden, George M. *The Evangelical Mind and the New School Presbyterian Experience: A Case Study of Thought and Theology in Nineteenth-Century America.* New Haven, CT: Yale University Press, 1970.

McCoy, Genevieve. "The Women of the ABCFM Oregon Mission and the Conflicted Language of Calvinism." *Church History* 64.1 (March 1995): 62–83.

McLoughlin, William G., ed. *The American Evangelicals, 1800–1900: An Anthology.* New York: Harper and Row, 1968.

———. *Champions of the Cherokees: Evan and John B. Jones.* Princeton, NJ: Princeton University Press, 1990.

———. "Cherokees and Methodists, 1824–1834." *Church History* 50.1 (March 1981): 44–63.

———. *Cherokees and Missionaries, 1789–1839.* Norman: University of Oklahoma Press, 1995.

———. *Revivals, Awakenings, and Reform: An Essay on Religion and Social Change in America, 1607–1977.* Chicago: University of Chicago Press, 1978.

Merritt, Jane T. *At the Crossroad: Indians and Empires on the Mid-Atlantic Frontier, 1700–1763.* Chapel Hill: University of North Carolina Press, 2003.

Meyer, Roy W. *History of the Santee Sioux: United States Indian Policy on Trial.* Lincoln: University of Nebraska Press, 1993.

Morgan, David. *Protestants and Pictures: Religion, Visual Culture, and the Age of American Mass Production.* New York: Oxford University Press, 1999.

Murray, Laura J. "Joining Signs with Words: Missionaries, Metaphors, and the Massachusetts Language." *The New England Quarterly* 74.1 (March 2001): 62–93.

Nichols, David A. *Lincoln and the Indians: Civil War Policy and Politics.* St. Paul: Minnesota Historical Society Press, 2012.

Noll, Mark A. *A History of Christianity in the United States and Canada.* Grand Rapids, MI: William B. Eerdmans Publishing Company, 1992.

———. *Protestants in America.* New York: Oxford University Press, 2000.

Nord, David Paul. *The Evangelical Origins of Mass Media in America, 1815–1835.* Columbia, SC: The Association for Education in Journalism and Mass Communication, 1984.

Olmstead, Clifton E. *History of Religion in the United States.* Englewood Cliffs, NJ: Prentice-Hall, Inc., 1960.

Oshatz, Molly. "No Ordinary Sin: Antislavery Protestants and the Discovery of the Social Nature of Morality." *Church History* 79 (2012): 334–58.

———. *Slavery and Sin: The Fight against Slavery and the Rise of Liberal Protestantism.* New York: Oxford University Press, 2011.

Peacock, John. "An Account of the Dakota–US War of 1862 as Sacred Text: Why My Dakota Elders Value Spiritual Closure over Scholarly 'Balance.'" *American Indian Culture and Research Journal* 37. 2 (2013): 185–206.

Perdue, Theda. *"Mixed Blood" Indians: Racial Construction in the Early South.* Athens: University of Georgia Press, 2005.

———. "Race and Culture: Writing the Ethnohistory of the Early South." *Ethnohistory* 51.4 (Fall 2004): 701–23.

Peyer, Bernd C. *The Tutor'd Mind: Indian Missionary-Writers in Antebellum America.* Amherst: University of Massachusetts Press, 1997.

Phillips, Clifton Jackson. *Protestant America and the Pagan World: The First Half Century of the American Board of Commissioners for Foreign Missions, 1810–1860.* Cambridge, MA: Harvard University Press, 1969.

Plane, Ann Marie, and Gregory Button. "The Massachusetts Indian Enfranchisement Act: Ethnic Contest in Historical Context, 1849–1869." *Ethnohistory* 40.4 (Autumn 1993): 586–617.

Pointer, Richard W. *Encounters of the Spirit: Native Americans and European Colonial Religion.* Bloomington: Indiana University Press, 2007.

Porterfield, Amanda. *Mary Lyon and the Mount Holyoke Missionaries.* New York: Oxford University Press, 1997.

———. *Sacred Language: The Nature of Supernatural Discourse in Lakota.* Norman: University of Oklahoma Press, 1986.

Price, Catherine. "Lakotas and Euroamericans: Contrasted Concepts of 'Chieftainship' and Decision-Making Authority." *Ethnohistory* 41.3 (Summer 1994): 447–62.

Prucha, Francis Paul. *The Great Father: The United States Government and the American Indians.* Vol. 1. Lincoln: University of Nebraska Press, 1986.

Pruitt, Lisa Joy. *"A Looking-Glass for Ladies": American Protestant Women and the Orient in the Nineteenth Century.* Macon, GA: Mercer University Press, 2005.

Putney, Clifford. *Missionaries in Hawai'i: The Lives of Peter and Fanny Gulick, 1797–1883.* Amherst: University of Massachusetts Press, 2010.

Reeves-Ellington, Barbara. "Women, Protestant Missions, and American Cultural Expansion, 1800 to 1938: A Historiographical Sketch." *Social Sciences and Missions* 24 (2011): 190–206.

Robert, Dana L. "From Foreign Missions to Missions to beyond Missions: The Historiography of American Protestant Foreign Missions since World War II." *International Bulletin of Missionary Research* 18:4 (1994).

Salisbury, Neal. "Red Puritans: The 'Praying Indians' of Massachusetts Bay and John Eliot." *The William and Mary Quarterly* 31.1 (January 1974): 27–54.

Satz, Ronald. *American Indian Policy in the Jacksonian Era.* Lincoln: University of Nebraska Press, 1975.

Seat, Karen. *"Providence Has Freed our Hands": Women's Missions and the American Encounter with Japan.* Syracuse, NY: Syracuse University Press, 2008.

Sheehan, Bernard W. *Seeds of Extinction: Jeffersonian Philanthropy and the American Indian.* Chapel Hill: University of North Carolina Press, 1973.

Siems, Monica L. "How do you say 'God' in Dakota? Epistemological Problems in the Christianization of Native Americans." *Numen* 45 (1998): 163–82.

Spack, Ruth. *America's Second Tongue: American Indian Education and the Ownership of English, 1860–1900.* Lincoln: University of Nebraska Press, 2002.

Spector, Janet D. *What this Awl Means: Feminist Archaeology at a Wahpeton Dakota Village.* St. Paul: Minnesota Historical Society Press, 1993.

Stanton, William. *The Leopard's Spots: Scientific Attitudes Toward Race in America 1815–59.* Chicago: University of Chicago Press, 1960.

Sterling, Everett W. "Moses N. Adams: A Missionary as Indian Agent." *Minnesota History* (December 1856): 167–77.

Sweet, Leonard I. *The Minister's Wife: Her Role in Nineteenth-Century Evangelism.* Philadelphia: Temple University Press, 1983.

Takaki, Ronald T. *Iron Cages: Race and Culture in Nineteenth-Century America.* New York: Alfred A. Knopf, 1979.

Tinker, George. *Missionary Conquest: The Gospel and Native American Cultural Genocide.* Minneapolis, MN: Fortress, 1993.

Vaughan, Alden T. "From White Man to Redskin: Changing Anglo-American Perceptions of the American Indian." *The American Historical Review* 87.4 (October 1982): 917–53.

———. *Roots of American Racism: Essays on the Colonial Experience.* New York: Oxford University Press, 1995.

Wacker, Grant. *Religion in Nineteenth Century America.* New York: Oxford University Press, 2000.

Waziyatawin. *What Does Justice Look Like? The Struggle for Liberation in Dakota Homeland.* St. Paul, MN: Living Justice Press, 2008.

Waziyatawin Angela Wilson. "Decolonizing the 1862 Death Marches." *American Indian Quarterly* 28.1–2 (2004): 185–215.

Welter, Barbara. "She Hath Done What She Could: Protestant Women's Missionary Careers in Nineteenth-Century America." *American Quarterly* 30.5 (Winter 1978): 624–38.

Westerman, Gwen, and Bruce White. *Mni Sota Makoce: The Land of the Dakota.* St. Paul: Minnesota Historical Society Press, 2012.

Whaley, Gray. "'Trophies' for God: Native Mortality, Racial Ideology, and the Methodist Mission of Lower Oregon, 1834–1844." *Oregon Historical Quarterly* 107.1 (Spring 2006): 6–35.

White, Ann. "Countering the Cost of Faith: America's Early Female Missionaries." *Church History* 57.1 (March 1988): 19–30.

White, Bruce M. "Give Us a Little Milk: The Social and Cultural Meanings of Gift Giving in the Lake Superior Fur Trade." *Minnesota History* 48.2 (Summer 1982): 60–71.

———. "Indian Visits: Stereotypes of Minnesota's Native People." *Minnesota History* 53 (Fall 1992): 99–111.

———. "The Power of Whiteness: Or, the Life and Times of Joseph Rolette, Jr." In Anne R. Kaplan and Marilyn Ziebarth, eds. *Making Minnesota Territory 1849–1858.* St. Paul: Minnesota Historical Society Press, 1999.

———. "A Skilled Game of Exchange: Ojibway Fur Trade Protocol." *Minnesota History* 50.6 (Summer 1987): 229–40.

Widder, Keith R. *Battle for the Soul: Métis Children Encounter Evangelical Protestants at Mackinaw Mission, 1823–1837.* East Lansing: Michigan State University Press, 1999.

Willard, Jon. *Lac qui Parle and the Dakota Mission.* Madison, MN: Lac Qui Parle Historical Society, 1964.

Wilson, Angela Cavender. "Grandmother to Granddaughter: Generations of Oral History in a Dakota Family." *American Indian Quarterly* 20.1 (Winter 1996): 7–13.

Wilson, Angela Waziyatawin. *Remember This! Dakota Decolonization and the Eli Taylor Narratives.* Lincoln: University of Nebraska Press, 2005.

Wozniak, John S. *Contact, Negotiation and Conflict: An Ethnohistory of the Eastern Dakota, 1819–1839.* Washington, DC: University Press of America, 1978.

Zabelle Derounian-Stodola, Kathryn. *The War in Words: Reading the Dakota Conflict through Captivity Literature.* Lincoln: University of Nebraska Press, 2009.

Index

Italicized page numbers indicate a photo or its caption.

mission stations, 36–40, 109–13, 138–39

monogenetic theory, 9–10

Morgan, David, 19

Murphy, Robert, 130

Myrick, Andrew, 183

Napesniduta, Joseph, 80, 105, 168

New Divinity, 22–23

Newell, Harriet, 19–20, 28

New Englander and Yale Review, 178

New Hope/Hazelwood mission station, 36–37, 135, 137–38, 156, 158–59, 186, 188

New York Evangelist (newspaper), 199

Nicollet, Joseph N., 71

Nix, Jacob, 181

Nord, David Paul, 19

Oak Grove mission station, 36, 37, 109, 111, 125, 146

Oceti Sakowin (Seven Council Fires), 36–37

"Old Hundred" (hymn), 216

Old Rail Fence Corners (Morris), 3

Other Day, John, 188–89, *189*

Paganism, a Demon Worship (Pond), 31

Pajutazee/Yellow Medicine mission station, 36–37, *59*, 135–36, 138, 159, 161, 186, 188

Panic of 1837, 42, 64

Peacock, John, 5, 186

Perdue, Theda, 32

Pettijohn, Eli, 109

Pettijohn, Fanny, 28, 59–60

Pettijohn, Jonas, 28, 109, 134–35, 139, 141, 157

The Pilgrim's Progress (translation), 50

Pioneer and Democrat (newspaper), 190, 198

Poage, Sarah, 28

Pointer, Richard, 4, 6

polygamy, 82, 84, 86–87, 143, 147–48, 213

Pond, Agnes, 58, *115*

Pond, Cordelia, 28, 42, 103, 113–14, 115, 119–20

Pond, Edward, 117

Pond, George, 117

Pond, Gideon H.: and ABCFM, 42, 109; on conversion, 44; counseling Williamson, 93; on Dakotas, 31, 105; demographics of, *26*; family of, *115*, 117, 118; and founding of Dakota mission, 33–35, 38, *111*; on fur traders, 80; missionary work of, 20; on mission schools and boarding programs, 125, 157; non-missionary work of, 13, 110, 121, 173; and the post-war period, 199, 206–7, 211–13; resignation of, 134–35, 138–39, 144–46; translations by, 48; on treaties, 100, 126, 129, 149

Pond, Ruth, 118

Pond, Samuel W.: on conversion, 44, 94; on Dakota language, 47–48; on Dakotas, 3, 30–31, 33, 54, 69, 72, 104; on Dakota War, 182, 196; demographics of, *26*; disillusionment of, 120; and founding of Dakota mission, 33–35, 35, *111*; on fur traders, 81; on land purchase, 149; on location of mission stations, 108–9; on marriage, 26–27, 28; on mission schools, 88, 90–92, 125; non-missionary work of, 13, 46; on polygamy, 82, 86; and the post-war period, 199; and relationship with other missionaries, 61–64, 92–93, 121; resignation of, 123, 134–35, 139, 146–47; translations by, 48–49, 51; on treaties, 99, 100, 103, 126, 132, 148

Pond, Sarah, 115, 117, 118

"Pond alphabet," 48

Pope, John, 190, 193

Porterfield, Amanda, 19

Potter, Joshua, 109, 121

Powers, William, 48, 50

Prairieville mission station, 36, 37, 109, 111, 125

Presbyterian doctrine, 13, 20–24, 26, 87
Price, Catherine, 105
prison schools, 204, 213, 215
Protestants, evangelical. *See* missionaries
Provencalle, Louis (Le Bland), 110

racism, 32–33, 65, 80
Ramsey, Alexander, 127–30, 132–33, 171–72, 190, 192
Rankin, Sarah (Hancock), 28, 109
Ravoux, Augustin, 198
Red Wing mission station, 36, 37, 109, 111, 133–34
Renville, Gabriel, 204–5
Renville, John B. (Jean), 79
Renville, Joseph: and Catholicism, 82; and conflict with missionaries, 94, 107; and conversion, 68–69, 77–81, 84–87; and founding of Dakota mission, 35, 41; on polygamy, 143; translations by, 48
Renville, Mary, 78–79
Renville, Michel, 106
resignations, missionary, 123, 134–35, 139–47
revivals, Protestant, 21, 25
Riggs, Alfred, 116–17
Riggs, Anna, 28
Riggs, Anna Jane, 117
Riggs, Isabella, 117
Riggs, Martha, 117, 182–83, 185, 189
Riggs, Mary Ann Clark Longley: on child care, 115–16, 118; on citizenship campaign, 171; on conversion, 85; on Dakota language, 50, 51; on Dakotas, 32, 57–59, 69, 71–72, 74–75, 76; demographics of, 26; disillusionment of, 7, 57, 60, 118–19; duties of, 55–56, 114; and founding of Dakota mission, 36, 39–43, 109, 112–13; marriage of, 18, 28–30; on mission schools, 90; and the post-war period, 193, 198,

200, 203; on soldiers, 45; on Treaty of 1837, 99–100, 106
Riggs, Stephen R.: citizenship campaign of, 171–76; and conflicts with other missionaries, 61–64, 141, 144, 145; on conversion, 77, 94; on Dakota language, 50–51, 54–55, 153–54, 170–71, 176; on Dakotas, 31–32, 65, 69–72, 74, 76, 82, 86–87, 89, 93, 143, 161; on Dakota War, 179–84, 186–87, 188–90; demographics of, 17, 26; and founding of Dakota mission, 36, 39, 41–43, 109–13; on marriage and family, 18, 27, 28–30, 118; on mission schools and boarding programs, 88–90, 157–60, 214–15; morale of, 120, 149; and the post-war period, 190–93, 196–201, 204–10, 212–13; and relationship with U.S. government, 45–46, 135, 156, 168–69, 180, 196–98, 210; on remaining at Dakota mission, 135–38, 151; and sawmill conflict, 154–56; on Semi-Jubilee, 176–78; and Spirit Lake Massacre, 164–65; on treaties, 98–103, 106, 126, 128–34, 162–67; writings/translations by, 13, 17, 49–51, 53, 174, 216
Riggs, Thomas, 116–17
Roberts, Benjamin S., 210
Robertson, Andrew, 156
Round Wind (Tatemina), 84
Running Walker, 156

Sacred Language (Powers), 48, 50
Sacred Nest, 195
St. Paul Financial Advertiser, 158, 171
St. Paul Pioneer, 181, 197–99
St. Peter's mission station, 36, 37
Salisbury, Neal, 8
sawmill conflict, 154–56
The Second Dakota Reading Book: Consisting of Stories from the Old Testament, 50